DANIEL HELL

SOUL HUNGER

THE FEELING HUMAN BEING
AND THE LIFE SCIENCES

*Daniel Hell*

# Soul Hunger

The Feeling Human Being and the Life Sciences

**DAIMON**
VERLAG

Title of the German original:
*Seelenhunger – Der fühlende Mensch und die Wissenschaften vom Leben*
Verlag Hans Huber, Bern, Göttingen, Toronto, Seattle, 2003


English translation by Dr. Julius Heuscher

Edited by Dr. Nicholas French

ISBN 978-3-85630-730-1

Copyright © 2010 Daimon Verlag, Einsiedeln, Switzerland

Cover illustration: © Ulrich Elsener, ulrichelsener.com
"Donna romana," 2007, acrylic, 50 x 35 cm

*Spricht die Seele, so spricht ach! schon die Seele nicht mehr.*

*When the soul speaks, woe! already the soul speaks no more.*

– Friedrich Schiller

# Contents

## *Part I:*
## *Historical Development*

Don't tire
but gently hold out
your hand
to the miracle,
like to a bird
– Hilde Domin

## Prologue

Who would wish to say that he or she lacks a soul? Yet how many speak of themselves as being "soul-filled"? To be soul-filled is an expression reserved for unusually intense sensations and experiences. Indeed, it takes an extraordinary occasion for most people to begin speaking of the soul. This often obscures the fact that most people are deeply interested in how they experience life, and feel anxious when their psychological awareness is diminished.

Martha S., age 40, is single and has studied law. She has had an excellent education, displays a keen intellect and has good self-awareness. She has fought episodes of very severe dysphoria for two decades, and during this depressive despair, she has repeatedly tried to kill herself. It's hard for her to saying anything positive about herself, even when she feels better. Self-love is unknown to her, and she has commented, "I know neither my reason for living, nor who I really am. How can I love myself, if I don't know who I am?"

Her lack of self-confidence does not cause her any significant problems during the periods when her mood is balanced. She generally goes to work without complaining, and often spends time with a few good women friends with whom she can share her cordial and sympathetic side.

But it is a different matter when her vitality wanes and she is blocked by depression. At those times, she condemns herself as a failure and says she would rather die than be the way she is. "A person like me has no right to live. I'm becoming a burden to everyone, especially my father and my siblings."

Such comments indicate an idealistic goal that she is unable either to embrace or even approach when in depressive distress. Blaming herself, she expresses bitter disappointment about a sense of personal irresponsibility and a feeling of being unfit to lead an effective life. While independence and efficiency seem to be her primary goals, they do not represent values with which Ms. S. actually identifies. However, as a child she was pressed to accept those values, and they have an ominous power precisely because they were continually reinforced family dictates. They control Ms. S. to such an extent that she would prefer to end her life rather than simply admit that she cannot live up to those introjected expectations of herself. While those values are not clearly voiced or defined, they are nonetheless capable of discrediting her feelings and perceptions, thereby reducing her soul's experience, as well as her physical life, to something utterly worthless.

As she was growing up, Ms. S. developed a pronounced aversion to her body. She is uncomfortable in her own skin, and at times experiences feelings of disgust when she touches her body or looks at herself in a mirror. She has tried to starve herself on several occasions, and has inflicted burns on her hands and arms. While Ms. S. feels embarrassed about these self-inflicted injuries because they are obviously viewed as abnormal, they do result in short periods of reduced psychological tension. Her body appears less offensive to her when it is wounded and in pain, and it is only by inflicting such suffering on herself that she can briefly relinquish her resistance to her own body and feel "at home" in it.

This pronounced rejection of the body began early in her life. She had been pushed, even in childhood, to act like an adult, and she was often punished by her mother if she expressed enthusiasm, joy or deep sadness in what was considered a "childish" way. In later years, she also suffered physical abuse by people she knew and trusted. All of this contributed to a growing sense of unworthiness and the experience of her body as dirty.

In light of her experience of others' disdain for her emotions and the abusive insults to her body, it is understandable that Ms. S. now rejects her body and tries to suppress somatic sensations. However, acknowledging these correlations does not help Ms. S. to reconcile with her body; her fears of being newly wounded if she expresses her feelings are buried far too deeply.

As a result, to avoid a terrifying loss of self and to cope with her increasing sense of fragmentation, her only means of escape seems to involve abusing herself. By causing the injuries, she feels she has prevented the kind of punishment that followed her childhood experiences of intense feelings. By punishing herself, she is also able to experience her physicality without having either to submit herself to other people, or to yield to her erotic desires.

Self-inflicted injuries also fulfill another purpose linked to her efficiency-centered education. Ms. S. was raised with very powerful emphasis on using her head as well as her body to achieve efficiency. She has observed, "What is hardest for me is that my willpower is too weak to successfully command my body. A major part of this failure is that my body can do whatever it wishes, and I'm forced, helplessly, to watch it." Her awareness is divided between a spiritual realm she considers pure, and a bodily realm she views as dirty. She would like to get rid of her body and continue to live only "like a little cloud in the sky." In her suicidal fantasies, Ms. S. pictures the destruction of her body, but not the dissolution of her spirit.

From this vantage point, we can see that her painful self-injuries demonstrate a dual meaning: on one hand, Ms. S. deals with her body as a foreign object; at the same time, the wounding allow Ms. S. to experience her body intensely. As one who injures herself, she is simultaneously object and subject. That is, since she both plans and is subjected to these procedures, her self-injuries can be seen not only as destructive actions, but also as a way to anchor her to her bodily existence, namely her "soul experience."

*Note concerning book citations: The page numbers listed in the text and in the footnotes refer to the German book editions. Not all of the German books have been published in English. If they are available in English, they are also listed in the bibliography. If they are not available, the German titles are translated mostly word by word and marked with "tr."*

And this is the wonderful aspect of life:
that all human beings who observe
themselves know what no science knows,
since they know what they themselves are.
                                    – Søren Kierkegaard

# Chapter 1.
# Homo Sentiens Newly Discovered

*No Place for the Soul?*

The origin of the German word "Seele"[1] is obscure. It contains the root word "See" (lake), recalling the ancient Germanic idea that the souls of the unborn and deceased live in the water. Other cultures also link what is 'soulish'[2] (pertaining to the soul) to the image of water. Soul-like qualities were recognized in the mirroring effect of still water, as well as in the unexplored depths of lakes. In an early Greek philosophical text, we find the statement that the soul is too

---

1. (Translator:) related to the old high German terms "sela" or "seula." Thus Prof. Hell's remarks about "Seele" apply also to the English "soul."
2. (Translator:) This translation of 'seelisch' is found in the unabridged Webster's dictionary; soulish is a somewhat awkward, little used word, not even listed in my shorter dictionary. "Soul-like" is an easier but far less accurate rendition of the German adjective "seelisch," for which my German/English dictionary offers "psychic," which could be rendered by the slightly better but cumbersome "having qualities of soul." "Psychic" is less desirable, as it has a Greek root and is not as precise. Thus, reluctantly, I will use "soulish," with an occasional substitute. As is indicated later, the precise translation of many terms related to our emotional and spiritual life is often impeded by various cultural, i.e. fundamentally different, ways of perceiving and experiencing. An in-depth study of these differences might yield additional insights into features of the "soul." Translating such terms can prove frustrating, yet we are challenged not to cling so tenaciously to either the terms or their translation that we cannot appreciate them as offering other, even richer meanings.

deep to be discovered. Also, the rough translation of a saying attributed to Heraclitus, occasionally called the dark, or
weeping philosopher, states, "You will certainly not find the
limits of the soul, however far you may go, even if you have
walked each and every street, for it has the essential presence
of "logos" [Ed.: Often rendered as "universal mind."][1]

These days, the image of the soul as "hidden in a lake"
has lost much of its symbolic power, for in our scientific-
technological age it's assumed that we are close to decoding
its veiled meaning. No longer do we commonly experience
the emotion of mythological images of deep waters; now
one tends to conjure up modern images involving cerebral
processes. An immediate and unique human quality has been
made into a scientific object that can be analyzed.

The more the soul is viewed as recognizable, the more it
becomes a common object. The "immediate" and "unique"
become something to be examined; the "original" and "hidden" become a quantity that can be made comprehensible.

Has soul thus lost its enigmatic presence? Has it become a
kind of "thing," a product that can be analyzed and perhaps
even manufactured? Is it no longer worthwhile to concern
ourselves with what is soulish, since it is ultimately nothing
but impulses coming from our cerebral neurons? Must the
glorious elevation of the soul in the Romantic Age now be
reduced to the simplistic literalism of our digital age?

Or perhaps there is quite a different possibility. It is as
impossible to turn the human soul into a thing as it is to nail
soup to a wall. Is the de-emphasizing of the soul a modern
phenomenon, since what is soulish can neither be quantified
nor dissected? What, then, does this mean for psychiatry and
psychology as sciences of the soul? Have they simply lost their

1. Fragment 45, modified by H. Diels 1985

object, or does an entity with the qualities of soul require a different approach?

Such questions must be raised at the beginning of this book, because in the mainstream of psychiatry, the human being is considered "soul-less." Anything "soul-like" is seen either in material terms, or is viewed as an unimportant side-product of energy processes. Psychology (literally, the study of the *psyche*, or soul), and psychiatry, the treatment of the soul, have largely evolved into applied natural sciences. While there still is, here and there, some esteem for what is soul-like, hardly any place for the soul is made available in the leading professional textbooks, or in scientific psychiatric publications.

This attitude rests on the accurate scientific observation that the soul cannot be studied and measured like an organ or any other localized object. The brain, rather than being an "organ of the soul," is now seen as an extremely complex regulatory apparatus. It is, therefore, not surprising that what is soulish has lost significance in proportion to the degree that the brain has gained in significance.

Yet it is not possible to ignore the evidence of the qualities of soul in human life. Psychology and psychiatry must deal with the challenging experiences of the soul, or they will distance themselves from the human beings who seek their help. What, then, constitutes that which is termed soulish? How can a modern medical science of the soul that concentrates more and more on details of the neuronal requirements of human life deal with the painful experiences of people who seek help without turning their distress into a solely material affair? Must the scientific method make soul into an essentially unimportant side-effect of a cerebral process and thus a figment of an archaic imagination?

Here is where we must begin the discussion in this book: the premise that the decline of the traditional view of the soul is not the end of its history, but the beginning of a new chapter. While 'soulish' will not perish, the traditional picture of a soul-substance – an eternal essence that is not dependent on the body – must give way to new conceptions of what pertains to the soul, i.e., what is 'soulish.'

I propose the following theses: 1. people cannot be reduced to soulless functioning beings, even if the soul does not lend itself to being analyzed and turned into some sort of object; 2. the experience of being human remains a phenomenon that cannot be explained in terms of physics and chemistry; 3. the experience that presupposes "body"[1] and "life," but is more than anatomy and metabolism, has always been called 'soulish'; it manifests its various effects even when it is not produced or carried by something that is easily identifiable. The human race has tried repeatedly, without success, to define this "soul," to be able to reduce it to something else.

The history of our culture is full of attempts to add to the idea of soulish (i.e., whatever reveals the qualities of soul) a supporting substance that can be defined clearly.[2] Psychology and psychiatry have continually attempted to verify disturbances of the "personified" soul[3], but practical knowledge of it eludes direct observation. It is simply illogical for an objectifying science to try to analyze the experience of soul. Scientifically, we can examine only what human beings report *after* their experience, or how the experience manifests itself in bodily changes. Thus scientific scrutiny is always secondary to the experience and always arrives one step too late. It is only the subject himself who perceives what occurs and

---

1. (Translator:) The English language does not distinguish between what the German language describes as "Leib," the life-carrying body, and what it describes as "Körper" the purely physical features of the body.
2. See Ch. 2: "A Short History of the Soul."
3. See Ch. 3: "Diseased Soul?"

what he experiences, feels, or wants.[1] Internal experience cannot possibly be replicated from an external point of view. It consists of what I refer to in this work as having the qualities of soul (soulish).[2]

It would, however, be a mistake if we were not to attribute any power to the soul's experiencing simply because it is apprehended exclusively by its subject. Soulish phenomena clearly influence various biological and social circumstances, just as they also need a body and an outside world in order to realize themselves and find a means of expression. The power of the soul experience is most especially manifested in psychological and psychiatric treatment. Psychotherapy, for example, is largely based on having empathy for the pain, suffering, joy, desire and lust of those who seek help. Such empathy does not interfere with the experience of the affected persons, but seeks to reveal problematic emotional patterns, along with other, more beneficial ways of dealing with them. Psychological problems arise mainly because there is an irreconcilable contradiction between the experiential perspective and the ideals of an individual (intrapsychic conflict), or because the experiential viewpoint of one person cannot be reconciled with that of another important person (interpersonal conflict). These conditions will be illustrated using the examples of shame (social phobia) and dejection (depression) in chapters 6 and 7.

*Speechless Soul*

One might ask if it would be simpler to discard the idea of soul, and simply speak of "subjective experiences," "ego-con-

1. See Ch. 4: "The Body of the Soul is Emotional."
2. The consequences of this observation for the understanding of psychiatric illness will be presented in Ch. 5: "Overwhelming Self-Assessment – an Attempt to reach a New Understanding of a Feeling Person's Illness."

sciousness," or "mental condition," terminology that might not be seen as "backward." Any opposition to the concept of soul and the diverse associations awakened by it could then be circumvented.

However, ideas have their own history. They are not interchangeable like pieces of clothing. That which seems objectionable in the term "soul" is precisely that which makes it necessary. It emphasizes as no other term would the uniqueness and special quality of human experience (without, moreover, limiting experience to an "insight"). The concept of soulish (*seelisch*: having qualities of soul, or, less common: psychological) is historically linked with vegetative and animal aspects, whereas modern, surrogate concepts such as "subjectivity," or "ego consciousness" do not have the same appeal to our senses, and thus appear artificial.[1] They are rational attempts to get control of soulish experience by means of abstractions. They lack, so to speak, "the meat on the bone," and therefore are in need of a crucial element of the soul's quality, namely the primacy of direct experience, feeling and will.

The substituting of more reasoned words for "soul" does not seem to have come about accidentally. In the attempts during the Age of Enlightenment to identify soul with subject, we recognize the demands of modernism to promote a higher consciousness and to see the human being as a "spirit-soul,"[2] emphasizing spirit and consciousness. What was hidden in the soul was now to be brought to consciousness and ex-

---

1. (Translator:) The connotations of the terms "subjectivity" and "soul" seem to differ somewhat less in English than do those of "Subjektivität" and "Seele," both because "subjectivity" has less of a scientific flavor and because "soul" is rather less familiar than "psyche." In fact, Freud used mostly the terms "Seele" and "seelisch," whereas English psychiatry is more comfortable with "psyche" and "psychological."
2. (Translator:) The term "spirit," the closest translation of the German "Geist," tends to suggest a somewhat spooky connotation. In German, "Geist" is understood as something intellectual, whereas "soul" suggests feelings, impulses and wishes.

plained rationally. This enthusiasm for "enlightenment" arose concurrently with the idea of the human being as a subject capable of cognition, and it increasingly reduced the soul and the soulish to entities that were practically interchangeable with other objects. As a consequence of this nineteenth century attempt to reduce our inner life (along with our physical surroundings) to a few natural scientific laws, "soul" gradually became the technical expression "psyche." It was believed to be possible to examine it much like any physical event, such as the fall of an apple from a tree. The law of Fechner, according to which a certain increase of stimulus was required for every significantly increased intensity of perception, superseded the laws of Newton.

At the beginning of the twentieth century, psychoanalysis took a further step, when Sigmund Freud elected to view the psyche as a device. At first he, too, considered a mechanical solution. He envisioned the psyche as rather like a steam engine, a mechanism capable of usefully channeling the physiological drives, mainly sexual libido, with the help of the "ego" and "super-ego."

Eventually, both in- and outside of the realm of psychoanalysis, talk of the "Self" began to replace the apparently obsolete terms soul and psyche. In this way, immediate experience increasingly dwindled in importance, whether the Self was seen as the unconscious breeding ground of the ego,[1] or as a superordinate entity encompassing the ego.[2] In its place, to satisfy the desire for a comprehensive system, adding the experience of one's Self into the theoretical model soon gained in importance. Even the Enlightenment's image of the conscious subject, which had replaced the idea of the soul, could no longer maintain itself as a result of this development.

1. H. Hartmann 1964
2. C. G. Jung 1994

The claim that there was an ultimate, subjective knowledge faded and gave way to the thesis that even the processes of such perceptions are subject to the complex organization of the human organism.

Even further from the idea of soulish experience was a behavioral theory, developed in the middle of the twentieth century, which viewed the soulish as a black box that defied investigation. In line with the natural sciences, it restricted itself to what could be observed externally. According to prevailing behavioral theory, human beings act in response to specific external stimuli that impel conditioned responses even in the absence of conscious experience. This view establishes the human being as an organism primarily controlled by environmental conditions. Perception, feeling and will, if they have any role at all, are considered secondary phenomena. Since behaviorism, dismissing personal experience, is interested exclusively in observable behavior affected by varying environmental conditions, it claims to have an advantage, because its observations can be verified by including biological data and by linking human behavior with genetic or organic preconditions.

Behaviorism sees the human being as a stimulus-response system even when the biological preconditions of the organism are inserted as links between stimulus and response. As a result, its model is based on the idea that the organism responds predictably to certain environmental stimuli because of its biological structure and its conditioned learning; thus, for example, the creature, depending on its degree of hunger, pushes a certain pedal when it has learned that the action will produce food.

This view, which has increasingly been shaping modern psychology and psychiatry, does not include soulish experience. It does not take into account the fact that a human being can also attribute to a stimulus (such as the offering of bread and wine) a symbolic significance (such as the religious meaning of the Last Supper). Neither does it consider that "Aha!" experiences, or other *personal* experiences, will disrupt this stimulus-response pattern. It does not take these phenomena into account because that kind of disruptive personal experience cannot be reduced to a chain of externally observable events. Disorderly influences can also originate in the imagination, or they can be conveyed linguistically. However, the retreat of psychology and psychiatry from the idea of the soulish experience is consistent with their ongoing endeavor to display a scientifically objective quality in their statements. As a result, they are compelled to concentrate on the observable body and its behavior, and to turn away from the key experiences of the soul's life.

This sort of neglect of the qualities of the soulish, a predictable result of methodical materialism, should not lead to the erroneous conclusion that soulish properties do not have substantial content, no matter how easily the allure of a promising hypothesis might cause such a misunderstanding. Rather than being offered a new way to integrate the corporeal (the observable) and the soulish (the experienced), we are faced with a worldview that gives serious consideration only to what is corporeal, material. The threat of such a loss becomes even greater with the tendency to confuse the reality of soulish experience with a misunderstanding of the subjective, thereby reducing the experience, even in the sciences, to merely subjective views. It is no laughing matter that ever since the Age of Enlightenment, popular confusion of soul and subject has generated in scientists and even theologians as much fear of the concept of soul as the devil has of holy water. Soulish becomes suspect whenever one views the term as merely subjective or irrational, or whenever the impossibility of directly observing the experience of the soul is misunderstood as the lack of cooperation of the subject. One then discounts the soul and speaks of it as unsuitable for scientific understanding, or even as a carrier of soul-processes. In this way one can overlook the fact that soulish perception, feeling and will are not theoretical constructs like the term subject. They are a fundamental human experience that is just as real as the observation of an object, even if they cannot be visualized like a table, or observed through a microscope like a microbe.

> Soulish experience is unique in that it is not only sensual, but it also evokes meaning that cannot be grasped physically or by natural scientific means. As the philosopher Georg Schulte remarked, "My happiness and my pains are more real than all material reality, weightier than all the sand of the sea."[1] The soulish is closer to the arts than to sciences interested in a measured assessment of what is present, because the arts manage with words, sounds, colors, touch and movements to communicate a perception of experience, the kind that can elicit a similar soulish experience in the observer.

One characteristic of soulish experience is that it can be understood only through other soulish experience. It always comes as immediate experience, and can never be imitated or produced by even the most refined electronic instruments.

This characteristic of the soulish makes it impossible to believe that one could conceive it as equal to an activity of the brain or any other material processes. People who focus on their experiences see themselves from a different perspective than do those who observe brain processes, whether their own, or as patterns on a monitor. No soulish quality is seen in the tracings of the brain waves of an emotionally distraught human being, but the rendering of her emotional status in a

1. G. Schulte 2000, p. 234

painting, a poem, a film or a play might portray an intense conflict that comes far closer to soulish.

Ancient Greek philosophy equated life and soul, and contrasted both of them with the body. Thus Plato came to say that, "The body is the grave of the soul."[1] In modern times we find that existential philosophy equates life with *being* (German: *Sein*).[2] Erich Fromm separated this *being* that can only be experienced from a *having* that can only be appropriated like a thing.[3]

What I have and what I am – though both pertain to the same person – refer to two fundamentally different perspectives. In one case, the word designates what is physically observable: the human being has a body. In the other case, it indicates the soul's experience: I am that which I sense, feel or will. The difference between having and being, or body and soul, enables a distinction much like the sciences that are interested in whatever can be examined as objects. However, we, like the arts and the cultural sciences, respect the realm of the soul and work from personal experience.

In scientific texts, words related to presence are impersonal. There is no narrator who speaks using the term "I," who has experienced something; everything is presented as "it," following the desire to exclude any personal bias. On the other hand, the first person (the self) is central to the description of personal experience. Yet the two modes of speaking do not exclude each other. While they differ, they are nevertheless part of a common play of words that makes it possible to shift from the "I" that experiences to the "it" that is the subject of

---

1. In "Phaidon" it is Socrates who presents the image of the body as the prison of the soul.
2. (Translator:) 'Being' is a difficult philosophical term used primarily by Heidegger, referring to the creative support and origin of everything of which we have largely become forgetful. Here, however, I use it more in line with the connotations of Fromm's comment.
3. E. Fromm 2000

the report. This capability, however, presupposes that human beings have learned to understand themselves in symbolic ways. In this case, however, they are more than a body that is recognized by others and responds to environment stimuli. They also recognize themselves as experiencing persons, each an "I am" whose environment has given them specific names. "He/she has," and "I am," words that testify to having both bodily and soulish being, does not, in this case, separate the object into a dual entity nor clone it physically. Instead they create a symbolic unity of body and soul. Within the context of these symbolic images of speech, beings become able to understand themselves as persons who experience themselves simultaneously both as individuals *and* as members of a group or society.

In the twentieth century, few studied language as thoroughly and deeply as did Ludwig Wittgenstein, who developed a comparison of language and play. Play, as he pointed out, requires rules but offers an enormous variety of possibilities in their application. He illustrated this by using the picture of a European city, its center a swarm of small, narrow streets and town-squares, and at its periphery, suburbs with straight streets and uniform houses.[1] Just as with such a city that has grown over many centuries, we can also distinguish older and newer styles in language. Concepts that have developed throughout history – like the word "soul" – have undergone transformation and become multilayered, not unlike the irregular centers of old cities. The newer, geometrically planned suburbs, though, illustrate the more modern and sharply defined concepts of science. Wittgenstein remarks:

---

1. Wittgenstein: Philosophische Untersuchungen, p. 18

"Language is a labyrinth of paths: coming from one side, you recognize clearly where you are; yet coming from another side to the same point, you no longer know your way."[1]

Such an image may well describe those who have grown used to the terminology of the natural sciences and who, figuratively speaking, being accustomed to the suburbs, must now approach a building at the boundary of the interior city. They know their way as long as they can see the outer perspective, but after venturing into the interior city, when they come upon the same building they do not recognize it because they now see it from a different aspect. The well-known writer Max Frisch expressed this concisely in his diaries, stating, "The most unfamiliar viewpoint a person can experience is what is his own, seen from the outside."[2]

Now, what happens when the idiom of the inner district is gradually lost, and that of the sharply drawn outer districts takes over? What becomes of human beings when the expression "I am" is replaced in everyday life by the scientific, technological expression "it has"? Might this not explain the increase in those seeking the help of psychotherapists because they cannot relate to life as a "thing"? Could their pain be related to those models that are shaped not by human feelings, but instead reflect the statistical norms based on external observations of others? Is the increase in compulsive and manipulative behavior the effect of trying to avoid anxiety and sadness?

Walker Percy, prize-winning author of *The Moviegoer* raised similar questions in a literary form:

"There is an astronomer working at night on Mount Palomar. He observes, collects, shapes hypotheses, writes equations, makes

1. Wittgenstein: Philosophische Untersuchungen, p. 203
2. M. Frisch 1985, p. 111

predictions, scours the sky, corroborates findings and writes articles for astronomers. During the day he comes into the town in order to satisfy the requirements of his organism and as a social being; he eats, sleeps, enjoys wife, family and home, plays golf and takes part in other social and spare-time activities."

"He remains one of the more fortunate (and privileged) contemporaries, since he functions both like an angel (as scientist) as well as like an animal (as social organism)…"

"Yet what about the less privileged inhabitants of the town? What happens to human beings in the twentieth century who have to eke out a living without being able to participate in the sovereignty and authority of the sciences and art? How does it feel to be just a lay person and consumer? Do such consumers suffer from a sense of being deprived, even though they be the richest in history? What are the symptoms of this lack or deprivation?"[1]

Almost half a century has passed since Walker Percy wrote those lines. The situation he described has become more acute since then. It has become increasingly difficult to live a kind of a double life by neatly separating professional research and personal experience. Those in the sciences must find a way to integrate the observable body and the less visible soul that can be experienced. There are ever more human beings who sense that the drive only to consume and to own leads to a deficient state of the soul.

### The Human Being – a Message?

Nevertheless, this problem doesn't appear to present the greatest difficulty that our species has been challenged to overcome. Body and soul do not necessarily exclude each other, even though different perspectives are appropriate to

---

1. W. Percy 1995, p. 21

them. It is possible to work toward solutions involving potential links between these differing viewpoints. There have been earlier, encouraging attempts to do so. The physical body and the less easily defined soul have been viewed as two aspects of a "life-body,"[1] the physical body being its material, the soul its phenomenalistic aspect.

Is it possible that the stubborn resistance against the soulish has nothing to do with biology and natural science, but instead comes from an entirely different direction? Could it be that soulish phenomena incite competition from a science that seems quite similar to psychology but is, in truth, incompatible with it?

It is probably not an accident that the technical concepts that have evicted the soul from psychology and psychiatry originated within the cognitive sciences. The term "cognition," although not very precise, refers to "what can be recognized" (its Latin origin refers to conditional perception). It emphasizes reason over empirical experience. The cognitive sciences attempt to reduce experience to observable "spiritual" elements or fragments of information. These sciences have their origins in the first seminars on psychological research at the end of the nineteenth century. Experimental psychologists like Wilhelm Wundt were trying to explain the process of sensory stimulation and the appearance of thoughts by means of specific, informal rules. The orientation of this research caused the idea of the soulish to increasingly recede into the background in favor of units of information that could be pictured as some kind of "spiritual" atoms that could be isolated. This research trend achieved additional impetus in the twentieth century, and over the last few decades, computers have enabled an incredibly rapid growth of informational analysis,

1. Please see footnote 1 page 16.

thereby nourishing hopes of explaining human consciousness using models of artificial intelligence.

In the middle of the last century, Norbert Wiener, a pioneer in the field of computer science, stated this formula: "The human being – a message". This quote proclaims in the clearest possible way the liquidation of what is alive, turning it into consciousness, into knowledge about information. Since then we have seen the genome, viewed as the carrier of a person's information, deciphered to a large extent. Intelligent robots are widely used throughout the world in both business and science. Information no longer exclusively serves the need for communication between human beings, but is also used to advance the increasing independence of artificial systems, including machines that can, unassisted, develop themselves.

As Ray Kurzweil, a well known computer scientist wrote: "When we dare make the leap and position ourselves within our computer systems, we find that our identity begins to base itself on a constantly growing 'consciousness-bank.' Eventually, we will no longer be hardware, but software."[1] Cybernetic scientist Kevin Warwick, who allowed the implantation in himself of some computer chips, is convinced that man-made mechanical intelligence will one day surpass ordinary human intelligence. Therefore, he states, "We must become one with the machines, and thus partake of their power."[2] In these blends of human being and appliance we find that the dividing line between organism and machine has become fluid. In such an exchange of information, one is no longer sure where the human being ends and the apparatus begins. Yet along with the soul, the body is also lost if the self loses its sense of the limits perceived as the body. As

---

1. R. Kurzweil 2000, quoted from G. Kalberer 2000, p. 2
2. Quoted from G. Kalberer 2000, p. 2. Already in 1956, Günter Anders spoke of people becoming antiques. The "Promethean shame" felt by human beings in the face of the machines they've created allegedly leads them to try to become similar to the machines.

a result of moving away from soulish experience and turning to rational cognition in a virtual cyberspace, life itself
becomes artificial. Outspoken computer specialist John Perry
Barlow writes, "Nothing could be as deprived of body as is
cyberspace. It is as if everything of you were amputated."[1]
He envisages existence in cyberspace as being closer to the
existence of an angel than that of a human being. "When the
longing for human flesh ceases, what remains? The 'spirit,'
floating in the cybernet, floating in an ecology of electrical
tensions that is just as intent on and capable of keeping him/
her alive as was its carbon predecessor."[2]

In this kind of glorification of a body-less and soul-less
existence we can see reflected a new version of the Gnostic
teachings pertaining to the victory of the luminous spiritual
domain over that of dark, earthy corporeality. Barlow and
his fellow devotees of pure consciousness may represent but
a small, peripheral group of computer freaks, while the large
majority of computer users remain rooted in our earthy life;
nevertheless, the increasing sophistication of information
systems presents an enormous challenge. They touch on our
fundamental understanding of the human essence, because
along with soul and body, they question the very basis of
soulish identity and bodily integrity.

Considering this state of affairs, it does not seem accidental that there are more and more people reflecting on their
bodily/soulish experience and trying to appreciate it, in part,
through meditation. For it is in bodily soulish' experience
that meaning and sensuality are joined. The old German
word 'Sin' contains the sense of both sensual perception
and meaningful striving. However, what is perceived with
the senses and is filled with meaning cannot be reduced to

---

1. J. Barlow 1996, quoted from E. Käser 1998, p. 81
2. Ibid.

abstract consciousness. It does not limit itself to containing of information, and it cannot be achieved as a "virtuality." The significance of meaningful sensuality presupposes a body that experiences with bodily senses, and simultaneously produces soulish substance (felt sense). Nothing will oppose more fiercely any breaking down into digital information that which is human as will the experience of feeling and acting that is tied to the individual's body. Just as Gnosis (the experience of direct spiritual knowledge) was suppressed in early Christianity in favor of renewed emphasis on the sensual body – the physicality of the soul-infused body of the Christ – so today, in our era of computer-based information technology, it is the human physical experience that guards against the soulless image of the virtual human we see in computer screens.

### The Cult of Experience as a Counter-Movement

The significance of soulish experience in modern life becomes especially obvious in light of the growing culture of experience, in which the unemotional quality of even impressive technological "virtuality" is confronted by a hunger for more intense personal experience. A geometrically progressive increase in hazardous treks, extreme sports, stock market gambles, gambling itself, and talk shows that feature explosive emotions obviously expresses a universal longing for an intensification of experience. The modern world's hunger for experience is often glibly called a symptom of superficial craving for "happy events." However, this hunger also represents a powerful reaction against any process that reduces our society to the merely technical and rational, and thus can be viewed as a desperate attempt to amplify bodily experience rather than see oneself as a mechanistic unit that simply absorbs information.

Recently, a hypothesis pertaining to risk-compensation was developed based on the observation that humans require a certain degree of intensity of experience in order to feel comfortable. This hypothesis contends that one instinctively takes risks when one's sensory systems are insufficiently challenged. In other words, when the daily routine seems too casual, or perhaps too secure in terms of material needs, people may deliberately stir up risk to evoke a thrill. In this way, the sort of suspense found in movies is courted as a thrilling experiment in one's life; in order to experience oneself more intensively, the body is challenged to extreme limits in sports, or is even disfigured and decorated by piercing and tattooing. Who would have imagined forty years ago that people would voluntarily drop three hundred feet on a rope, brave torrents in rafts, climb the walls of skyscrapers, or steal from stores for sport? Whether by altering the body, using drugs, or unprotected sex, we see others try again and again to heighten their experience of life. The thrill that they seek corresponds directly to a bodily soulish experience, since physical stimulation and the soulish experience of danger result in a mixture of fear and pleasure. This hunger for intense experience, for a "high," does not arise casually. Indeed, seeking the intoxication and intensity of high risk threatens to become a way of life unless – according to Peter Sloterdiyk – such people are capable of sensing spaces within themselves of which physics know nothing.[1] When security based on one's foundation in life fails, and the traditional sense of how things came about can no longer be perceived, people begin to create a

---

1. Søren Kierkegaard remarked in 1849 on the phenomenon of desperately wanting to be oneself when there no longer is a sense of personal ground (or inner space).

sense of themselves in which external events are substituted for internal experience. These artificially provoked episodes of fear, pleasure and pain eventually can replace the kind of inward-directed search that once found heart's ease in the silence within.

This new way of searching for one's sense of being seems typical for an era characterized by mobility and flexibility, and in which continuity and faithfulness are no longer considered enduring values.

## From Social to Psychological Deregulation

Now, at the beginning of this new millennium, human beings of the industrialized West find themselves in an extraordinary situation; they have, in many ways, lost the certainty of living on an earth created by God and influenced by divine forces. Even their faith in a rational power that controls the events of the world with the help of wise, insightful beings has been shaken. More than anything else, they have been deprived of the social utopia in which it was hoped a universal, classless society would be established. Theories emphasizing the relativity of knowledge have replaced laws once thought eternally valid. Computer sciences have opened up a virtual space that lacks the familiarity and constancy of our previous everyday world. No longer is it possible to detect what is real on the television screen and what is fiction. Worse yet, other forms of modern communication create a world of information in which it is difficult to separate reality from illusion.

The postmodern human being is constantly confronted by the sense of an acceleration of time that no prior generation has known. While at one time it was the position of the sun or the ringing of church bells that regulated the rhythm of work and life, it is hours and minutes that count today. In sporting events, mere fractions of seconds determine success or failure. In travel, the factor of acceleration makes it a commonplace occurrence to cross numerous time zones in a single trip, something inconceivable in previous eras.

Thanks to the widespread electronic transmission of data, our culture has reached the kind of speed that effectively cancels space and time, because it is possible to exchange information instantaneously anywhere in the world. This ability to reach others electronically, irrespective of where they are or what time it is, has led to a state of affairs in which it is more of a luxury *not* to be available than to be constantly accessible.[1]

Such changes result in both admiration and fear. The global collection of data, impressive as it is, also results in the dread that the human being will increasingly be regulated from outside: medically, in terms of genetic code and bodily functions, commercially in terms of behavior at work or as a consumer, in leisure activities as well, and politically, in terms of social standing and position.

This technological and scientific revolution goes hand in hand with profound changes in the socioeconomic structure, and many people find themselves faced with demands for which they are insufficiently prepared. As a result, increased existential insecurity receives little help from an increasingly fragmented culture.

One who impressively describes the consequences of society's neo-liberal upheaval regarding the conduct and attitudes of its modern citizens is sociologist Richard Sennett. In his

---

1. (Translator:) The ease of contact has led to electronic devices for blocking direct accessibility. For example, a phone call is answered by a machine which asks what we want, and then offers a number of options. The caller responds by pressing numbers, and the machine then asks again and again for our patience because "All the agents are busy." We may eventually get to speak with a representative of the person we wanted to reach, who then insists that we tell him or her what we wanted, and so on.

book "Der flexible Mensch" (tr. *The Flexible Human Being*), with its very appropriate English title *The Corrosion of Character*, he uses the example of the USA, presenting data that prove how deeply the life plans of people in western industrial nations has changed over the past 25 years. Sennett points out that the professional career which traditionally shaped a person's occupational life "like a straight road" has broken down into short-term commitments, and that typically firm family and friendship ties have tended to increasingly drift apart. At the same time, he describes how workplace and home are losing their distinct meanings. Employment has become temporary, mostly a short-term enterprise. Work projects are limited, and increasingly undertaken without long term perspective. The values of continuity and loyalty in regard to one's profession and colleagues is replaced by the demand for flexibility, teamwork and rapid comprehension, which serve the pursuit of short-term goals and adaptation to a rapidly changing economy.

Sennett illustrates his theses not only with statistical data but also by using the examples of Enrico, a representative of the post-war generation, and his son Rico, who represents a younger generation (those 25 to 40 years old).

Enrico emigrated from Italy to the USA in the nineteen-fiftys. He realized the American dream, saving the money he made in cleaning jobs so he could buy a house in the suburbs of Boston. Living among his suburban neighbors, he remained a quiet, inconspicuous citizen. But when he returned to his historic Italian surroundings, he achieved considerable recognition as a man who had achieved a great deal in his world. He was a respected, committed father and family man who went to mass every Sunday. His life seemed quite predictable. He measured his success by the various additions and improvements that he was able to complete on his wood frame house. By the age of forty, he already knew when he would be able to retire and how much money he would have available when that day came. In order to plan his time in a useful way, Enrico required what Max Weber called a "Gehäuse," the kind of bureaucratic structure that allows one to navigate and control his course. "The system of his union wages and the regulation of his federal pension established in his case this firm structure... He had shaped for himself a clear life history within which he assembled his material and psychological experiences; in this way, his life took on meaning as a linear narration."[1]

However, things were entirely different for his son Rico, who followed the wishes of his father and became the head of a consulting firm. Rico despises people who, like his father, do as they are told and seek the protection of a bureaucracy. "Instead he is convinced that one must be open to change and to risk."[2] He graduated from a business school in New York and married a classmate. After graduation, he worked as a consultant in various firms in Los Angeles, Chicago and Missouri before establishing himself as an independent following a painful dismissal from his former position. In fourteen years of work he has moved four times. He tries, by means of electronic communication media, to establish the sense of community that he knew in his childhood, but he finds this online communication too short-lived and hurried. "The inconsistency of friendship and local community underlies the context of Rico's deepest concern, his family."[3] Though he is able to sustain himself successfully in his circle thanks to the flexibility he's developed, troubling questions arise when it comes to the education of his children. How will they be able to find themselves when the people they relate to change constantly, and they must move every few years? How can they develop faith in themselves and others if there is no permanence? The motto "Nothing is lasting," while a professionally rewarding attitude for Rico, sounds ominous to him now for the way it touches on the development of trust and of self-assurance in

---

1. R. Sennett 1998, p. 16f.
2. Ibid. p. 19
3. Ibid. p. 23

his children. He foresees catastrophic consequences if his work ethic – "Keep moving," "Don't get tied up in relationships," and "Don't make sacrifices" – were transferred to and applied by his family. "How can a human being weave his identity and life history into a coherent story while he is in a society that consists of short episodes and fragments? The preconditions of this new, modern, commercial organization favors far more the kind of experience that shifts in time from place to place and from one activity to another."[1]

In light of Rico's dilemma, Sennett concludes that capitalism based on short-term actions threatens especially those character traits that bond human beings to each other and provide the individual with a stable sense of self. More important than globalization and the diffusion of technology, he argues, are the consequences of the flexibility promoted by new economic structures and which profoundly touch the emotional life of human beings outside their workplaces.[2] His conclusions are echoed in Rico's words: "You have no idea how stupid I appear to myself when I tell my children of my obligations. For them, these are only abstract points, because they can't see them."[3]

Sennett's analysis of the upheaval in the workday and the everyday world is likely to be reflected in the average psychological problems of the population. There are also numerous indications that the way psychiatrists pose questions has been profoundly influenced by these socioeconomic changes. In Sennett's book we find Rico in psychological crisis because he fears his children will become emotional and ethical "drifters" or deteriorated spendthrifts. So far, no author has systematically followed, as Sennett did with healthy human

---

1. Ibid. p. 31
2. Ibid. p. 29
3. Ibid. p. 29

beings, the analogous conditions of psychiatrically ill human beings and their various ways of coping.

As far as my specialty in the treatment of depression is concerned, I find a noticeable shift in the relevant problematic issues during the past thirty years that cannot be ignored. On one hand, the number of cases of depression requiring treatment has increased dramatically; in the last ten years, the number of depressed persons treated in the Canton of Zürich, Switzerland, has doubled.[1] On the other hand, depressive symptoms today exhibit noticeably different expression than just a generation ago, which has also led to different therapeutic strategies.

The following two cases illustrate this impressive change:

In the seventies, I treated a man I shall call Peter, then 45 years old, who suffered from a severe depression. Peter blamed himself for being responsible for ruining his family. Thanks to a frugal lifestyle as a teacher in a high school, and with some secondary jobs, he had managed to accumulate substantial savings and so had, shortly before his depressive illness, obtained a mortgage and bought a home. The decision to buy a house caused him many sleepless nights, partly because he was able to separate himself from his place of origin only with a heavy heart, and partly because the real estate market seemed to him insecure. Though Peter was severely blocked and unable to experience either sadness or annoyance in his depression, it was not that lack, nor the low morale, but rather the severe problem of his guilt that stood in the foreground. He kept torturing himself by brooding over his decision to buy the house, and he was convinced in a delusional way of having driven himself and his family into ruin. He therefore interpreted his depressive affliction as justified punishment for his personal failure. None of the comments of his relatives who saw the purchase of the house as

---

1. The increase of treated conditions is also due to various populations' changes of attitude towards these ailments, and towards psychiatric treatment in general.

reasonable and right could change his mind. Because he believed
it reasonable that he alone had caused such misery, Peter did not
consider himself ill in a medical sense.

Only after Peter had gradually recovered (during inpatient psychiatric treatment) was he able to recognize what he had experienced as an illness. Yet even then he continued to believe that
he was the cause for it, and he considered the required therapy
to be his responsibility.

By chance, twenty-five years later I became acquainted with
Peter's 32-year-old son, who also suffered from severe depression.
He, however, did not question himself the way his father had;
for him, suffering from the depressive blocking was the primary
concern. He experienced himself as limited in his thinking and
his ability to remember, and complained of a profound loss of
feeling, diminished appetite, insomnia and absence of sexual
desire. Though the son considered any hope for improvement
to be illusory, he cooperated passively with all the therapeutic
approaches, and did not in principle question the diagnosis of
depression.

After many weeks, when he finally felt better, he wanted very
much to leave the pain and suffering behind him without
any introspection. He believed the depression was caused by
a chemical imbalance in the brain, and therefore accepted the
prescribed medication as a preventive measure that would reduce
the likelihood of any recurrence of the purely chemical malfunc-
tion. Some doubt, however, did surface: could his history and
his life circumstances have something to do with his depression?
Just prior to the depression, Peterson had to deal with a major
change in his job environment – could there be a connection?

This brief comparison of the depressive experiences of
father and son is meant to illustrate what one could call a
radical change in the manifestation of depressive suffering
from one generation to the next. In my experience, the usual
problem of guilt has increasingly given way to the dread of

being unable to experience and perform. The sense of personal responsibility and the self-referred depressive suffering that once were typical of depression have shown a tendency to recede in favor of a sense of "illness," with focus on the body. An increasing number of subjects consider the suffering experienced in their soul as a medical problem that should be removed by some manner of fast, effective treatment. Their disorder is increasingly seen as a genetic or biological phenomenon, which disturbs the patient's personal sense of responsibility far less than his ability to make decisions.

I do not mean to say that the problem of guilt has disappeared altogether. Even today, we can find depressive suffering similar to Peter's. Yet statistics show quite clearly that ideas of guilt, and especially forms of depression resulting from obsession with guilt, have diminished. In their place we encounter a growing population of those who approach the medical establishment with the expectation of being repaired. The individual's suffering distress is presented as a thing that demands a technological solution. Now the over-riding concern of the depressed is not the shattering of their hopes for achieving their dreams, but the fear that being blocked by depression is a disadvantage in some material way. At the same time, we see an increase in the number of people with less predictable depressive disorders. The latter often go hand in hand (as we have seen with the earlier case of Ms. S.) with personality problems related to a borderline disorder, presenting a combination of depressive and addictive problems in which the character problems and the dependency problems increasingly cover up the depressive picture.[1]

---

1. The concurrence of the abuse of alcohol, medications and drugs with depression increases the resistance of these disorders to therapy (H. G. Guscott and P. Grof 1991). A concise review of cultural influences on depressive disorders can be found in D. Hell 2002.

It thus appears that upheavals in our current society have left their mark in the shaping of depressive illness. There is abundant evidence for this conclusion: first, the more frequent occurrence of borderline symptoms (reflected in examples of living on the edge, unstable identity and frequent self injuries, as well as eating disorders) plausibly related to the increased adaptability demanded by business and our economy; next, the growing dependence on technology along with the diminution of the problems of guilt; furthermore, the growing emphasis on consuming and the increase in addictive disorders, along with rootlessness, and an increase in the number of illnesses. Viewing the social and psychiatric developments as being parallel is, however, much too one-sided, because different forms of suffering of the soul do not reflect merely the consequences of social development. They are also a protest, an outcry, the potential birth of a counter-movement that is no longer content to conform itself to external events. In the history of human thought there have always been individuals whose very suffering led to insights that energized their ability to emancipate themselves from the domination of mere social and biological events. We, too, can discover in modern forms of psychic suffering a protest against the prevailing norms, and though it is clearly linked to those norms, emphasizing them even as it simultaneously caricatures them, one must not overlook the fact than it is from just such suffering that the protest arises.

The manifestation of personality problems mainly characterized by instability and a diminished sense of identity due to periodic loss of ego boundaries is labeled as a borderline disorder.[1] This problem is clearly linked to an epoch that only

---

1. In 1991, the World Health Organization (WHO) designated as borderline those personalities with characteristics of continuing problems of emotional instability and unclear self image: "The inclination to enter intensive but unstable relationships can lead to repeated emotional crises with threats of suicide and self-damaging actions." (WHO 1991)

barely continues to hold a unitary view of the world, and in which there are fewer and fewer stable family structures. This epoch can also be seen as a time when people attempt to experience themselves as integrated persons, at least temporarily, by intensifying their experiences and relationships, hoping thereby to avoid a threatening sense of emptiness, or of the lack of meaningful history. The modern passion for physical slenderness is related to this, being a caricature of the ritual of "breaking bread" in a traditional family by seeking to oppose the intoxication of eating through the ascetic struggle for a new bodily consciousness. Even though it causes great suffering, widespread dependency on alcohol, medications and drugs draws attention to a consumer attitude in our society that reveals itself as a protest against the paradise promised by technology.

What points most directly to the mutinous independence of soulish experience is the greatly increased number of depressive disorders that have become the most frequent, most painful and costliest illnesses of our time. While economics and science push for a rational exchange of units of information, and while global commerce insists on unhampered transactions of material goods (because personal and national feelings appear to get in the way of free trade), we note that the depressive condition manifests as emotional numbness, but that the very suffering from this lack of feeling reveals a hunger for genuine experience.

That it is neither the intellectual nor the cognitive disturbances that seize the attention of modern human beings, but rather that emotional issues such as depressions have become the prominent disturbance of the postmodern human being seems a paradox of our times. In the misery of depressive emptiness a kind of longing emerges that cannot be appeased with information or fabricated data. The painful awareness of one's restricted feelings is set against the technological and virtual world that is, ultimately, unfeeling. The continually quickening pace of our era is countered by depressive incidents and the impairment of efficiency, both of which arise from a slowing of the mental functions required for problem solving. Is it surprising, in view of such a situation, that depressive distress has become the arch enemy of a society based on flexibility and mobility? No other disturbance unsettles the confidence of our epoch as painfully as this depressive blocking, which opposes the expected, rapid professional and private adaptation by demanding that the affected individuals simply slow down or stop.

> It brings to mind a well-known African fable that tells of a white explorer who each day, by means of additional pay, coaxes his African bearers to carry him to his goal more rapidly. On the fifth day, however, the bearers refuse to be persuaded to continue. Asked the reason for their refusal, they answer, "We walked so fast that now we no longer know what we are doing. We must wait until our souls have caught up with us again."

> The essential difference between the message of this fable and the events in a depression is that the depressed human being is not forced to stop by an insight, but by an intolerable physical reaction. This is very like the biblical story of Balaam, who keeps beating his donkey because he is determined to reach his goal, while the animal does not move, stopped by an obstacle Balaam does not see; similarly, our physical organism often seems to be aware of more than that which is recognized by human reason.

## A Rediscovery of the Soul

Utilizing the body's perceptive faculties makes excellent sense in times in which, thanks to technological virtuosity, we are presented the possibility of replication, making it possible that even the human being can potentially become a clone of him/herself. Being anchored in sensual perceptions and rooted in one's body takes on new importance in the face of arbitrary, almost casual, virtuality. There is a real need for sensuality and for sense experience, and its relevance is closely related to what was called, at an earlier time, *Gemüt* (warmth of feeling).[1] "*Gemüt*" (middle-high German "*Gemüte*," derived from "*Muot*" meaning bodily excitation or mood), meant originally to convey the totality of soulish experience and thought, and later, the seat of inner experiences and images as well. Thus *Gemüt* implies a penetratingly soulish experience, the sort of experience that constitutes the essential core of a human being. Other languages express the German term with *coeur* (French) or heart (English). Those who have heart, or *Gemüt*, are able not only to live intensely for themselves, they are also heartily linked to their world. Therefore, this "warmth of feeling," this "heart" represents an inner and outer unity that provides the person with a way to integrate both personal history and environment.

These days, we find the term *Gemüt* (heart) no longer fashionable. It is being replaced by expressions such as "affective level," "emotionality" and "mood." Yet none of these substitutes is able to render what is characteristic of *Gemüt*, namely what, for many, is at the very heart of their lives.

It is probably no accident that in times of rushed living and emphasis on performance the focus is less on *Gemüt* than on relearning goal-oriented features of emotions (that is, the essential intelligence of emotions).

---

1. (Translator:) "Gemüt," an essential, recurring word in this book, is one of the many terms that can be translated only with some approximation. "Warmth of feeling," or "a disposition with warmth of feeling" may come close. This, like a number of terms dealing with our subjective responses to our world – few of which I comment on in footnotes – challenges the reader to enter the world of a different culture while simultaneously becoming aware of a wider wealth of human experience.

During the past few years many psychological studies have addressed the significance of the role of emotional processes in understanding one's life. In these studies it was possible to demonstrate the emotional origin of many decisions and actions.[1] Clinical studies have shown that life cannot be mastered exclusively by the rational intellect. Thus, for example, it has been shown that the activity of reasoning (in the sense of processing information) is in no way sufficient for a realistic adjustment to life. Success in life depends much less on performance during academic examinations or a high intelligence quotient than it does on emotional maturity.[2]

Most of the studies that have followed the lives of university graduates for decades have disclosed the not too surprising fact that diplomas and high IQ's do not guarantee prosperity, status, nor happiness. The prestige of IQ tests has faded as far as social competence is concerned. What seems far more important is personal intelligence supported by *Gemüt*, that is, warmth of feeling, or, in a word, heart. This combination helps in understanding others' motivations and learning how to work cooperatively with them. The intrapsychic capacity for a well-tuned, appropriate model of oneself is essential, and it is based on a well-differentiated feeling function.[3] Neuropsychiatric case histories of brain-injured patients have shown quite clearly that logical skills alone are insufficient in saving one from feelings of helplessness. Neurologist Antonio Damasio, his wife and a group of co-workers spent several decades studying the consequences of prefrontal and right-sided brain-injuries.[4] Patients injured solely in those regions showed normal linguistic behavior, unimpaired memory and good performance in the standard intelligence tests, but they were impoverished emotionally, and were frequently socially inappropriate and unable to make practical decisions in

---

1. An introductory review can be found in L. Ciompi 1997, p. 93f.
2. An example is offered in a long-term study of 450 young people by J. K. Felsman and G. E. Vaillant (1987)
3. D. Goleman 1996
4. A. R. Damasio 1997

their lives. Particularly impressive is Damasio's description of a patient who, in spite of his high IQ, was no longer able to appropriately evaluate social conditions and so, for example, often failed to fulfill prior agreements, or to meet people with whom he had scheduled a meeting.

These and other observations have contributed to the concept of "emotional intelligence." The fact that this notion spread like wildfire is not entirely due to Daniel Goleman's successful book on the subject. Rather, the idea, as well as Goleman's book of that title, met the needs of a culture based on rational organization but seeking relationship to the senses and the emotions. The very expression "emotional intelligence" speaks of the combination of emotion and reason, feeling and intellect, as if they were sorcerer's words; notice, however, that in the verbal formulation feeling is secondary to intellect. Feeling must be seen as intelligent, so its irrational side is pushed offstage. Emotionality thereby loses its true value; it no longer stands for itself, but is forced to serve a rational goal.

To provide the condition for a rebirth of the warmth of feeling and heartfulness of *Gemüt*, one must understand that emotions are more than painful and pleasant reactions that serve a need to survive. It is simply inadequate to add to intellect and reason an emotional intelligence believed to regulate human experience successfully.

To feel means one is involved in something.[1] During any heartfelt experience, one finds a degree of familiarity that no rationality can ever provide. Only our emotional attitude toward the world, toward the "thou," and toward ourselves can establish the identity and uniqueness that is ours, and no other person's.[2] This highly personal experience cannot be grasped logically.

1. A. Heller 1987, p. 33
2. C. Meier-Seethaler 1997, p. 170

It is the soulish experience that makes a human being human, and even natural scientists are guided in their everyday life by personal experience, as much as their theories might maintain this to be an illusion. Inward experience makes it possible for all of us to become aware of a personal consciousness, the unmistakable center of personhood. Neither brain potentials nor any other objectified, neurobiological factor can separate us from the flow of phenomena, and only conscious, inner experience will transform mere physical existence into an occasion of happiness or suffering.

Yet what is soulish today no longer fits yesterday's definition. Today's view must come to grips with the shadow of nihilism. What is soulish today cannot claim to be either transcendentally nor concretely absolute. Natural science and postmodern society join in avoiding any firm point of view.

Modern science presents us with "a view from nowhere," attempting to see things objectively, i.e., just as they are, independent of any specific perspective. This way of seeing also demands that one consider the relative aspects of whatever is perceived by each subjective human being. "We flee from anything subjective, driven by the conviction that all that exists must exist *as such,* namely, independent of any emotional perspective. To be able to achieve this by distancing ourselves farther and farther from our personal perspective is the unattainable ideal toward which our endeavor for objectivity is directed."[1]

This "view from nowhere" is an abstraction. While that does not exclude a concrete perspective, it nevertheless means it exists only in correspondence to other perspectives, and so is relative. Yet it is just such relativizing that demands we make allowance for a real understanding of the soul. One cannot expect that the soul can be caught like an image in

1. T. Nagel 1991, p. 119

a mirror. The long list of theological, psychological, psycho-analytic and neurobiological attempts to establish a reliable image of the soul can fairly be seen as fruitless. In effect, the positivistic mirror of the soul is shattered. Recognizing the failure to establish a dependable representation of the soul, we must resume the search at the point where the soulish manifests itself: in personal experience. However, one must not attempt to do this by positing the representation of the experience as something absolute, but rather by carefully avoiding the temptation to draw sharp lines, instead paying close attention to the boundaries in which the soulish shows itself in all its diversity. This manner of experiencing what makes each person unique and different should not be allowed to play a secondary role in psychology and psychiatry. It must not be swept under the carpet in favor of observable behavior and measurable organic change.

In this book I shall try to do justice to the soulish by working from the assumption that it is *personal experience,* and by examining it through its individual, social and biological effects.

*Suggestions for the Reader*

The first part of this book offers a review of the historical development of the understanding of psychiatric illness, and it tries to show in a "short history of the soul" the stages through which the understanding of the soul has gone in the West. The different ideas about the soul that developed are not dusty history, for they exert an influence to this very day. Knowledge of them helps us to better understand the various aspects of psychological illness. This will be illustrated with individual cases at the end of Chapter Two.

The second part of the book presents fundamental reflections pertaining to the understanding of the soul, and explores the biological and social prerequisites of soulish experience. It also deals with the connection that exists between the manifestation of psychiatric suffering and the cost of soulish experience. The product of these reflections is a concept of illness based upon emotional experience and the evaluation of its significance.

In the third part, the theoretical considerations will find their practical application in examples of the problem of shame and depression. This is not an arbitrary choice. The shame that often accompanies the stigma of psychiatric problems, and the view of depression as a "discouraged heart (*Gemüt*)," not only represent additional complications, they also express the kind of emotional judgements that are characteristic of the era. The book ends with a review of the arguments to address once more the viewpoint of a late postmodern understanding of the soul.

The three individual parts are written so that they can be read separately. One is not required to read the historical development in part One to understand the conceptual development in part Two. The practical application in part Three illustrates the basic concepts employing examples of modern disorders; this, too, can be read as an independent entity. All the chapters are concluded with summaries. While in chapters Two to Four some fundamental questions are addressed from the aspects of both the cultural and natural-scientific viewpoints, chapters Five to Seven are reserved for setting forth the practical challenges of everyday life. Part Two separates a more theoretical chapter Four from a primarily practical chapter Five. In this way, readers who are oriented primarily to practical application will be able to approach the subjects in a less logical manner.

*Part I:*

*Historical Development*

In order to become aware of time and to be able to
speak of time, one must be aware that something
has changed. And one must be aware, too, that in
or behind this change there is something that was
there before.

– Peter Høeg

# Chapter 2.
# A Short History of the Soul

*Symbols of the Soul*

In his philosophical investigations, the Austrian philosopher Ludwig Wittgenstein argues that there is no private
language for the internal experience of the soul, and that we
can describe such perception only by employing the values of
everyday speech. However, this everyday speech is based on
the observations of others, and is therefore based on an external perspective. So it is impossible, according to Wittgenstein,
to convey directly one's personal experience; this implies that
one must remain on the irregular ground of a given language
and grapple with a mind that is bewitched by artificial concepts. He emphasizes that what cannot be said renders words
useless, and that one can only allude to an experience by
stating clearly that which can be said.[1]

Wittgenstein concludes: "One must remain silent regarding
things one cannot talk about."[2] This oft-quoted conclusion
does not devalue the unspeakable, nor does it exclude personal
experience. Yet it is clearly states the fact that our immediate

1. Tractatus logico-philosophicus 4.115
2. Ibid. 7th section

perceptions cannot be captured by means of a description. In 1931, Wittgenstein stated: "The unspeakable (that which appears mysterious to me and which I am unable to put into words) may offer the background against which that which I was able to say gained significance."[1] This thought parallels the sort of language used by mystics; by means of what can be said, it evokes an image that refers paradoxically to that which is unspeakable.[2] In effect, this approach offers a mental image to convey foreground that will also point to what is hidden in the background; a the same time, what is hidden in the background is essential to the meaning of what is in the foreground. In this way, Wittgenstein manages to remain silent regarding the unspeakable, allowing it to find expression in a form antithetical to the speakable.

It is possible that being restricted to the "speakable" may also have influenced the earliest views of the soul. Initially, terms such as soul (the Greek *pneuma*, or Hebrew *ruah*) were not intended to convey an immaterial substance, but rather something visible about the living human being, such as the breath that ceases when one dies. The Hebrew term *ruah* and the Greek word *psyche* both represent breath. The German term *Atem* is related to the ancient Indian term *atman*, which is also used to indicate the soul. Thus the history of expressing the idea of a soul does not begin with a spiritual message of soulish experiences. Its origin is more closely related to precise observations of living and dying human beings. Soul, therefore, did not necessarily refer to something spiritual or transcendent. Yet it is also likely that from the very beginning, any talk of a soul (*psyche, ruah,* or *atman*) was not understood solely as an observable, concrete indicator of life; the terms achieved as well an additional, metaphorical meaning. Later

---

1. L. Wittgenstein 1977
2. (Translator:) The word "unsagbar" carries a slightly more negative connotation of the English "unspeakable," indicating something so ugly or scary that one cannot mention it. Here the word is used in its immediate sense, referring to something that cannot be put into words.

use no longer describes the soul as the observable breath of a human being. Instead, the soul comes to express something that is alive, a symbol of life. As symbol, the concept of soul reflects not only a given concrete reality, it also becomes part of the world of language which can carry imaginary forms.

> This does not occur arbitrarily. Symbolic speech is based on principles that allow one to say in an understandable way the things that are possible given the current rules of a particular language. The French psychoanalyst Lacan described as a "symbolical treaty" that which establishes the limits of what can be said, just as concrete objects limit the use of words describing them. But in contrast to descriptive terms for concrete objects, symbolic language has a broad scope that permits statements that differ from one culture to another, as well as from one epoch to another, and that separates itself in different ways from what is "unspeakable."

The history of the soul can be read as a series of attempts, influenced by the cultures of those times, to put the experience of life into words. What is accepted in one cultural setting may seem to be rejected in another. Individual experience can never be fully expressed in words, and personal experience can never be separated completely from the cultural background in which it is rooted, and by which it is shaped. "Words gain their meaning only in the flow of life."[1]

Wittgenstein was also of the opinion that philosophical examination of languages had a therapeutic function: that of cleansing oneself of misunderstandings and ideas that, on the basis of linguistic analysis, are untenable, so one could then expose oneself to the "unspeakable." In the beautiful and mysterious language of Wittgenstein: "My sentences make sense when he who understands me recognizes the words as senseless after, as a result of them and on top of them, he has

---

1. L. Wittgenstein, Werkausgabe (Published Works) Volume 7, p. 468

climbed beyond them. One must overcome these sentences; only then does one see correctly."[1]

Does the same system apply to those ideas that pertain to the soul? Are they the rungs of a ladder that one must discard after using them to climb? Do the portrayals of the soul in various epochs and cultures represent ever new attempts to get closer to the "unspeakable"? What if they are indispensable in directing our attention to the goal and the journey to the goal, but a hindrance to reaching the goal that will allow us to make progress on our own journey?

In presenting a brief overview of the historical development of ideas pertaining to the soul, I do not intend to assess the different individual views, nor to play one against another. Instead, I wish to present them as individual creations that attempt in different ways to convey basic human experiences by means of visual images. Just as a work of art cannot be judged by criteria of right or wrong, but must be viewed in terms of whether it appeals to a person or not, we can appraise linguistic images of the soul by how powerfully they touch a person. In this way we will find that diverse ideas of the soul can be either quite helpful and stimulating, or rather foreign and strange.[2]

## Representations of the Soul

The oldest known portrayals of the soul express in powerful images the vitality of human experience. In addition to the soul being described as "breath," history shows that the

---

1. Tractatus logico-philosophicus 6.54
2. Along with the primary and secondary references cited, Hans-Peter Hasenfratz's theological book "Die Seele" (tr. *The Soul*, 1986), as well as Charles Taylor's socio-psychological treatise "Quellen des Selbst" (*Sources of the Self*, 1996) were of great help. The important work of Austrian psychiatrist Hartmut Hinterhuber, which seems closest to my concerns, was published too close to the original printing of this book to allow for any comments.

experience of soul was quite early associated with a bodily organ or a concrete living being. Thus the soul is frequently shown in animal form and as an altered human shape (a "living corpse," for example).

Among the early illiterate cultures, it is the tribe of the Ugren,[1] residing east of the Ural mountains on the shores of the Ob, that has been researched most thoroughly, making them quite relevant to my introduction into the linguistic world of the soul.[2] The Ugren people had different images of the soul, all with concrete form, such as a bird, a turkey, or the shadow of a living human. In fact, the diversity of the tribe's images resulted in the formation of different, coexisting ideas of the soul.

The natural experience that the influence of a person on others does not immediately fade after his or her death is portrayed by the image of a "shadow-soul," which corresponds to a "death-ghost" who remains as "living corpse" (or grave-soul), mainly around the grave or in the vicinity of the deceased's previous range of activities.

The realization that human beings can have various experiences in dreams while visibly being completely motionless finds expression among the Ugren in the image of a "wandering soul." When the person is awake, this sort of soul dwells in the head in the shape of a bird or a mosquito and, when the person sleeps and dreams, it leaves in order to roam around.

A third form of experience among the Ugren finds its pictorial expression in the image of an "external soul," most often in the shape of a turkey. This soul lives in the vicinity, mainly the forest, while the person is awake; when he falls asleep, this external soul flies to him. This "external soul" symbolizes the relationship of the living human being to his

---

1. (Translator:) Ugren is the German term; no comparable English term was found.
2. H.-P. Hasenfratz 1986

or her surroundings, and if it is killed, the person related to it dies, too. One might ask oneself, as the theologian Hasenfratz did, whether modern people would misuse and destroy nature as thoughtlessly, if they retained the image of an "external soul" as the environmental component of their personality.

The Ugren's fourth category of the soul is also the most modern, namely the one that survived all the way to the social structure of our times and is still present in the ideas of many contemporary people. This "ego," or "vitality soul" that the Ugren associated with the breath (therefore also called "breath soul") reflects the experience of one's self, of a center of emotional forces as well as reason. Though we, if we still believe in a "soul," are most likely to relate this sort of soul to the brain, the Ugren localized it in the hair of the scalp. For this reason, they were intent on scalping their enemies, so depriving them of the possibility of being born again by capturing what they viewed as linked to the personal soul (while we restrict ourselves to simply wishing that our worst enemies would drop dead).

In our culture we have inherited bodily soul images that existed in similar ways in other primitive tribes; we find them mainly in traditional fairy tales and fables. In German stories, for example *Grimm's Fairy Tales*, there is a profusion of animal figures and celestial and underworld beings such as witches and trolls that ultimately symbolize corporeal images of souls. Granted, it requires considerable effort and exploration if we want to grasp the wisdom that such sagas and fairy tales contain. As we have become "sophisticated" human beings, shaped by the education provided by a scientific-theological age, we have largely lost our access to such somatic representations of the soul.

This is related to the fact that ideas of the soul, in the high culture of the West as well as of the East, have largely been freed of any corporeality. The soul is no longer a bird. Even the "spirit" in form of a living corpse appears nowadays only in a miserable horror movie. Yet the power of verbal impressions of the body has continued to shape our modern images of the soul.

Humanistic psychology thus offers such expressions as "parental ego" or "child-ego," thoroughly personified aspects of the soul that keep working in us and influence our inner lives. However, such concrete images are no longer seriously viewed as actual living beings, but rather as metaphors for symbolic images. They can nevertheless be imagined as internalized presences with whom a dialogue is possible, even when in fact they mostly serve to unite learned attitudes and ways of thinking as a single factor. This applies similarly to graphic depictions of a "starter within myself" that keeps pushing me to maximal performance, of a "protector within myself" that rejects excessive demands, thus seeing to it that I do not overdo, or of the "child within myself" that needs protection. All such metaphors have retained their power because our language draws on bodily experiences. Even the language of natural science cannot ignore its roots in the personified sphere of life when immunology speaks, for example, of killer cells and helper cells.

Therefore it is probably more correct to say that physical representations of the soul have been turned into symbols, rather than to assume that they have vanished altogether. By turning them into symbols, however, a radical change occurs: the soul as a tangible portrayal of a living being now gives way to an abstract, symbolic image of what is soulish, i.e., reflects the soul.

## The Soul as an Organ

Another line of development follows depictions of the soul from the point of being seen as a complete living being to where it is expressed through the image of a specific organ of the person. Considering the Ugren, we met the idea of the soul as a bodily organ, for example in the image of the scalp that incorporates the life forces. Among early Germanic tribes it was primarily blood that assumed an outstanding role as substance and carrier of the soul. In the blood brotherhood rite of the Germans, two persons would intermingle their blood, thus establishing a bond in which they placed their entire personal *beings*. Blood remained a very "especial juice" with Goethe; as Faust deeds his soul to the devil, he signs the pact with his blood. The similarity between Goethe's Faust and the old Germanic blood bond lies in the fact that in the old traditions the soul actually resided in the blood, whereas the so called enlightened people were able to see blood only as a symbol of life. Yet the persistence of the archaic traditions was revealed with unspeakable barbarity during the Nazi Reich when the blood myth again became very real as part of the glorifying of the "Aryan race."

In the Old Testament, blood is the carrier of the life force:

"For the soul of the flesh is in the blood...
therefore I speak to the sons of Israel:
Each of your souls must not eat blood
Because the soul of all flesh, his blood is with his soul."[1]

In the earlier texts of the Bible, we find that soulish functions are attributed to a large number of body parts. The heart, for example, is the seat of "spiritual attunement" and inner center of the person. Solomon speaks thus: "Only the

---

1. Lev. 17.11 – 17.14 (according to the Buber/Rosenzweig translation)

heart knows about the bitterness of itself. And a foreigner is unable to intrude in its happiness." (Sayings 14.19)

The image of the heart as seat of the soul is common also in the Christian West, for example in the widely known blessing: "May the peace of God protect your hearts and senses." Jesus of Nazareth taught: "Do not store up for yourself treasures on earth, where moth and rust destroy... For where your treasure is, there your heart will be also" (whereby the heart is understood as the soulish center of a human being).[1]

In keeping with this description of the soul as an organ, we find that the Judaeo-Christian tradition hardly ever imagined a separate life of the soul after death. On the contrary, in that tradition human beings must resurrect at the time of the last judgment as complete organisms in order to truly live. In early Judaic times, the bones of the dead were collected in special containers so that they would be available together at the time of the resurrection. Why especially the bones? One reason is that they are exceptionally durable. Yet a deeper reason might be that the bones were seen as being tied to soulish emotions with the value of "organ souls." Thus we hear that bones, in the sayings of the Psalms, are able to "die of thirst,"[2] "become frightened,"[3] "rejoice,"[4] or be "burned by fire."[5]

The Judaeo-Christian understanding of the soul is not exhausted with the image of "organ-souls." In Biblical texts we find further developments in imagery of the soul. Quite early, the soul is understood to serve also as the nucleus of a moral personality. As a result, there is a close connection between the image of the "body soul," ethical behavior, and the demand of the deity. Not only are the people expected to follow Moses' commandments, they are also to commit themselves

1. Math. 6.19 – 6.21 (according to the translation of the International Bible Society)
2. Psalms 31.11
3. Ibid. 6.3
4. Ibid. 51.10
5. Ibid. 102.4

to the care of their fellow human beings, especially the weak and the orphans:

> "Whoever is hard on the weak sneers at He who created him. Honor him who favors the one in need, thus says a saying of Solomon."[1]

The interpersonal and moral questions raised in the Bible find probably their most moving portrayal in the story of Job. He whom God allows to be afflicted with diabolical suffering fights for justice. He argues with his friends as to what degree doing the right thing and soulish well-being belong together. Job reproaches God for causing the righteous to suffer ("like a slave he longs for shade"[2]) and for no longer being on the side of the unhappy and offended. From this it becomes clear that according to the story of Job, well-being and justice are at least partly independent of each other, for reward does not necessarily follow good actions. He who does the right thing receives no bonus. God allows the sun to rise over both the just and the unjust, and worse, He also allows the just to suffer.

The extraordinary quality of Job thus is shown less by his correct behavior than by his steadfastness in face of the suffering he endures. Job not only rejects the view of his friend that his suffering should be viewed as punishment for prior failures, he also disputes the idea that his suffering is a trial sent by a tyrannical, ruling deity.

In the story of Job, the "genuine heart" manifests itself in his holding fast to ethical values – even while suffering – as well as in his insisting on a given promise. The proper attitude toward the unfortunate and offended, and a fair-minded relationship to one's neighbor, now become fundamental issues of human beings trying to understand themselves.

---

1. Saying of Solomon 14.31 (according to the translation of Buber/Rosenzweig)
2. Job 7.2 (Ibid.)

In view of this ethical dimension, the distinction between bodily and soulish suffering becomes of secondary importance. In the language of the Bible we find that the soulish is always included in bodily pain. The Bible sees no clear separation between body and soul, even though at certain places either bodily or soulish aspects of suffering may appear in the foreground. The Bible appears committed to the idea of an holistic "aliveness" in the sense of a "body soul." This bringing together of bodily perception and soulish experience finds expression in formulations such as "a stubborn, discouraged or defiant heart," or "a happy bone."

We do observe a difference between the Judaeo-Christian understanding of this essential point, and ideas that developed in the ancient Greco-Roman period (as well as in the advanced cultures of Asia). Both have influenced our current understanding of the soul, a development that will be taken up in what follows, by considering the example of ancient Greece.

## The Rational, Eternal Soul

Because of the lack of written documents, one can only speculate about the origins of all conceptions of the soul in the time preceding the classic Greek epoch. However, in the Homeric epics we can still find presentations of the soul that reflect animistic ideas. Thus the "psychai" (Gr. souls) in the last song of the Odyssey are portrayed as bustling and fluttering like bats. They leave the dead body through the mouth or an open wound and follow Hermes, the guide of the souls to the nether-world, in the guise of shadows, breaths, or smoke figures. When Odysseus descends to Hades, he offers them blood to drink, strengthening them with this juice of life so that he is able to converse with them on a person-to-person basis.

It is only with the pre-Socratic philosophers of early classical Greece that we find a tendency to oppose to the material body – or bodily images of the soul – a uniform and more abstract image of soulish forces.

> It must be stressed in this regard that in the period preceding classical Greece, there was just as little distinction between body and soul as in the Old Testament. We modern mortals, however, experience considerable difficulties thinking of the material body and the spiritual soul as one. This comes from our tendency to picture the body as soulless and the soul as immaterial. The preconditions for this modern picture of the soul were developed in Greece.

The pre-Socratic nature philosophers searched for a unified explanation of nature and the soul. Just as in Judaism, the entire world was seen as having been created by *one* God, so the earliest Greek philosophers, Thales of Miletus (ca. 625-547 BC), Heraclitus (550-480 BC) and other pre-Socratic thinkers searched for *one* origin of nature. They first believed they had found the principle that unifies nature in water (Thales), then in fire (Heraclitus), or in other elements. The general search for a comprehensive explanation was more important than the particular choice of element, though, so the disparities took a backseat to the focus on a singular unifying principle rather than the various theories.

"One and the same is what is alive and dead, and what is growing and sleeping and what is young and old; for one changes in the other, and the other again changes into the first," writes Heraclitus[1] . He cites the *Logos* as the highest principle. With *Logos* Heraclitus apperceives a universal law that underlies all happening.

---

1. Heraclitus 1965, p. 29

This tendency to abstract and to unify, characteristic of pre-Socratic philosophy, also includes an understanding of soulish perception; psyche becomes an essential factor of life. The soul no longer is a figure imagined to live inside and outside of the body. Thus the soul is not a separate body, a specific organ, a "breath," nor a "shadow," it is an expression of the whole, part of a universal truth. The soul can therefore no longer simply leave the body, and no longer is it capable of appearing to the living as a "death-spirit" (as, according to Homer, the deceased Patroklos, who continued to appear to his friend, Ulysses).

Within certain limits, the soul in Heraclitus' thought becomes *Logos*[1]: "The soul owns the logos, which increases by itself." Whatever possesses the qualities of the soul turns into the legitimate, formative principle that to some extent becomes accessible to our cognition. "If one intends to speak with reason, one must strengthen oneself with what is shared by all."[2]

Rational truth became the dominant theme of classic Greece. It was Socrates and his disciples who developed this subject to its highest point, and Plato pushed this comprehensive thinking to the point where his image of the soul transcends any temporal limits. In the soul he saw motion that moves itself. "When that which moves itself is nothing else but the soul, this leads to the necessary conclusion that the soul is neither something created nor something mortal."[3]

Yet inasmuch as he categorically attributes to the soul the capacity of grasping immortal ideas, Plato also concedes to the soul, and especially to the soul's upper layer (*nous*), the possibility of becoming an observer of that which is behind what exists, and of grasping its laws. However, to be able to

---

1. Fragment 29, quoted from H. Diels 1985
2. Ibid. Fragment 24
3. Phaidon 246 a (quoted from H.-P. Hasenfratz 1986, p. 63)

see the ideas in their full purity, the soul must not allow itself
to become corrupted by the body. With this comment Plato
separates the ultimate essence of the soul from the body. He
compares the soul to something like an ideal external guardian of our bodily existence. This guardian can do justice to its
task only by distancing itself from all bodily greed.

It was overlooked for a long period that it only became
possible through Plato's teachings on the soul to objectify and
make concrete an external perspective of what is corporeal
and, along with this, all that exists. As long as there was not
a strict separation of body and soul, that is, as long as what
was body was seen as soulish and what was soulish was seen
as bodily, it was only the gods who could observe human life
from the outside. Thus there was no human authority that
participated in establishing the lawful and proper ideas that
ruled the world. With the Platonic conception of a soul that
was a sort of external guardian of heavenly origin, a separation was created between what existed bodily (ruled by laws)
and the absolute world of ideas. This doctrine, transmitted
by way of the Roman empire, profoundly influenced (in a
somewhat popularized form) the Christianity of the Roman
church. Thus our occidental view of the soul is unthinkable
apart from this Platonic influence. It was only with Platonic
philosophy that the image of a uniform, immaterial soul,
distinct from the material body that is *not* uniform, arose in
the occident.

### How did the First Upheaval in the Understanding of the Soul come about?

The "first revolution of the soul" may be described as the
departure from an integrative body-soul conception to the
separation of body and soul. How did this come about, a

division which imprinted on the occident for more than two thousand years the thinking that even today is hard to overcome? We can think of several explanations. It is certain that the deeply rooted image of a body-soul unity was not dissolved by something like a mutation. Quite the contrary; the image of a body-soul wholeness continued to exist at a subcultural level even while the classic Grecian doctrine prevailed, and during the Middle Ages it resurfaced in cultural consciousness.

From the viewpoint of social history, this separation of the "body-soul" into a body and a soul occurred during the transition from matriarchally to patriarchally organized cultures. In this transition, the holistic and natural way of thinking is devalued in favor of a rational, supernatural perspective. Worshiped no longer are the fruitful soul and the mother-goddess, but rather the eternal laws and the all-powerful father in heaven. With this came a tendency that had existed two thousand years before Christ in all the high cultures of the Near and Middle East. It no longer explained natural phenomena as unforeseeable consequences of the arbitrary actions of the gods, but instead defined them with concepts and explained them abstractly.

This profound transformation was probably given a strong boost some thousand years before Christ by the introduction of new forms of information and management. For around that time a new system of numbers, the so called "positional number system," was introduced, replacing the stringing together of equivalent numbers. The new system, which is still in use today, provides the individual numbers – for example 1, 2 and 3 – different values depending on their position in a row of numbers (for example 123 or 321). A number can increase its power depending on its position by a factor of $10n$ (in the first Babylonian system of numbers, even $60n$). Thanks to this system of numbers that favors calculations, it became possible to include in one's calculations quite large amounts of data. Simultaneously, however, the individual and material dwindled in importance compared to the calculable and abstract (that is, positional).[1]

It is probable that even greater influence on the spread of rational thought was exerted by the introduction of the alphabet, which closely preceded the Jonic Greek revolution of pre-Socratic thought around 800 BC. The Greek alphabet consists of consonants and vowels (in contrast to earlier Semitic alphabets that lack vowels). Thanks to the Greek alphabet, it became possible to shape a flexible, basic structure of letters into many ideas and thoughts using words and sentences that allowed one to formulate dissimilar ideas and thoughts without becoming ambiguous (as was the case with earlier alphabets that lacked vowels and so had to use an individual sign for each concept, as with Egyptian hieroglyphs). This Greek discovery of an alphabet with vowels proved so successful that it has been used all the way to our modern era.

The communication offered by this style of alphabet also facilitated the sort of rational thinking that attempts to reduce reality to a few fundamental elements.

> Modern critics of language take even a further step: they not only view the shaping of occidental logic as related to the development of a Greek alphabet with its consonants and vowels, they also trace the development of occidental logic back to other aspects of the Greek language, pointing out that the subject-predicate model of Aristotelian logic corresponds to the grammatical structure of the Greek language. The emphasis placed on *the* righteous, *the* beautiful and *the* good is, according to them, emphasized by a use of the specific article which is lacking in the languages of other cultures.

---

1. The history of knowledge and technique has been collected in a fascinating manner by Charles van Doren (1929).

The combination of numbers and letters is the basis of mathematics, a kind of number-language that becomes understandable only in the spirit of alphabetic speech. Like letters, numbers can be brought into relationship with each other. Higher mathematics greatly transcends counting with rows of numbers. A few decades before Plato's birth, Pythagoras (540-500 BC) was able to show that various musical notes are related to each other in terms of specific numbers, thus recognizing hidden numerical relations in the harmonies of music. He then reckoned that the entire cosmos was based on a spherical harmony of numerical relations. Granted that we now know that constellations move only in a limited way in terms of numerical relationships, it was nevertheless Pythagoras who showed us a path to the understanding of nature by using mathematical laws. How much the high culture of the Greeks was influenced by reason can also be seen in the fact that so called "irrational" numbers that cannot be expressed in precise, rational numbers (such as the square number of 2) greatly bothered Pythagoras and his disciples. Such numbers were, for the school of Pythagoras, an expression of the chaos that stands in contrast to the pure harmony of numbers.

We have stated that in the millennium before Christ a strong rationalist tendency in Near East cultures contributed to the "spiritualization" and increasing abstraction of the idea of the soul. This rational spirit underlay the Platonic and post-Platonic teachings pertaining to the soul. Identifying the soul with eternal law allowed Plato to regard human behavior in a new way. Only one attitude was seen as exemplary: that which follows reason and observation. Probably influenced by Pythagoras and Persian images, Plato combined his doctrine of rational thought with the belief in rebirth. According to that view, souls that continue to yield to bodily greed and who do not orient themselves towards the immortal world of ideas will find no redemption in the beyond, but will have to endure another life on earth in a new bodily form.

## The Soul as Formative Principle

The evolution of the image of the soul from an holistic view to one in which the soul is separate from the body has had a significant influence upon the self-concept of the people of the West. The picture that people have of themselves is not self-generated, nor is it inborn; it is imprinted by cultures shaped by the requirements of nature.

In the history of Western culture there has probably never been a change in the image of humanity and the world to equal the transition in Greek culture from the holistic body-soul experience to the rational concept of a spiritualized soul.

Julian Jaynes, a professor of psychology at Princeton University, has studied this revolutionary change using numerous sources.[1] Briefly, he is of the opinion that human's knowledge of themselves, in the form that is common in our days, began to develop only about 3000 years ago. Faced with crucial situations, the people of that era were not aware of an inner capacity to decide, and thus experienced themselves as guided from without. Thus, in the most critical situations they experienced "voices," mostly from gods who pronounced tasks and orders. One example is Achilles, who heard the voice of Pallas Athena, not unlike Moses hearing God's voice coming from the burning bush.

> According to Jaynes, the hearing of voices was so common to the people of earlier generations that they never questioned it. As a result, they were rarely bothered by self doubt or exaggerated feelings of personal responsibility. They relied on the voices that they heard, or those that were communicated to them

---
1. J. Jaynes 1988

by priests. Jaynes mentions, among other examples, the Greek commander Agamemnon who, in the Iliad, explains his hostile attitude toward Achilles by stating that God had afflicted him with madness. According to Jaynes, this sense of the external control of human beings changes only in the Odyssey, a later epic Greek poem in which Odysseus makes some of his own decisions, no longer depending exclusively on the voices of the gods. Here, then, are the first indications of a consciousness of self that was foreign to the heroes of the Iliad.

Today, Jaynes' thesis that this pivotal change in human consciousness occurred around the beginning of the millennium before Christ is no longer scientifically contested. One might question the extent to which being guided from the outside and hearing voices can be equated to an absence of consciousness of oneself. One could also see in such circumstances a different form of experiencing oneself, for the heroes of Homer are likely to have had some sense of ego, even if they had the impression of being guided by gods. If so, the sense of ego probably corresponded to a preliminary stage of the consciousness of themselves that came later. Greek literature documents the degree to which this consciousness evolved during the centuries following Homer. Archilochus, a seventh century BC poet, claims the right to place himself in the center, writing exclusively of his own anxiety, rage and love, subordinating everything else to his personal feelings. It becomes evident that nothing is as important to him as his own life. In fact, he freely admits throwing away his shield during a battle to save his life. With this, a more modern understanding of oneself – one that was foreign to Homer's heroes – manifests itself. Archilochus no longer listens to the voices of the gods; instead, he seizes the right to express his judgments about both the gods and the myths.[1]

---

1. K. Steinmann 1998

Archilochus, unlike his philosophical contemporaries, anchors his experience of himself in a conscious perception of his feelings. Yet these reflections about himself link him to the philosophers of his time. Thus he becomes the poet of the post-Homeric period, the champion of a soulish experience that is fully conscious of itself.

This shift of perspective changed the way people viewed themselves and their fellow human beings (and as well, their ways of living together). Additionally, the prevailing view of life was profoundly altered as a result of the influence of Plato's school, and with Aristotle, Plato's most important disciple, the new concept of the soul also shaped the doctrine of life: biology. In About The Soul, Aristotle writes: "The soul causes us to live, to feel and to think. The soul is, to express it in modern terms, the organizing principle of what is alive. It is the formative force, it is what forms our totality." According to Aristotle, everything alive exists for one purpose, a purpose determined by the formative soul. Inasmuch as Aristotle separates matter from form, it is the power of the soulish that introduces us to nature. The soul becomes part of nature, not in the sense of an animistic soul-body, but as a superordinate function that shapes matter.

The soul is then what provides the organism with identity, with its "self." This individual entity that is characteristic of the living organism cannot be created exclusively from matter. Instead, it can only keep recreating itself. According to Aristotle, it has the force to move itself, and it has the power to create itself. By ascribing to the soul (among other roles) the function of metabolism and reproduction, he presents it as characteristic of what is alive in the body.[1]

Like Plato, Aristotle understood the soul as something primary, a quantity that cannot be reduced to something

---

1. This thought is developed in detail by A. Gierer 1998.

else. This leads to the uniqueness of living beings and, quite especially, human beings; the soul dwells in the body (Plato) or forms the body (Aristotle) and simultaneously partakes of the eternal. Therefore, according to Aristotle, "Without knowledge of the soul there can be no comprehensive understanding of anything, and this is true especially in regard to nature, for the soul is in a certain way the principle of all animated beings."[1]

## Turning Inward

The Greek view of the soul as rational and self-forming contributed to our modern understanding of humans as beings who are conscious of themselves; yet the ancient is not identical with the modern. The earlier understanding lacks both the capacity for self-reflection and the development of the concept of personhood. These two came about in the Christian West.

The Platonic soul is not introspective. It sees an external, cosmic order of which it is but a part, an image. According to the Platonic view, people do not need to look toward the inside to perceive this rational order, they must turn their view outward, toward the cosmos, where they can discover ideas as fundamental forms.

Plato expressed his ideas about discernment with the grandiose symbolic portrayal of a cave. Here human beings are trapped, and see before them only the *shadows* of what is real projected onto the walls of the cave. As long as they do not turn and see the reality of what is outside, their limited ability to know truth corresponds to the darkness of the cave. Only turning toward the light brings true insight. The sun, in Plato's parable, provides the light that is the source of true

---

1. Quoted from A. Gierer 1998, p. 89

cognition, and the cave symbolizes humans' life on earth and their impaired vision of reality.

Plato's views, accepted in part by Christian theologians, were then reversed by Augustine through a magnificent inward turn. The "bodily mortal" of Plato becomes instead the outward, the "soulish-eternal" to the inward aspect.

According to Augustine, recognition of the absolute is not to be found in observing the outward, but in observing the inward features. The human is able to see only the earthly facsimile of the eternal. "Do not turn outward, return to yourself; the truth dwells inside the human being."[1]

The soul is not a reality that allows itself to be recognized from without. It alone can recognize itself.

Augustine justifies this inward journey by stressing that God is the fundamental principle of our ability to recognize anything: "He is the inner light."[2] In doing so, he directs our attention as much to the process of cognition as to that which is to be recognized. He turns to the self in radical self-reflection.

However, looking into the inside can be blocked. Not unlike Plato, who sees recognition of the eternal impaired by bodily greed, Augustine believes that the desire for insight can be stubbornly blocked. He is convinced that humans can turn their backs to the good even when they see it before their eyes. In his autobiographical "Bekenntnisse" (*Confessions*), Augustine returns over and over to what Paul said in Romans: "For the good that I want, I do not do, but the evil I do not want, that I do."[3]

---

1. Quoted from C. Taylor 1996, p. 238
2. Ibid. p. 293f.: "Different is the light that we perceive with the eyes, different is the light that enables the eyes to feel; and this second light that glows in the inside is the light of the soul."
3. Rom. 7.19

Augustine relates the stubbornness of the will to the human selfishness. He calls it selfishness when human beings turn themselves into the "navel of the world," and appropriate everything to themselves, locating such stubbornness entirely in the very soul of the person. Because of this, he believed it impossible for the soul to reach insight by meditation and reflection about itself alone. Rather, the soul requires the grace of God, because one alone is incapable of finding this path to the inside. There is an established limitation in this view of God's world.

According to Augustine, the soul has two aspects: on one hand, it is prey to selfishness in the absence of grace, and on the other, through grace it becomes capable of the most magnificent insights. The Christian West has been shaped by this polarized vision for a thousand years. It was only in the Middle Ages and the Renaissance that a liberating way of viewing the internalized soul began to prevail.

## The Soul of the Mystics

During the thirteenth century, both within and without the realm of the Church, a mystical movement began to spread that equated turning inward with becoming free of compulsions. According to Christian mystics, humans were capable of uniting themselves in their innermost essence, in naked being and beyond all reason, with the divine. Meister Eckehart recommended freeing the soul of all wishes, and not trying to grasp everything with reason. Only then would one be able to discover in the depths of the soul something utterly secret and hidden, something that will and intellect are unable to reveal, something without name or form, without time or space.[1]

---

1. Meister Eckehart (Publ. J. Quint) 1963, Sermon 7

Teresa of Avila describes the journey toward the innermost region of the soul as walking through many rooms of a castle until one reaches an innermost chamber that cannot be understood in terms of logical concepts.[1] As a result, a topology of the life of the soul is created that leads to the innermost, yet at the same time is the most external; into the lonesomest that is at the same time the most communal or, in mystical language, the union with God.

The soul turns into "Something that no one knows," (Eckehart), because "A power is contained in the soul that cannot be touched either by time or by the flesh." This cosmic understanding of the soul distances itself from rational attempts at description, and thus attempts to convey the experience in paradoxes that exclude each other logically. It does so not with the aim of being irrational, but in order to give voice to the inconceivable.

### The Soul as Recognizing Subject

While mysticism represents an approach resulting from the inward turn initiated by Augustine, we see on the other hand a search for enlightenment based entirely on reason and logic. The latter finds its leading representative in Descartes. In this focus on rationality, we find at its center not trust, but doubt. It does not originate in grace but in knowledge. By detaching itself from the religious presentations, it is able to turn even more radically to the inside.

It was Descartes (1596-1650) who, in the beginning of the Age of Enlightenment, propelled this internalized, reflective depiction of the soul to its highest peak. To do so, he used the method of radical doubt. Asking himself what in life cannot be doubted, he answers, "Cogito ergo sum (I think, therefore

---

1. Teresa von Avila (Publ. F. Vogelsang) 1979

I am)." Nobody can take away his thinking or his doubting. Even if all other experiences were dreams, delusions, or inspired by a devil, "I think and therefore exist" manages to oppose effectively all doubt. (It did not occur to Descartes that, as Wittgenstein suggested much later, it is possible that he erroneously became victim of a play of words.)

The soul is not just the center of life in the thoughts of Descartes; it also becomes the ultimate authority to which all other things must subordinate themselves. The soul does not discover itself prior to rational organization, so it creates it. The world is understood purely as a mechanism that is grasped by the soul. The body is no longer a medium in which the soul can appear (as it does according to Aristotle), it is pure matter.

However, Descartes' soul does not free itself of the body by turning away from it. On the contrary, it focuses its attention upon it so it can study and control it.

According to Descartes, the soul is also, in a certain sense, no longer animated. Feelings are understood more as devices that promote survival rather than as shapers of the soul. Descartes therefore states, "In fact, sense perceptions are provided to me solely in order to indicate to my spirit whatever is advantageous and what is bad for the whole of which it is a part; as such they are sufficiently clear."[1]

It may be more correct to designate Descartes' soul as spirit. One would thereby get closer to the "disengaged perspective" (Taylor) that conceives of Descartes' "soul-spirit." For Descartes, distance and clarity are preconditions that enable the human being to control all that is alive and dead. This rational control must ultimately determine also one's dealing with oneself. A truly rational relationship to oneself is free of emotions. Individuals must view themselves as rational

---

1. Sixth meditation, quoted from C. Taylor 1996, p. 267

human beings. They are to protect themselves through the use of stoic equanimity when overcome with passion. Bearing their suffering with firm patience turns them into human beings with great souls.[1]

Charles Taylor finds in Descartes (probably quite correctly) a newly assumed, antique, bellicose, or knightly ethic of honor. However, this new ethic of honor is no longer meant to serve the acquisition of public life – as it did before with warriors and knights – but is now charged with the internal task of sustaining the individual's sense of self worth. The scenario has turned from the outside to the inside; Descartes' soul observes from within what is happening outside of it.

The move to the inside that began with Augustine has now led to the solitude of a rational and isolated soul. With the beginning of the Age of Enlightenment, the question of how to integrate death into life is raised less and less; instead, the modern question of how to live in the face of a mechanized and functional world is raised more and more. No longer is what is dead "the foreign," it is the living that turns into a riddle because it is no longer self-obvious in relation to the vision of a lifeless world.[2]

> The modern era, beginning with the Age of Enlightenment, raised the idea that humans must realize themselves by means of disciplined and methodical actions within a world that is viewed as rational.[3] For the English philosopher John Locke, the soul then turns into the 'point-shaped self.' There is nothing outside of rational consciousness that belongs to the self, yet consciousness can address itself only to something else. As a

---

1. Letters – as above, p. 278
2. H. Jonas 1997
3. This idea was developed primarily by Michel Foucault and became the starting point of his fundamental critique of the humanistic sciences ("Psychologie und Geisteskrankheiten" [*Mental Illness and Psychology*] 1962), of medicine ("Die Geburt der Klinik" [*The Birth of the Clinic*] 1973) and especially of psychiatry ("Wahnsinn und Gesellschaft" [*Madness and Civilisation*] 1963).

result, empiricism, the science of experience, gains the upper hand. The point-shaped soul, unable to expand, essentially exists only to process sense-impressions. At a later point even this is questioned.[1]

### Renewed Turn toward the Outside? – The View from Nowhere

Our modern science of the nervous system no longer has a view derived in regard to an inward location of the soul. The conscious subject has yielded to a "view from nowhere."[2] Along with this, the very idea of "soul" has began to evaporate. The disillusionment of the world has now taken hold of the soul itself. The modern science of neurology no longer asks about the soul. Instead, it is determined to understand consciousness physically and functionally as a kind of "mind-machine."

Two main trends can be identified in this regard. One is physically oriented and tries to equate soulish-spiritual events in humans with physical (chemical) processes of the central nervous system. The brain thus comes to resemble an organ of the soul. The other trend is functionally, or in other words, informally oriented. It considers mental processes parallel to software programs, and so interprets spiritual-soulish events in terms of digital information processes. From this viewpoint, the brain serves only as the hardware that allows an independent process of information – the software – to be effective.

In the first case – reducing soulish processes to physical attributes – one starts with the idea that only physical-chemical processes can affect aspects of life, while on the other hand, life experiences have no effect upon material processes. As a

1. C. Taylor 1996, p. 288
2. See Th. Nagel (1992) in the book with the same title *(The View from Nowhere)*

result, there does not seem to be value in concerning oneself any longer with soulish experiences. Those have become a mere relic, a "turn of phrase," or are even considered illusory by some representatives of *eliminative* materialism.[1]

In the second case – seeing in the soulish a function of providing information – the meaning of experience does not extend beyond being a principle of organization. Thus the experience of pain is viewed as a protective function, furthering survival by drawing attention to any current danger. Inasmuch as such situations can in principle be analyzed and reduced to their basic elements, it is possible, according to the proponents of this so-called functionalism, to build a machine that uses artificial intelligence to satisfy soulish functions without experiencing anything consciously.[2]

Recently, this sort of physicalism and functionalism merged in order to become a pairing of body and spirit that excludes the third aspect of the soulish. Now we find in the domains of the neurosciences the tendency to link physicochemical events in the brain with functional analyses of behavior, the intent being to study the human as a purposive, organized unit based on the body.

In these varied neuroscience approaches one no longer focuses interest on a unique, single individual, but rather on a "something," on a person *qua* "thing." The attention is no longer directed toward a being with a unique history and experience, but toward a functioning physical presence with observable patterns of behavior.

This depersonalization of experience carries far-reaching consequences for the understanding of human beings. Inasmuch as the neurosciences have been successful in show-

---

1. Feyerabend and Rorty put forward ideas suggesting that soulish-spiritual conditions as such did not exist. One prominent present-day representative of "eliminative materialism" is B. P. M. Churchland.

2. D. Dennett, going a step further, defends the theoretical possibility of "conscious robots" (1993, p. 431f.)

ing a close connection between cerebral function and mental performance, i.e., specific modes of behavior, we find that the inner world of the human is being equated more and more often with neurological processes that can be technically conceptualized and measured. It would seem that there is no longer any inner experience that cannot be understood outwardly.

A soulish vacuum has grown out of this radical revision of the inner search for truth of Augustine and Descartes. Thus Descartes is mostly misunderstood, and is accused, by modern students of consciousness and systems who have not read his work, of having conceived of the world as a Cartesian theater.[1] In this theater, the soul of the spectator is alleged to observe what happens on the stage of the world, and they object that there are in fact no spectators. They add that the world plays itself while humans are but part of this world and their consciousness, also part of the world, obeys physical and chemical laws.

In this modern period, a disenchantment of the world has occurred that involves large numbers of the population. This disenchantment (the removal of a spell) reveals itself most clearly when we observe how grim is the fight for the preservation of a self that is no longer self-understood. The attitude of many who insist that they want to know the "self" probably does not so much reflect their selfishness as it does their deep questioning of the forgone conclusion that they are individuals. I shall return to this in the fourth chapter.

### *What led to the Second Upheaval in the Understanding of the Soul?*

To explain the first Greek revolution, I mentioned the introduction of the alphabet and the development of serial

---

1. Ibid. p. 99f.

numbers with multiple positions. Writing and mathematics changed the world of that time. Their development into a medium of information helped to formulate and spread the transformation of Greek thought.

The second revolution in the understanding of the soul coincided with a period of great scientific and geopolitical discoveries. Descartes not only created a revolution in the understanding of the soul, he also developed mathematical methods such as analytic geometry in order to turn questions in the realm of ideas into practical problems (a form enabling it to be solved using algebra). The mathematical method he developed did not generate as much attention and resistance as did his doctrine of the soul, yet its success was striking. Thanks to this method, his way of thinking prevailed even among those who resisted the complete restructuring of the soul. Whoever adopted Descartes' scientific method had to restrict it to mathematical problems, its only application.

Regarding the geopolitical situation, it is worth noting that the diminishment of the idea of the soul to an imaginary point coincided with the unseating of Earth as center of the cosmos. The dominant thinking during the Age of Enlightenment was that the universe was a realm of matter and soulless forces.

Copernicus (1473-1543), born just one hundred years before Descartes, broke (albeit carefully) with the idea that the earth was the center of everything and that the sun rotated around it. Tycho Brahe (1546-1601), born half a century before Descartes, observed new stars that no longer fitted into the existing world image of the structure that Aristotle had proposed. Johannes Kepler (1571-1630), a slightly older contemporary of Descartes, discovered deviations in the trajectory of the planets that demanded a new understanding of the cosmos. Galileo Galilei (1564-1646), also an older contemporary of Descartes was able, thanks to a newly developed telescope, to observe movements on the surface of the sun. He furthermore observed that the planet Jupiter had its own center of gravity enabling the rotation of moons around it. His discoveries led him to the conclusion that the laws of nature had to be calculated mathematically.

Discoveries made in the following centuries – from Newton's view of the cosmos as mathematically regulated, to Lemaître's widened universe, all the way to the "big bang" – caused the earth as home of human beings to shrink further. Enormous achievements in science and technology rewarded people's skill for abstract thinking to such an extent that the disregard for all that is soulish could progress much further.

It is quite likely that other factors were involved in this process. The explosive spread of commerce probably contributed to the sense that humans were increasingly viewed as quantifiable objects of the economy, i.e., objects related to the production and consumption of merchandise. It is probably no accident that Descartes' birth fell in the century of the first globalization of commerce. The birth of worldwide commerce was made possible by the discovery of America and of the sea lanes to Asia. The subsequent industrialization of the eighteenth and nineteenth centuries, as well as the intrusion of technology into our daily life in the twentieth century, contributed to raising the rational powers of humans to an unimaginable degree. By contrast, in the first half of the twentieth century two world wars and the holocaust served as proof that human life and soulish experience were treated as worthless. Faced with this evidence, it was obvious that what pertained to the soul was increasingly repressed and reduced to a small, imaginary dot.

However, does what is soulish actually allow itself to be reduced to the vanishing point? Do we simply no longer notice it because we have explained that it is dead or something imaginary? Shall we disregard what is soulish because we still expect it in a form that belongs to the past?

Could the soul reveal itself today in a new form? Perhaps it is doing that by cultivating certain forms of experience, such as a longing for action and excitement in adventurous sports (e.g., rock-climbing, parachuting, river-rafting etc.), in the growing appeal of meditation and bodily therapies, or in various arts that appeal to the senses?

If this is so, we may find ourselves at the beginning of a fresh understanding of the soul that, though it expresses itself in bodily terms, ultimately represents an attempt to define itself in respecting the body without falling into the trap of either materialism or mentalism.

*Summary*

In this chapter I have focused on some of the essential lines of development in an attempt to succinctly present historical shifts in the conceptions of the soul during the last one hundred generations.

Magical, holistic ideas predominated in the earliest cultures. Not only the people, but also their surroundings are endowed with soul. The souls present themselves concretely in a variety of forms, such as animals, shadows, or bodily organs.

| Table 1: Changes in the Conceptions of the Soul | |
|---|---|
| Early Cultures | The soul is concretely presented as a living being (e.g., a bird) or an organ (such as blood).<br>– Animistic, concrete model |
| Ancient advanced cultures | Soul/spirit is understood as immaterial, as a formative principle such as "Logos."<br>– Abstract-rational model |
| Modern (since the Age of Enlightenment) | Soul/spirit becomes the cognitive subject and is associated with being conscious of oneself. The identified object stands out in contrast to the subject that identifies it.<br>– Subject-oriented model |
| Late modern | Heterogeneous models, with a tendency to render soulish phenomena as concrete, seeing them as material events of the central nervous system.<br>– Tendency toward an object-oriented model |

In the times of ancient Greek and high Roman culture, the soul was viewed, according to Plato, as *Logos*, or which Aristotle saw as form separated from the body. The first revolutionary understanding of the soul consisted of focusing on an abstract idea of the soul. This went hand in hand with the notion of the world as a body-soul unity in which inside and outside, human and cosmos were, to a large extent, interwoven. Simultaneously, a separation of body and soul/spirit announced itself. The second upheaval in the West's understanding of the soul occurred two thousand years later with the Age of the Enlightenment. A rational concentration on the central nervous system is followed by a turn toward the inside. This inner location of the soul as begun by Augustine and completed by Descartes. With this was established the image of a self-confident and responsible individual who forms a personal identity and makes his or her free choices from within.

Another revolution in the understanding of the soul began in the twentieth century, as we have reached a point where the image of an inward soul appears to dissolve and cede its place to a new externalization.

Soul is a concept that, in the history of the West, took on very different meanings as each epoch struggled for an appropriate understanding of it. Today we have almost insuperable difficulty in attempting to overcome the dualistic separation of body and soul.

Up to this point, my description of the chronological development might give the impression that the portrayals of the soul in any one era were quite uniform, and developed continuously along a straight line. This idea needs to be corrected. In various periods we find that differing views of the soul have intersected and collided with each other, nurtured or fought with each other, become mutually interwoven, and finally separated, displaying different syntheses and different implications. Nor do all the mentioned portrayals of the soul belong to the past; many have survived with some of their main features to this day, albeit adjusted to our world.

What is the moral of this history? I understand this "short history of the soul" as a kaleidoscopic presentation of sundry views of the soul that shape people in various ways. The experience of body-soul wholeness remains important for many people. Viewing the soul as an organ has left deep traces in our modern language. Plato's portrayal of the soul continues to live on as a parallel to the Judeo-Christian image, just as the rational, uninvolved spirit-soul lives side by side with the vegetative and animal soul.

## Aside: Effects upon Today's Therapeutic Situation

Their differing views of the soul are a likely reason why today so many social and scientific groups are unable to understand each other. Religious Christian circles influenced by the Jewish Paulus and the Roman Christian Augustine have both semantic and philosophical challenges when in discourse with neurologists or psychotherapists of humanistic orientation. Practitioners of alternative medicine – fond of more holistic and Platonic ideas – can find no common language with the traditional medicine that seeks to objectify the human. Aesthetically oriented people, more interested in the defining form than the mere physical substance, feel like strangers in treatment situations that are firmly based on matter and function.

Differences between attitudes regarding the soul are found not only between various groups but also between couples and in families, indeed, even within some individuals. It is possible for one person to hold two different images of the soul as a result of upbringing and profession. So, for example, a technician whose work is oriented to a picture of the world characterized by physical presuppositions may, as a faithful Christian, believe in the physical resurrection.

In completing this chapter on the history of the soul, I would like to add more emphasis on the possibility that the formation of psychiatric problems can also be an expression of a particular understanding of the soul. It is likewise possible that any therapy might be rendered more difficult if there are family or others involved with the patient who have very different opinions of the soul. It is particularly hard these days to fathom modes of experience that maintain belief in magical influences from their surroundings, or that attribute animistic significance to an organ of the body (e.g., the lung). People who speak of these experiences are frequently misunderstood; from a rational viewpoint, they appear crazy (psychotic).

One may, of course, approach such apparently psychotic experience from the view of a magic-holistic or animistic understanding of the soul, but there are limits to the efficacy of such attempts.

The rational experience of knowing oneself and one's world from a single point of view turns into an entirely different form of experience in a psychosis. Here, as we like to explain to the patients, the world does not necessarily dissolve but it is brought into a different relationship to the person. In the psychotic experience, there are no longer sharply distinct external and internal worlds, but rather, the external and internal are mutually intertwined. Outward aspects of the world acquire an inward meaning; one's experience of self turns on sensations that are organ-related.

> The following recollection of a psychotic episode by a woman who had suffered from acute schizophrenia may serve as example: "While I was psychotic, everything had a special meaning for me. Every object I noticed communicated a message to me. So I sat myself down in a restaurant when a truck bearing the sign "Sit" passed. Birds pointed out to me the direction I was to follow by means of their flight, or I would orient myself by the direction that pine cones seemed to indicate. Then again, it could be the colors of a flower that indicated the direction to me. Cigarette butts, globs of chewing gum or discarded pieces of paper also gave me directions."

Many psychotic patients hear voices and experience themselves being led by foreign powers, an experience of being guided by external forces that recalls Homer's description of the heroes of the Iliad. Even if such comparisons are valid only within certain limits, this questionable relating of psychotic experiences with ancient representations of the soul may help us get closer to what otherwise seems almost inconceivable.

There has been an attempt to describe the psychotic way of experiencing as being magically concretized. In this case, the magical element is linked with a variant of the soul that is able to step outside the person and affect – as a kind of "excursion-soul" – external events and other people, while conversely it, too, can be affected by external powers. This implies that the world is not viewed abstractly and rationally from an independent perspective, but that it remains firmly interwoven with concrete and local influences.

In this form of experience, the rational centering that was established with Plato's portrayal of the soul is apparently withdrawn and gives way to a magic-holistic understanding of the soul. This soul no longer occupies a single position. Instead, it is experienced as something that can inhabit a number of places and is also able to find a home in a variety of organs. The modern observer thus is given an impression of fragmentation and dissociation.

Clearly it is very difficult for those who suffer from a psychosis to orient themselves within a rationally ordered world. If psychotic patients nevertheless manage to survive in our society and find in their own way a path through life, it may occur to a psychiatrist that these sick people are living under a good star, or that they are protected by an angel. This manner of speaking is noted even among physicians of the soul, and points to magical, irrational roots, although the physician applies it symbolically.

Language incorporates various levels that carry different images of the world and the soul. Linguistics teaches us that in modern European languages there are many concepts that refer to the body and show their roots in organic conceptions of the soul. For this reason, psychotic patients, in their understanding of the soul, often take the language literally; they are able to grasp the original meanings even of words that have undergone symbolic distortion in their modern usage.

Thus one patient complained about the heartlessness of his mother using the following words: "She has a heart defect and should see a physician." Another psychotic patient understood the term "heart-touching" in the sense that some invisible hand was touching his heart.[1]

Anyone who carefully "Watches people's mouths," that is, takes language seriously, will frequently notice expressions that are soul-organic in origin, such as, "My heart is getting warm," "A chill is going down my back," or "This makes my diaphragm shake." Yet the German and English languages are also shaped by magic-holistic images; doesn't one speak of being "beside oneself," "ecstatic," "blown away," "in another place," or "under a different star"? Isn't it possible for people to turn into "furies" when they hate, or turn into "angels" when they are in love?

Many people hear voices. According to reliable polls, that is the case in varying degrees for ten to fifty percent of the population, though most tend to keep quiet about it, fearing they would be considered insane. These inner voices come from an internalized understanding of the soul, whereas the voices that come from the outside and are diagnosed as hallucinations fragment the modern understanding of the soul.

In this difference an important indication of the modern understanding of the self becomes evident. The *individuus* (Latin: the indivisible), or individual is self-contained and autonomous. As a result, thoughts are no longer initiated from outside, or worse, are heard as voices, but instead correspond to an inner means of speech. Language, whether thought, heard, or spoken is always related to the individual who has control over this linguistic skill. For this reason, most people would consider any words heard without being spoken by another person to be delusional. Language is no longer a sea into which one can dive the way Francis of Assisi dove, find-

---

1. (Translator:) These and expressions that follow are taken directly from the original German, in which they are common, so in translation they may be awkward. My hope is that they convey the author's point accurately.

ing a world where he spoke with fishes and birds. Language is now commonly understood as a learned skill and presupposes the speech centers of the nervous system.

Psychotic experience is not only of a magic-animistic nature (in the sense of being a receiver to whom everything becomes a message), it is also possible to lose all external connections, a loss that threatens to bring one's known world to an end. This difference alone makes it imperative to distinguish between a psychotic illness and one who instead has a magic-animistic understanding of the body/soul. While a psychotic condition may indeed find expression in a magic-animistic manner, it is important to keep in mind that the psychotic experience blocks any possibility of integrating that special manner into the prevailing culture.[1]

If one feels one's very sense of self is threatened, it is possible, as long as the psychosis has not yet manifested itself, to fight the onset by living an exceptionally rigid life and adhering to fixed ways of behavior. Of course this can result in the problem of a compulsive condition that could be likened to an extreme, ego-driven defensive strategy of one's rational presence.

> A patient, Roberta C., suffered from the fear of not being able to shield herself against external influences that could cause her being to dissolve. This thirty-year-old woman had worked as a secretary until she developed an increasingly strong impulse to control both her personal actions and her immediate surroundings. Eventually, her compulsive desire for control, and obsessive washing rituals occupied her to such an extent that she became incapable of working. Now she must painstakingly regulate her

---

1. A psychosis is "privative" (C. Scharfetter 1996). In other words, it disengages one from his or her sense of community with other people. This is contrary to the animistic-magic ideas of earlier cultures. According to H. Tellenbach (1987, p. 268), the delusions of the psychotic patient express "the destruction of the shared 'in-betweenness' which enables a person to understand a fellow human being."

day and keep herself away from anything she suspects is dirty, for she is afraid that otherwise she'd be overwhelmed by external influences and lose her identity. Whenever she fails to keep out the "unclean" outside world by means of washing rituals, she panics. She has very precise ideas of how she must order things, will not tolerate any casual behavior and especially abhors disorder. Any deviation from her personal ritual results in even greater efforts to keep herself clean. If her defenses exhaust themselves, she is overcome by panic, fearing she is at the mercy of an overwhelming, filthy environment. Ms. C. fights a nearly inescapable battle that rages between "a pure internal soul" and an "unclean external world." Clinging to her principles, she strives to avoid the constant dread that she will become soiled and will disintegrate.

One might see in this inner struggle a parallel to the gnostic battle between the ideal good and the earthly evil. The battle is waged at the point of transition between a magic-animistic union with the world, and the rational focus on the self that became predominant in the West following Plato's teaching about ideas. The gnostic concept of a pure, immaterial soul that must maintain itself in the midst of a spoiled world, and that in this conflict tries to follow eternal truths, again reminds us of the defense against an animistic body/soul portrayal. Even if this parallel between historical and personal problems is possible only to a limited extent, it nonetheless offers a theoretical basis of comprehension for the problem of compulsiveness that is one expression of a basic human struggle. Without such understanding, pathology threatens to become a soulless mechanism.

> The example of Roberta C. allows us to interpret another psychiatric disturbance – the dissociative disturbance – as a struggle between different images of the soul. Ms. C. experienced a dissociated state of consciousness when the mechanism with which she tried to control her existence failed. She could no longer

express her distress in words; instead, she cried convulsively or tried to express herself with mechanical defensive movements. This behavior appeared phony and hysterical to the staff personnel who were not acquainted with her condition. In such moments, one could not make contact with Ms. C. (Charcot would have used the expression 'belle indifference'). Even her compulsive crying had a theatrical tone, because one could not sense a corresponding inner emotion. As a result, her behavior was seen as being oriented towards some purpose, i.e., manipulative. It seemed to be pure form or pure function.

Actually, in such moments the patient in truth experienced an overwhelming fear, but was no longer capable of communicating it. The form of expression therefore became independent of the inner experience. What was exhibited was merely the functional aspect of what she felt. As a result, Ms. C.'s expressions lost their symbolic content, so it seemed that her manifestation of distress was only a show. There was no perceptible substance behind the crying spasms and her stereotypical movements; because the experience rang hollow to others, no sympathy was elicited, leaving those around her with no emotional response.

Is it conceivable, in attempting a cultural and historical comparison, that Aristotle's emphasis on the form as well as the function represented a rational attempt to overcome the magic-holistic idea of a "body-soul" without having to pay homage to Plato's ideas? Of course, this also raises the possibility that the *Gestalt* or mode of expression can represent the soulish without tying it to an idea or a symbolic representation. This manner of expressing oneself enables people to point to their distress without revealing their inner experience. Thus a dissociative disorder that earlier was seen as hysterical could represent a soulish experience that cannot be allowed expression in words nor, considering the seriousness of the predicament, can it be suppressed. The anxiety finds expression in screaming, becoming silent, or in mechanical movements without revealing the inner experience. Thereby the sufferer does not give herself up, but can nevertheless draw attention to herself by expressing her feelings through various physical actions. Can it be accidental that women who have been so socially disadvantaged and suppressed have resorted to a body language that cannot be grasped physically or intellectually?

The problems of the modern person show up differently in depressions. In the depressive person, a threat is not merely present (as in anxiety); rather, a part of life already appears to be lost. While anxiety may find an outlet in flight or a desperate attack, most depressed people remain focused on what they have lost. Today's depressed patient is less afraid of dying than despairing over the thought of not knowing how to continue in life. In this regard, a depression may reflect most typically the plight of our times. Depressed individuals long for a felt experience of life that they can no longer find, whereas addicts try desperately to put new magic into a burnt-out world. The depressed person's own body may even be experienced as lifeless matter, like a wrapper. They perceive their consciousness to be empty, circling around a point without energy, without ever finding access to what was once important to them. Many no longer show the problem of guilt that at one time tormented many depressed people. They experience themselves as "nothing," as groundless and lifeless.

What makes their situation even worse are the restrictions on their ability to think. Ever since Descartes, it has been important to self-understanding that one have control over an autonomous, personal view of the world. Because of this, mental blocks hit modern people in a very vulnerable spot. It is the perception of a personal ego, a mental image of themselves that defines the modern human. Yet the ego belongs to one only as long as memories and thoughts permit it. In a depression, however, what occurs is that which the modern person can tolerate the least: thoughts and memories are now difficult to remember. Planning and decisions are blocked, as are vigorous movements and body language. At the most vulnerable point, the ego is experienced as questionable. Yet at the same time, the ego – unlike during unconsciousness – remains fully aware of its situation. Depressed people clearly and consciously experience that their ability to make decisions or express influence is blocked.

In such a situation, the modern ego experiences itself as being confronted by nothingness, a dreadful void. It no longer can achieve meaning by experiencing itself as a part of the whole world, something the Renaissance conception of melancholy made possible by relying on pre-Socratic and Pythagorean models. Nor is the modern ego able to understand what comes of being derived from a soul-organ, such as the black bile (melancholy); it cannot see what is happening as a natural change, as was possible in the era of Hippocratic medicine in classical Greece. The modern ego arose out of the dualism of the Age of Enlightenment. Its only choices are to place the source of its suffering in either the body (that is the brain), or into consciousness. Both of these possibilities, however, lack precisely what depressed human beings are seeking; they are too lifeless, too rational.

Medicine seeks to find in depression a psycho-chemical cause. The psychology of consciousness tries to see it as the failure of a certain life plan, or as the consequence of defective thinking. Yet those avenues through the brain and consciousness are not able to replace the feeling of aliveness for which depressive people struggle. Even if one could successfully escape from depression by following either of those paths, the dread remains of losing vitality right in the midst of life.

Health as such does not exist,
and any attempts to define anything as such
have miserably failed…
In the end remains the great question:
whether we can do without the illness,
especially for the development of virtue,
and whether especially our thirst for knowledge and
self-knowledge has a need of the sick soul as much as
of the healthy one.

                     – Friedrich Nietzsche

# Chapter 3.
# Diseased Soul?
# A Comment Pertaining to the History of Psychiatry

## The "inferior" Illness

People who suffer from psychological disorders are not only afflicted by inferior health, but also by an "inferior" illness. This is how Robert Musil characterizes psychiatric disturbances in his monumental work "Der Mann ohne Eigenschaften" (*The Man without Qualities*). Many who are afflicted by psychiatric disorders will agree. Even now there are many who suffer as much from the stigma of their psychiatric problems as they do from the disorder itself.

Psychiatric diagnoses often have the same effect as disgrace, something that causes people to be viewed as being outside the normal borders of society. Those who are critical of psychiatry have been inclined to see its history as a one of stigmatizing suffering people. It is, however, unfair to view the development of psychiatry only from this angle, for part of its history is a battle against the stigmatizing of psychiatric patients. The founders of modern psychiatry, in the beginning of the eighteenth century, viewed themselves as representatives of a movement to liberate the insane. They wanted to free those suffering from psychiatric illnesses who were confined in penitentiaries and institutions of forced labor along with thieves, vagabonds and others who were thorns in the side of an absolutist social organization. For these founding representatives, the tragedy was that liberating these patients from prisons and other confinement led to their being locked in rigid rational and patriarchal institutions.

Nevertheless, these liberation movements shaped the history of psychiatry just as much as the thinking and establishments of society. Liberation and confinement not only shaped different periods, they also merged in complex ways. A widespread idea of illness can at any time serve, like an outmoded belief, to separate these two complementary basic attitudes (liberation and confinement). On one hand, one understands by "illness" a problem that interferes with a person's development and results in a flaw in that person's behavior and breadth of experience. This kind of diagnostic understanding of the problem aims to strengthen the individual. On the other hand, the illness is understood as a disorder that has harmful consequences to both the patients and their surroundings. In this case, the diagnosis of the illness is intended to correct the deficient functional adjustment rather than to broaden the patents' personal experiences. It can thus be useful for including them in society.

In what follows, I shall attempt to trace the historical evolution of what was defined as psychiatric illness, and to indicate which among the developing influences contributed to today's understanding of psychological disorders. The clarification of these historical conditions will, in the next section, serve as a foundation for the attempt to develop a person-based understanding of illness. The physical and social preconditions of psychiatric suffering are most thoroughly considered in a person-based thesis. However, the patients' personal experiences are not seen as exclusively dependent on biological and social conditions, but are also seen as starting points of the ongoing dynamic of the illness.

> The understanding of psychological suffering that will be developed later on also shows the history of psychiatry in a new light. Rather than speaking exclusively of social relations that are psychologically notable, one must also address the psychological attempts to introduce general social norms. Humans are not simply locked up, nor confined internally by means of stigmatizing opinions; they may also experience an internal process that opposes the shame that presses from without. From this ensures an historical dynamic that must be examined not only from the outside towards the inside, but also must be studied in the opposite direction.

## Psychiatric Therapy in Contrast to Pastoral Care

Just as ideas about the soul have changed substantially with time, so have convictions pertaining to what is "ill," or – in the wording of the WHO (World Health Organization) – what is "disturbed." As a science of the treatment of the soul, psychiatry is only about two hundred years old.[1] Yet previous epochs were aware of many problems that now fall within the sphere of psychiatry. Until the nineteenth century, these problems were viewed as magic, moral or religious rather than as medical issue to be healed. As a result, they were dealt with largely by ministers, not treated as medical illnesses.

---

1. The idea of psychiatry was introduced early in the nineteenth century by Johann Christian Reil (1759-1813), a German physician who was teaching as a professor in Berlin, and who recommended, in part, frightening methods of treatment for the ethical correction of mentally ill patients. (E. H. Ackerknecht 1985, p. 39)

The ancient school of Hippocrates was an exception to this. This movement, which presented a physically oriented view of illness in Greco-Roman antiquity, was willing to also include those who suffered from what we consider to be psychological disorders. In that school, terms such as melancholia (for depression and related disorders), mania (for excited or psychotic conditions) and phrenitis (for feverish, confused, or delirious conditions) were formed. These illnesses were attributed to an imbalance in the four fluids of the body (blood, phlegm, yellow and black bile), and were treated with dietary measures and natural remedies.

It would nevertheless be presumptuous to equate ancient Hippocratic doctrines with our modern natural-scientific understanding of psychiatric disorders. Although the Hippocratic school, in contrast to earlier priest-healers, rejected religious approaches to healing and favored measures based on natural medicines, it nevertheless paid homage to Asklepios, the god of healing, and remained strongly under the influence of soul-organ images. Thus, for example, the Roman physician Aretaeus of Cappadocia, a representative of that school, explained hysteria as being due to a migrating of the uterus inside the body. Melancholia (or depression), alluding to the darkness and depth of depressive conditions, was related to a bile presumed to be black (melan-cholia = black bile).[1]

Remnants of the Hippocratic ideas of illness continued into the Middle Ages and subsequently experienced a renaissance. Basically, however, until the Age of Enlightenment no bodily oriented medicine for the treatment of the psychiatrically ill could really prevail. The reason for this probably

---

1. The Hippocratic idea that the thickening, heating or cooling of the body's saps leads to various illnesses corresponds to a pictorial understanding of illnesses due to soul-organic influences. This probably contributed to the widespread use of blood-letting and laxatives (see R. Klibansky et al. 1992; J. Starobinski 1960)

lies in the initial cultural-historic situation, because among the Germanic tribes that conquered the Roman empire, any awareness of illness was under the influence of the local mythologies of the various clans. Later, this tradition became intermingled with elements from the Judeo-Christian faith.

Pre-Christian German depictions of illness followed an animistic interpretation of the world. Illness and death were understood, on one hand, as loss of the life-forces, and on the other hand, as God-sent fate. During the Christian Middle Ages, the practice of medicine was tied to theology. Christian doctrine taught that Christ was the physician of the soul who restores the soul to health by expelling evil spirits from the possessed.[1] It is not surprising that people believed that patients with psychological illnesses were controlled by spooks or demons. As victims of supernatural powers, these possessed people provoked compassion, bewilderment or terror. Cures were often sought from relics. Witnesses to this are the thousands of votive pictures in churches and convents.

> The bones of Saint Dymphna of Gheel (Belgium) were of exceptional importance for the mentally ill. According to legend, Dymphna was the daughter of an Irish king, and apparently refused to marry her father after the death of her mother. Persecuted for many years, she eventually died, mentally deranged, in Gheel. Ever since her death, her bones have attracted mentally ill people and their relatives. So many came that in the thirteenth century, Gheel became, in some measure, a center for psychotic people. Many mentally ill patients who did not experience a cure were left by their relatives, lacking payment, with local families.

The religious ideas of the Middle Ages also contributed to encouraging treatment of the sick in convents. Thus, in the thirty-sixth chapter of the rules of his order, Benedict

---

1. The healing of the sick by "Christus Medicus" is most impressively portrayed in the Romanesque church of Saint George on the island of Reichenau (Switzerland).

states, "The care of the sick is before and above all other obligations… For the care of the sick brothers a personal room has to be chosen and a God-fearing, conscientious and caring attendant must serve them." The first establishment of hospitals was a consequence of this convent-medicine of the early Middle Ages. The general population also were provided with care and treatment by priests in these hospitals.

The medical historian Neumann very accurately characterizes the medieval concept: "The concept of illness that was widely disseminated is ambivalent: being ill, on one hand, reveals personal guilt… yet on the other hand, one recognizes in being ill the suffering Christ."[1] In a negative instance, illness and suffering of the soul result in guilt and being ostracized; in a positive instance, in being tested and chosen.

### Psychiatry as a Child of Enlightenment

The development of a medical science of healing (Gr. iatreia) the soul (Gr. psyche), or psychiatry, is linked to the new ideas of the Enlightenment. Gerhard Rudolph, a specialist in the history of medicine, is of the opinion that modern medicine began in 1637, the year in which Descartes published his "Discours de la Méthode" *(Discourse on the Method of Rightly Conducting the Reason, and Seeking Truth in the Sciences).* At that time, he points out, a radical split took place between faith and knowledge. "It is Descartes' conviction that reason is so predisposed for the recognition of nature and the human being that it can separate the truth from what is false."[2] Until the time of Descartes, the opinion prevailed among physicians that the body functioned only as the servant of the soul: "The events of life are produced by the soul, in

1. J. M. Neumann 1996, p. 139
2. G. Rudolf 1996, p. 204

no case by the body itself, nor do they come about, so to say, by themselves."[1] Descartes reversed that view, stating that humans (and animals) are complete systems that obey mechanical laws and must be understood as a machines or automatons.

Descartes concluded that all processes of the human body must be reduced to the position, order and movements of its smallest parts. Position would later be studied by anatomy, the order of the parts by biochemistry, and movement by physiology. Instead of focusing on the purpose, as was done before the Enlightenment, one must research the causes. Medical science became a rational examination of the laws pertaining to cause and effect and their application to the humans.

The laws of the physical world must also be applicable to living organisms. Just as a machine cannot have a goal by itself, the physical body, according to Descartes, is also regulated by laws that are independent of it. This natural scientific picture of the world revolutionized medicine. That human beings receive implantations of heart valves or pacemakers is based upon a mechanistic understanding of the body that was developed in the Age of Enlightenment.

The new spirit of the time filled the physicians of that epoch with increasing optimism. Their confidence in a medicine based on a mechanistic model grew steadily with every additional success. Physicians now dared to tread in areas that were previously avoided, problems of a spiritual and soulish nature that had previously been left to the care of ministers and priests.

Yet the developing understanding of psychiatric illnesses was not furthered by the medical profession alone. The social upheaval engendered by the revolution of the middle class and the new thoughts of the Enlightenment led to evaluations

---

1. Ibid. p. 208

of the way the mentally ill had been treated up to that point. There was a growing conviction that it was not permissible to lock up the mentally ill with vagabonds and criminals, but rather that they needed a special kind of treatment in institutions directed by medical personnel. These medical aspirations were encouraged by the early capitalist economy, since they seemed to promise that the "crazy people" could be tamed and, to some extent, turned into productive forces.

Michel Foucault, teaching on the history of systems of thought at the Collège de France in Paris, believes that medical view of insanity developed as a result of the collaboration of the Enlightenment (reason versus unreason) and the new commercial interests (order versus disorder) of the population. In *Madness and Civilisation*, in which he questions psychiatry both critically and exhaustively, he begins with the observation that it was only with the totalitarian regimes' practice of confining people that both the creation of insane asylums and psychiatry itself became possible. During the seventeenth and eighteenth centuries, in countries with absolute rulers a wide assortment of people – homosexuals, criminals, those believed to be insane and others – were locked up together in penitentiaries because they interfered with the established order.

In Germany, these institutions were correctly named penitentiaries; in England they were called workhouses, and in France they were given the euphemism "hopitaux généraux" (general hospitals). In the seventeenth century, one purpose of the institutions in which people could be interned was to control social crises.

It is Foucault's opinion that the history of insanity can be understood only if the history of reason is considered at the same time, as he sees reason and insanity as a pair that cannot be separated. In his view, the higher valuation of reason has led to a system of order that despises life and condemns the voice of "counter-reason" (insanity) to be silent. There is no doubt that psychiatric institutions became coercive in following their intention of maintaining the established order in the name of reason. Yet psychiatric knowledge also developed outside such institutions.

The period of the French revolution is of particular meaning for the history of psychiatry. Between 1793 – 1795, the physician Philippe Pinel assumed the direction of the institutions in Paris that were handled like prisons: Bicêtre (for men) and Salpêtrière (for women). Within a short time, Pinel managed to abolish many restraints such as chains, neck and feet rings, and to introduce new treatment approaches.

> When Philippe Pinel is celebrated as the "liberator of the insane," one must take into account that his chief superintendent, Poussin, provided him with considerable support. It should also be pointed out that long before Pinel and the French revolution there were good places for the care of psychiatrically ill patients, for example in some religious order settlements, or in a Florentine hospital administered by Vincenzo Chiarugi (1759 – 1820). In 1796, the Quaker William Tuke, a businessman and medical layperson, did away with mechanical restraints and relied on "moral management" in his private insane asylum, "Retreat." Finally, it must be added that while Pinel and his disciples did abolish the chains, they later introduced new and technologically more advanced means of physical control, such as restraining chairs and restraining jackets.

Nevertheless, Pinel remains an important figure in the development of psychiatry. He is the embodiment of an historic turning point during which the socially outcast sufferer moved from being seen as troublesome and possessed to being viewed as ill. Pinel turned them, in large numbers indeed, into medical cases. In that era he created a type of institutional psychiatry that focused primarily upon the systematic observation and examination of both women and men patients. As a result of his exact descriptions of mania, melancholia, dementia and feeblemindedness, psychiatry established itself as a specialty in the field of medicine. All this was based on his case histories of the sick. The type of institution that he and his disciples called for soon spread, aided by the support of new laws and the foundation of new institutions all across France; by 1950 almost every French province had its own institution for the insane.

A similar proliferation of institutions for the insane also took place (given certain delays) in other European countries and in North America. It did not take long for psychiatry to be accepted as a medical science in Europe and in America. Chairs for the teaching of psychiatry were established in the universities everywhere in order to promote a medical view of psychiatric disorders.[1]

The history of psychiatry's development and its link to the political obligation to maintain orderly systems created some difficulties for this medical specialty that last to the present. Psychiatry's understanding of psychological illness developed from an historical perspective that attempted to overcome absolutism and its tendency to inclusiveness, but was not willing to renounce the appraisal of humans by rational means. So this generation of psychiatry's founders advocated a "moral therapy." Seeing problematic doubts in psychiatry was interpreted as an expression of spiritual confusion,while psychological health was characterized by moral insight and ethical actions. An enlightened understanding of psychiatric illness no longer meant a sin against the holy ghost, but a sin against reason.

---

1. A summary of the development of institutional psychiatry is contained in my inaugural lecture (D. Hell 1993)

The psychological treatment that characterized early psychiatry consisted largely of attempts to reestablish ordered reasoning in the mind of the sick person. The strongly hierarchic structure of the new Institutions of "welfare and maintenance" served this aim, as did a well-planned system of supervision. However, when deemed necessary, carefully planned punishments, such as the shock of a cold shower or bath, or some whipping, were also employed. For a long time, a kind of rotating machine like a carousel was popular. This machine, invented by Charles Darwin's grandfather, reflected the mood of the time because its effectiveness could be measured, and the physician was assured of proceeding precisely, mathematically and with proper controls.[1]

> The principle of treatment by the psychiatric method has been summarized accurately by Jean Starobinski: "One might cuddle the sick individuals as children, trying to tame them by means of pleasant things, but then one frightens them, terrifying them with things and brutalizing them."[2] All this is done with good intentions of changing the mind from its aberration. In addition, there are music, theater and other excursions intended to help wealthy patients amuse themselves with moderation and discover an "art of living." The methodical prescription of medicine for vomiting and laxatives used since ancient times also fell within the scope of this method of treatment. However, these herbal purifying medications were no longer introduced to reestablish a balance of the "saps," as advocated by Hippocrates, but in order to punish the sick persons for their confused thinking, hoping to get the self to disclose its rational awareness.

According to the way illness was understood during the Enlightenment, the soul was a subject capable of conscious-

---

1. Detailed presentations are to be found in K. Dörner 1984, F.G. Alexander/ S.T. Selesnick 1968, M. Foucault 1973, and in "Skizzen zur Psychiatriegeschichte" (tr. *Sketches for the History of Psychiatry*) by C. Müller 1998
2. J. Starobinski 1960, p. 67

ness whose rationality could become confused by passions and emotions. Being psychologically ill, then, implied a condition of licentiousness, confused thinking and internal contradictions. In addition, K. Ideler (1795-1860) a highly respected psychiatrist, viewed people with greatly intensified uniqueness as pathological.

In keeping with the spirit of the Enlightenment, the highest aim was to assist reason, considered the greatest treasure of the human being, to become freshly predominant. This is why approaches developed during that time have a moralistic taste. J. Henroth (1773-1843), the most prominent spokesman of romantic psychiatry, saw illnesses of the soul as related to unwise and sinful behavior.

Almost anything was allowed in the name of returning sick people to reason. The highest goal was a "life based on reason." Medicine, in the nineteenth century, appreciated reason so enthusiastically that it was willing to fight unreasonableness with pious fraud and false promises, or to fight one's passions with methods employing shock (e.g., cold showers, eels in the bathtub and other means of evoking disgust). What began in the name of reason grew, through arrogance, into unreason.

*Psychotherapy of the Soul versus Somatic Psychiatry*

We must concede that the methods introduced as "psychiatric cures" were not all new; the Greeks and Romans had, to some extent, tried similar approaches. However, the theoretical justifications for their use were adapted to the new times. In that connection, there were two different schools of psychiatry. Psychotherapists began with the opinion that each spiritual activity can be reduced to soulish, not somatic, factors. They consistently saw their patients as people who had become diseased in soul or spirit, namely in the organ

(Descartes' "res cogitans") that made them capable of recognizing things.

Opposite them stood the "somatic therapists" (Gr. soma = body), who took the position that there was no disorder without some activity of the nerves; they saw in psychiatric patients people who suffered from disturbances of the nerves.[1]

Psychotherapists and somaticists deliberated for a long time whether psychiatric disorders were spiritual (i.e., psychological or moral) or more of a bodily nature. Their exchanges seemed to be based on insuperable contrasts. The bitterness of the fight between psychotherapists and somaticists could, however, obscure the fact that these hostile brothers were ultimately children of the same fundamental view. In truth, both of them resolutely stood for Descartes' conviction that the human was a combination of a knowing, immaterial subject and a recognizable, material object. The problem lay in the fact that the psychotherapists saw the cause of the psychiatric suffering in the subject, while the somaticists saw it in the object. In a certain sense, the somaticists could claim to represent Descartes' doctrine in a purer form than the psychotherapists, because they were convinced that the immortal soul could not become ill and because of that, one had to study the body as the part of the person that is susceptible to illness.

Both the psychotherapists and the somaticists were children of the Enlightenment. They shared the rational view of their time that a disturbance of order was at the root of psychiatric problems. Their only argument, then, concerned the question of whether these disturbances were of a psychological or a physical nature.

---

1. In the seventeenth and eighteenth centuries, the concept of disturbances due to the nerves was new, since to that time, medicine had been dominated by the Hippocratic doctrine of the "saps."

We note that as time went on, different combinations of psychological and somatic factors determined the interpretation of psychiatric illness. Among the prominent representatives of more complete views were Wilhelm Griesinger in the middle of the nineteenth century, and Karl Jaspers in the first part of the twentieth century. Griesinger's medical practice persuaded him to take seriously the patients' subjective experiences and their objective data. Jaspers, both physician and philosopher, gained recognition for a psychiatry that was based on a theory of cognition. We shall repeatedly have to return to him.

> Griesinger (1817-1869) coined the frequently quoted sentence: "Psychiatric illnesses are illnesses of the brain." In spite of this example, he was no somaticist, but sought a synthesis of physiological, psychological and social viewpoints. He viewed psychiatric disorders such as psychoses not as aggregations of single symptoms, but as holistic processes in which hereditary factors, character development, intense affects and changes in the nervous system worked together. He taught that difficult psychological circumstances turned out to be the most frequent causes of psychological disorders, because they lead to conflict states in consciousness, and thus to a disturbance of the ego(!).

Unduly rigid diagnoses of psychiatric illnesses were foreign to Griesinger's nature. Adhering to the idea of a unitary psychosis, he not only espoused the idea that single psychiatric illnesses could change one into another, but also that health and sickness could not be sharply delineated. To illustrate that, he used the example of a dream and a psychosis, remarking that even in the dream of a healthy person, just as in a psychotic condition, there are involuntary responses to physical sensations. A full fifty years before Freud, Griesinger stressed the role of the unconscious in both health and illness; but he also supported the view that in mental illnesses, one should explore what part of the brain is affected.[1]

## What is Normal?

It is not just the scrutiny of different biological and psychosocial factors that have influenced our understanding of psychiatric illness. Developments in the understanding of what constitutes illness have been shaped even more fundamentally by the very question of what is "normal," i.e., what is normal and what is a deviation from normal. Later on, this question was superseded by the far more important question of whether "normal" is also "healthy," and whether "abnormal" is necessarily "sick."

Ethnology points to the fact that certain styles of behavior that are considered sick in industrialized nations are often considered normal in foreign cultures. To some extent, this is also the case with ideas of persecution and greatness, and with hallucinations and states of ecstasy. So, for example, hallucinations are not considered extraordinary among the Mohavies and Takalas.[2]

> Therefore, medical historian Erwin Ackerknecht, who otherwise follows a natural-scientific orientation, reached the following conclusion: "We can thus conclude that what is psychologically normal depends to a large degree on the views of a particular social organization… and that the decision by such a group as to whether a certain person is mentally ill is basically not dependent on certain symptoms that occur in a similar way everywhere, but on whether the affected persons display a minimum of blending and operating in their own society, or whether the psychological

---

1. E. H. Ackerknecht 1985, p. 67f.
2. according to E. H. Ackerknecht 1985

variations are so advanced that they become a 'foreign body' in that society.

The relativity of symptoms (in their pathological severity) can be seen not only through ethnological but also historical data. Henry E. Sigerist pointed out many years ago that the same medieval master-singer who was considered normal by his contemporaries would be viewed as insane today. The same applies to many other characters living in medieval times and later, for example ecstatic religious persons, persecutors of witches and ascetic puritans. There is little doubt that the "normal" person of the twentieth century would have been viewed as abnormal in many earlier centuries…"[1]

Differing from the tendency to view various behavioral standards as relative is society's adherence to rigid diagnostic standards. In the middle of the twentieth century it became known that in Russia, opponents of the government were given psychiatric diagnoses in order to intern and silence them. When, at about the same time, Rosenbaum's research showed that in large American psychiatric clinics, volunteer research patients pretending to have specific symptoms were diagnosed as schizophrenics, opponents of psychiatry began to ask for the abolition of all psychiatric labeling. American psychoanalyst Thomas Szasz, in *The Myth of Mental Illness*, described that as the resurgence of "possession in modern attire," comparing psychiatric diagnosis to the procedures of the inquisition in the 16th century, when "witches" were prosecuted for their deviant behavior.

Admittedly, this historical comparison is problematic. Nevertheless, it points to a fundamental problem in the evaluation of deviant behavior: diagnoses, at times, are not exclusively the basis of a helpful therapy; they can also be used to characterize people unfairly as punishment, or to protect authority. The history of psychiatry includes not

1. E. H. Ackerknecht 1985, p. 3

only diagnostic and therapeutic advances, but also a history of psychiatric abuse related to social goals. Historically, it has been the uncritical alliance of social norms and established psychiatric-biological norms that have lead to catastrophic consequences.

## The Unspeakable Mixture of Social and Biological Norms

As indicated, psychiatry, as it developed in early institutions designed for the internment of "disturbed" people, took on absolutist qualities. As a child of the Enlightenment it was committed to rational order both internally and externally. Its historical origins fostered hypotheses about psychiatric disorders that focused primarily on those who previously had been avoided socially, or forcefully interned in asylums as being abnormal. These patients were the raw material for the studies of Emil Kraepelin (1856-1926), who continues to strongly influence the classification of psychiatric disorders.

The methods used for separating people from society with diagnostic evaluations were made easier by a new understanding of illness that was shaped by ideas of social and biological norms.

According to the researchers Sarasin and Tanner,[1] medicine developed a new understanding of illness that viewed the body as a physical device little different from a thermodynamic machine. This went beyond an exclusively anatomical description of the body, and with this physiological belief it became customary to compare purposeful and normal events and to separate them from abnormal, that is, harmful events. This was formulated by Claude Bernhard, the leading physiologist of the nineteenth century, in the following way: "An understanding of pathological or abnormal conditions

1. Ph. Sarasin /J. Tanner 1998

can be gained only on the basis of insight into the normal condition." (Quoted by Sarasin)

Based on this understanding of the body, what is alive becomes an inner dynamic that serves external goals. The inner dynamic of metabolism follows patterns that can be reconstructed mathematically, and functional conditions in equilibrium are viewed as normal, while their imbalance is viewed as abnormal.

At the turn of the century this "inner system of regulation" of physiology was expanded into a "super-individual regulation." As Mendel's laws were newly presented, procreation began to be viewed as a process that could be formulated and controlled.

This natural-scientific model of an internal organic order was brought together during the shift from the nineteenth to the twentieth century with a very different, external ordering system. This ordering system is of a social nature, being based on a society's evaluation of human behavior. Because of this, it became possible for two different ordering systems – the social and the physiological – to be linked together in a very puzzling manner: the biological organization of the internal environment and the reproduction processes was expanded to include the entire human being and eventually, the entire social order. The laws of natural science were put forward to justify specific social value standards. Conversely, social norms were established in order to exemplify physiological events.

Hence we encounter the idea of eugenicist Karl Schneider, director of the psychiatric clinic of Heidelberg University, who stated that an organism consisted of a system of overlapping functions that not only encompassed the bodily and 'soulish,' but also determined the organism's interactions with its surroundings. Using this reasoning, Schneider concluded that questions pertaining to the body-soul and the integrated structure of the human were problems that could be solved with the proper method.[1]

Other physiologically oriented psychiatrists viewed the organism as a hierarchically ordered system that they compared to an business whose various jobs were related to making the enterprise successful.

Seeing social aspects in biological terms was also greatly furthered by social Darwinism. In his profoundly influential work *On the Origin of Species by Means of Natural Selection* (1859), Charles Darwin wrote on the "survival of the fittest."[2] Soon after this publication, the theory of evolution was shifted from a biological to a social level. Thus we find German zoologist Ernst Haeckel (1868) writing in a widely distributed publication about cultural selection, and drawing attention to the notion that it was a citizen's duty to eradicate the sick and undesirable in order to improve his genetic assets and survival chances.

This mixture of physiological function, genetic and social Darwinism drew broad interest before and after the First World War, but then spread faster as social misery became widespread. The greater the social distress, the more fervent the search for a simple, technological solution that would seemingly do away with all the problems in predictable, controllable ways. It was just this kind of rational and efficient solution that seemed promised by the science of eugenics that had formed under the influence of social Darwinism and psychiatric beliefs about degeneration[3].

---

1. G. Hohendorf et al. 1996, p. 939
2. Darwin, however, was not a eugenicist. The idea of "natural selection" clearly excludes selective breeding by human beings.
3. According to the "degeneration" theory of the psychiatrist B. A. Morel (1809-1873), mental illnesses developed on the basis of hereditary predisposition, which was believed to get more serious from generation to generation.

The concept of eugenics was developed in 1883 by psychologist Francis Galton as a science of the preservation and improvement of human hereditary assets by means of improved methods of propagation. For Galton, the term "positive eugenics" meant encouraging the propagation of genetically healthy people, and the term "negative eugenics" meant restricting the propagation of genetically unhealthy people.

Both conservative and progressive circles expected early successes in the fight against poverty and illness as a result of eugenic measures. Especially desired and – it is frightening to have to say so – promoted by the psychiatric community, was the eugenic campaign against alcoholism, mental illness, feeblemindedness and epilepsy.

The political success of this unholy partnership of alleged science and social programs intended to eliminate the "unhealthy" was enormous in spite of warning voices. By 1931, thirty-one states had laws enabling "hereditary detectives," and the sterilization of people with hereditary illnesses. In most of the European countries, the sterilization of mentally ill and feebleminded people was legalized in the years that followed. In Switzerland, the Canton Waadt accepted a law to that effect in 1928. In Germany, four hundred thousand hospitalized psychiatric patients were forcibly sterilized.

Eugenics did not stop with the suppression of the ability to procreate, however. In 1920, two German university professors, an attorney named Binding and a psychiatrist named Hoche, called for permission to euthanize not only sick people who asked for an end to their suffering, but also to do that – without the patient's consent – when incurably psychotic and feebleminded patients were involved, calling such patients "dead weights" and "empty human shells." In 1939, Hitler ordered the deaths of mentally ill and feebleminded patients after a committee of professors of psychiatry and neurology and directors of psychiatric institutions submitted precise suggestions for ways to terminate those patients. "In the fall of 1941, gas chambers which had been used for murdering psychiatric patients were transferred to concentration camps. Forced sterilization, euthanasia and the "final solution" were explained ideologically and, directly or indirectly, hygienic, racial motives were implied." (C. Ernst)[1]

Is there a connection between these historical developments and our way of understanding psychiatric illness? Yes, and it is significant! I cannot imagine that the euthanizing of severely psychotic patients would have been possible in the absence of a totalitarian regime and considerable social misery. At the root of those crimes is the connecting of "socially inferior" to "sick." The equating of social abnormality with biological abnormality branded psychiatric patients in two ways: first, social devaluation was justified by the biological argument, and second, the biological abnormality seemed to necessitate the social consequences. This led to a diabolically vicious circle that first was a factor in denying the mentally ill their right to procreate, and then, under Fascism, lead to their deaths as "unworthy eaters."

> Today, half a century after a holocaust that also involved the mentally ill, the collaboration of social emergency programs and eugenics practices may seem to be only a bad dream. However, some social scientists and historians, such as G. A. Allen, are of a different opinion. In a 1997 edition of the international journal *Genetics*, Allen drew attention to the fact that even now, medical and socioeconomic interests complement each other in analyses of cost-efficiency, and that discussions of who should

---

1. C. Ernst 1990, p 110. The most comprehensive and careful study regarding euthanasia was prepared by theologian and social academic Ernst Klee (E. Klee 1983). Zürich psychiatrist Cécile Ernst has covered in two impressive articles the connections between national socialism and eugenics, as well as between nationalism and euthanasia (C. Ernst 1985; C. Ernst 1990).

receive what help for how long are not new. Such discussions are impossible lacking value judgments regarding different attitudes to life. As to any likelihood that the United States would one day attempt to solve social problems with natural-scientific means, Allen answered, "I'm sorry to have to say that I think that my answer must be yes. It is self-evident that a new eugenics movement would be labeled differently, but a time of similar economic and social conditions and a similar political response – couched, for example, in our current philosophy of "cost-effectiveness" and the "bottom line" – is already at our doorstep."

One can counter this gloomy prediction with the argument that it was not natural scientific findings but rather insufficient biological knowledge that led to eugenics, and that it was, in fact, scientific advances that exposed the failure of eugenic measures. In addition, modern research in molecular biology shows that genes are not unchanging carriers of information that exert their influence apart from other internal or external influences. Thus it seems that the genes involved in human behavior are most strongly influenced by the environment. It must be noted, however, that in difficult social times little attention is given to skeptical objections against technological attempts to solve socially problematic situations. Also, one must not forget that it is especially a society with a one-sided orientation to efficiency and competition that risks discrimination against those who are not successful, as well as denying them needed assistance.

It was the darkest chapter of the history of psychiatry, in which human beings, seen through a filter of false certainty, were made into "things" that could be disposed of like any other object. The mixing of disparate standards, e.g., equating the individual and society with the biological and physiological sciences, has to do with the suggestive power of the word. The difference between what is meant biologically by "race," and what is meant by "race" socially becomes murky when the same word is used for biological and social conditions. It then becomes feasible to justify social and racial discrimination using biological arguments.

This historical experience should cause us to be very careful in our choice of words. If a modern term such as "cognition" can be applied poorly, it is possible that a psychological description of spiritual events might suddenly become a neuro-biological event if no distinction is made between the conscious mental process of thinking and remembering and its biological correlation. This sort of imprecision is unsuitable, and might make it easier in the future to treat a human being as "something" rather than "somebody."

### Sick Human Being or Sick Organ?

My final cautionary opinion may at first seem exaggerated and only theoretically grounded. The fact, however, that psychiatry did not submit its theories to a systematic critique seems directly related to its fair share of guilt for the age of eugenics. The same danger applies to the inexact term "illness." Eugenically oriented psychiatrists like Karl Schneider merged and confused different classifications, making no distinctions between a "sick brain" and a "sick person." There was even talk of a "sick population body" in the sense of a sick society.

Yet an organ or organism is not sick in the same way as a human being. The term "illness" that is applied to a human cannot be applied to an organ or the physiology of an organism, or even less, to a society. Admittedly, human illness has to do with changes of the organism or its organs, but it is only human judgment that makes possible the assessment of specific organic changes as one that is pathological.

Let me illustrate with an example: Since psychiatry, until rather recently, viewed homosexuality as an illness that required treatment, this evaluation led to the conclusion that hormonal and genetic deviations in the homosexual had to be considered abnormal and pathological. Yet when homosexuality was eliminated as a category of psychiatric illnesses, the genetic constellations in homosexuals, even though they had not changed, were no longer seen as abnormal.

Whenever an organ or a metabolic function is regarded as disturbed or sick, we must always remember that nature is not able to evaluate itself; it is only the human being – *qua* cultural being – who is able to assess him- or herself. For this reason, an organ or organism is never "naturally sick." It is only when the life of a person is negatively affected by an organic or metabolic change that deviations in the organs of affected people can be assessed as diseased.

> The idea that changes in organs directly determine, by themselves, the psychological illness of a human being, is an erroneous conclusion. In the first half of the twentieth century that idea led many psychiatrists to see eugenics as required by nature. My prominent predecessor at the Burghölzli Psychiatric Hospital, Eugen Bleuler, even tried to interpret eugenics and morality as unfolding from nature. He took a stand against the "hyper-Christian welfare" that would lead to a genetic weakening of humankind.[1]

The study of various theories of illness shows quite clearly how the definitions of illness are influenced by social conventions. The criteria for psychological illness have changed radically several times just during the past century. As mentioned above, sickness was first defined as whatever interfered with the external order, or disturbed the inner equilibrium. The pathological causes of hysteria and psychopathy that were diagnosed with great frequency during the transition from the

---

1. I have described these connections in an article: "Eugen Bleulers Seelenverständnis und die Moderne" (tr. *Eugen Bleuler's concept of the soul and our present one)* (2000). A review of Eugen Bleuler's life and work is found in D. Hell / Ch. Scharfetter / A. Möller 2001.

nineteenth to the twentieth century were seen as being linked to disturbances of family or social order. At the beginning of the twentieth century, the pathological view of schizophrenic psychosis became the prototype for illness characterized by being torn apart inside (schizophrenia = split mind).

This situation changed in the first half of the twentieth century as rigid diagnostic terms were shaken up by patients' deeply moving experiences during wars and social upheavals. One's ability to master difficult situations in life by means of appropriate skills in adjusting now occupied the foreground; in the definition of health, the criterion of maintaining stable order was replaced by that of demonstrating the ability to adjust flexibly. The increasing influence of psychoanalytic teachings supported this trend in its view of psychological disturbances primarily as expressions of inner conflicts that reduced human adaptability. Sigmund Freud defined psychological illness as a disturbance of the ability to work and love. The new diagnosis of neurosis that prevailed in the middle of the twentieth century implied not only diminished adaptability to external circumstances, it also referred to an individual's inability to adjust to conflicting inner demands. Soon, "Adjustment disorder" was accepted as a diagnosis in the international classification of psychological disorders of the World Health Organization. This was a result of the inception of behavioral theory, which reduces psychological disorders to changes in behavior.

Toward the end of the twentieth century, a third distinguishing criterion became prominent: in place of order and adjustment, it is now the level of one's well-being that decides whether a person is sick or well. The actual World Health Organization definition states that a person is sick when his or her well-being is disrupted. Individual experience is thus given priority over any other criterion. Feeling unwell – e.g., in a premenstrual state, or being shy – conditions previously viewed as normal, have thus become disorders requiring treatment. Even relatively minor depressive mood changes are given the higher assessment of "illness."

These trends have been reinforced by commercial influences: during the last decades, with the cooperation of an increasingly significant pharmaceutical industry, different disorders of well-being have been grouped together because they could be treated with the same medication. For example, the diagnosis of "Panic disorder," surfacing at the end of the nineteen-sixties, encompassed as uniformly treatable disorders such conditions as heart-neuroses and hyperventilation syndromes that manifest in very different ways.[1]

## From Convention to Deconstruction

As is true with all other medical branches, psychiatry is a practical discipline. It aims to treat states of suffering and disturbance. To this effect, it establishes diagnostic categories and clinical guidelines, aiming to distinguish different conditions of illness, intending to observe their development, and surveying their treatment. However, these categories are not absolute.

Every system of classifying diseases or disturbances is an attempt to meet, as well as possible, the practical requirements. "All classifications are expressions of viewpoints, perusing a heuristic principle (seeking, for example, to be useful for research, therapy, communication or even for administration

1. In *The Antidepressant Era*, using depression as an example, David Healy described the influence of science, health-department politics and industry on the understanding of illness (D. Healy 1998). Edward Shorter, for example, views psychosomatic disorders as an expression of the interplay of nature and culture, that is, of genetic predisposition and the current spirit of the time. (E. Shorter 1999)

and financing), and they are neither able to grasp nature as a whole nor to cut nature at its joints."[1]

All this boils down to the insight that in defining illness there is a temporary agreement among specialists on the smallest common denominator. As a result, ideas of illness correspond to "The actual situation of the error."

However, his insight is easily overlooked when a practical science such as psychiatry is less concerned about its foundations than its successes. In that case, *hubris* may broadly assert itself, more or less reflecting the following attitude: "Why should we be concerned about cognitive theories and basic philosophical questions? We are guided by our experiences, and leave to the theoreticians and philosophers the task of fitting our doctrines into a comprehensive whole." That attitude, and the conviction that one's ideas correspond to natural truth, contributed to the misuse of psychiatry for social purposes in the first half of the twentieth century.

Karl Jaspers once observed that every physician is also a philosopher. What he meant was that every physician behaves according to a personal view of the world and of values, whether she/he is aware of this or not, and that physicians thus are unable to avoid assessing the value of their patients. Thus he saw no course of action other than having a view, a philosophy pertaining to a human being, and renouncing that evaluation; in this sense, a physician has only the choice of being aware or unaware of this fact. Jaspers also made a carefully analytic attempt to methodically comprehend the body-soul problem.[2] He drew the sharpest distinction between inner psychological experience on one hand, and what can be observed externally, on the other hand. According

1. E. Wallace et al. 1997, p. 71. W. Wieland showed in his book "Diagnose" (tr. *Diagnosis)* (1975) that the concepts of illness are of a general nature, and that it is inaccurate to identify them with individual diagnoses.
2. In the ninth edition of the book "Allgemeine Psychopathologie" (*General Psychopathology*) *(1973)*, and in tr. *Collected Writings on Psychopathology.*

to Jaspers, whatever is observable from the outside can be explained biologically, whereas the "inner psychological" is approachable only through an interpretive (hermeneutic) understanding. Yet inasmuch the inner-psychological and the externally observable occur at the same time, and since the external can be shaped by the internal, Jaspers stressed that it is decisive for both diagnosis and treatment that the biologically explainable and those aspects that can be explained by interpretation be combined, but not mixed.

Karl Popper, another outstanding philosopher, has stressed this as a rule: "Clinical observations, like all other observations, are interpretations in the light of theories."[1] Meanwhile, a number of scientific disciplines have arisen (in philosophy, sociology and history) that follow the connections between social history on one hand and scientific views on the other. They clearly show that the search for natural laws in medicine is in no way independent from sociological evaluations. Research does not draw knowledge out of the body, but in essence transforms the body into a text, a living book that is read in a specific, culturally determined way.[2] In reading this "living book," the interpretations can be so complicated that the body recedes into ever more abstract ideas.

Looking at the past hundred years we find that physiology has "liquefied" and "electrified" the body by discovering the regulatory systems of hormones and neurons. Due to molecular biology, the body has turned into a setting of information exchange. The text which is sought in the body has become so abstract that the real body, that which can be touched and felt, is in danger of being lost in science.[3]

1. K. Popper 1963
2. Ph. Sarasin / J. Tanner 1998, p. 19
3. B. Müller-Hill 1981, p. 143

*The Overly-Quantified Human Being*

These conclusions confront modern medicine with special challenges. First is the challenge to do justice to the living human body, to its sensations and feelings, even though in our era of evidence-based medicine, the human being, viewed from the perspective of modern medicine, increasingly resembles a data bank. Digital recording of data collected about people facilitates the synthesis of a virtual human being in cyberspace. As a result, we must question what position medicine will take in the future in regard to the individual's intangible life space, that which has been, in the history of the occident, symbolically distinguished as "soul."

The likelihood of characterizing the structural composition of a human being by means of ever more information – in effect, the virtual person – goes hand in hand with the psychiatric attempt to also reduce character traits and the psychological, problematic questions of being human to single units of information. Such tendencies may easily cause academic society to lose interest in the testimony of the individual, namely in what people say about themselves and how they have knotted together their experiences into a meaningful story. Increasingly, academic psychiatry is focused on information about specific traits that can be recorded and assessed digitally.

The specific traits that one can establish by questioning refer, for example, to:
a) the level of consciousness (whether the person is fully awake or sleepy);
b) the memory (whether the person possesses clear or murky short term memory, or an intact or impaired long term memory);
c) the form of thinking (whether there is an unimpaired flow of thoughts, or if there are blocks in thinking); or

d) the mood (whether it is happy, balanced or depressed).
In combining such information into a grid of symptoms, a new "image" of the subject is drawn.

Made up of units of information and established with the help of computers, this picture of a human is a robot image. It is different from the overall impression of a person that I gather when we meet (the person's appearance, outward behavior and style of communication). The digitally created image has no real Gestalt[1]; it contains no personal message, no meaning. It is simply a made up fact, the digital calculation of various characteristics and figures. It gains its Gestalt, becomes a message and is meaningful only when an observer considers at this robot image and is able to create a corresponding likeness from personal experience. However, the observer's ability to create meaning can be misleading, if one does not recognize that the digitally created picture is artificial, not being based on personal experience. To gain that experience, one must have a genuine dialogue with the person to be evaluated, a conversation that goes beyond the digital recording of separate traits.

The problem in making a useful diagnosis is not just about measuring human traits by computer; it comes from the uncritical assumption that such a method could ever be a substitute for a dialogue with a person who is asking for help. One must be able to understand the individual's situation and history. There would, however, be no objections if the intuitive impressions that often occur in such personal discussions could be carefully validated by technical methods; proceeding that way would definitely improve the individual assessment.

---

1. (Translator:) A physical, biological, psychological, or symbolic configuration or pattern of elements so unified as a whole that its properties cannot be derived from a simple summation of its parts.

However, since 1980, modern psychiatry, with the guidance of the United States and with the introduction of *The Diagnostic and Statistical Manual of Psychiatric Disorders* (DSM III and IV) diagnoses psychiatric disorders based on specific signs and symptoms that can be established without knowing if the answers of the patients are related to their personal histories and actual circumstances. These symptom-oriented proceedings allow for easier diagnostic processing. They also satisfy a need for research, as with it, correlations can be obtained between several research efforts. However, they also lead to the unjustified conclusion that those objective observations can truly understand the subjective experience.

In psychiatry one acts more and more often on the assumption that the specific traits of a person that are found on a questionnaire correspond to a specific change in the brain. In this way, the unquestioned assumption that all experience and behavior have a physical origin will lead to a false conclusion that a fixed psychological syndrome, such as a depressive disorder, must necessarily be the expression of changes in metabolic and neural activity.

> One might assume that the psycho-social definition of illness involves the separation of physical conditions at their "seams." However, in truth, certain syndromes (such as dejection, fatigue, indecisiveness, disorders of appetite and difficulty falling asleep, representing a pattern of depressive symptoms) may be expressed by various kinds of physical conditions and do not need to display a consistent pattern of neural activity.
> The assumption that there are distinct patterns of psycho-social symptoms and disruptions of bodily functions is conveyed more by the suggestive power of language than by rationally grounded relationships.

Logic demonstrates that it is quite possible to think of clusters of symptoms that indicate very different bodily conditions. Just think of the state of feeling hot, accompanied by a loss of appetite and anxiety. This group of symptoms could just as easily be attributed to elevated body temperature due to various causes as to a disturbance of temperature receptivity in the central nervous system, or an excessive demand in terms of heat regulation in a very hot environment. For this reason, it has become important in the science of neurology to start by studying certain changes in the brain and following their consequences by consciously distinguishing them, than by reaching conclusions born from changes in experience or related to hypothetical bodily deficits due to a lack of more accurate knowledge of any underlying disturbance of neurological function.

> Paul Broca, the originator of neuropsychology, studied very carefully the psychological status of a Monsieur Lebrogne, a patient who had suffered an injury of the posterior left frontal lobe, and worked out the connection between the brain lesion and Lebrogne's speech disorder. Broca also analyzed his observations of other patients with left side frontal lobe injuries and, on the basis of these observations, was able to draw conclusions pertaining to the speech centers in the posterior left frontal lobe. This approach enabled him to avoid the problems of a purely statistical comparison of personal traits and changes in the brain. Had Broca restricted himself to merely establishing statistical correlations between verbal expression and brain structure, it is unlikely that he could have presented his important findings.

*Example: Schizophrenia*

By focusing on schizophrenia, I would like to clearly show what I have up to now presented theoretically as problems in the modern theory of illness. The idea of schizophrenia was introduced to psychiatry a century ago by Emil Kraepelin, who used a different term for the condition. Kraepelin said that he was able to differentiate one group of patients from other hospitalized patients based on the course of their illness. According to him, in this regard it was irrelevant that the patients presented very different disease features, for example, being totally withdrawn, or agitated, or having delusions with hallucinations, or were conspicuous because of their silly behavior. For Kraepelin, only the early onset during puberty and the unfavorable course of the illness were important. It was because of these prognostic criteria and the disintegration of the patient's psychological coherence that Kraepelin spoke of "dementia praecox," i.e., premature dementia. In 1905 he wrote, "I chose the designation dementia praecox because it did not contain anything other than the unfavorable prognosis and the onset of the disorder at a young age, traits that appeared to be central in the newly formed group of illnesses."[1] Kraepelin's list of the symptoms of dementia praecox, which included more observed features from one edition to the next, was increasingly accepted. His theory of dementia praecox was inseparably linked to his belief that – as in the case of general paralysis, a recently identified infectious disorder of the brain linked to syphilitic spirochetes – an anatomically identifiable origin of the disorder could be found. As a result of this conviction, in describing dementia praecox patients Kraepelin focused exclusively on the presenting symptoms and his observations of the course of the disorders, deliberately avoiding the inner emotional struggles of the affected patients.

These internal struggles were emphasized first by psychiatrist Eugen Bleuler, of Zürich. It was he who gave the disorder its current name: schizophrenia (Greek for divided spirit). For

---

1. Quoted from my article: "100 Jahre Ringen um die Schizophrenien" (tr. *100 years of struggling about schizophrenia*) (D. Hell 1995)

Blculer, it was not the course of the illness that was most important, but rather the psychological split, the inner tearing apart and the obvious discrepancies in the communications and behavior of these patients.

> Bleuler saw their internal ambivalence and confined focus on themselves (autism) as essential indications of the disorder. His focus on the tendency to turn inward was not just related to Bleuler's interest in Freud's psychoanalytic theories, but also to his much greater empathy for the patients he treated. In that regard, it is important to know that Bleuler's sister developed a psychosis at a young age, and that her illness influenced the choice of his profession and the subsequent course of his life.[1]

Austrian psychiatrist Leo Navratil recently drew attention to the peculiar fact that, "At just about the time the term "schizophrenia" appeared, the theme of fragmentation of personality and dissolution of the ego also frequently appeared in the arts and in literature. Was this parallel merely an accidental development, or were there cultural connections?" Navratil further, states, "One could get the idea that Eugen Bleuler was led to the concept of schizophrenia not only by the messages of his patients, but that the image of a split soul in the literature of that time had also reached psychiatry and contributed to the establishment of the new term."[2] Anyone who explores this notion will find fascinating parallels between the schizophrenic's forms of expression and specific stylistic expressions of modern art in Louis Sass' rather striking book *Madness and Modernism*. Never before were ambivalence, fragmentation, depersonalization and loss of identity themes as dominant they became in the literature and art of the twentieth century.

1. Bleuler's beginnings and youth are described in D. Hell et al. 2001
2. L. Navratil 1992, p. 16

By employing the unifying feature of dissociation to group previously unrelated illnesses into a coherent perspective, Bleuler seemed – or was – able to gather variations under the same denominator. After that, patients' varying manifestations – "silly", "excited," or "delusional" – no longer occupied the foreground; it was the dissociative element that, like a paper clip, united those different forms.

Bleuler's concept of a "group of schizophrenias" had the advantage of opening the way for the evaluation of patients' inner experiences, and of allowing the inclusion of attempts at psychodynamic interpretations. Yet it also had the disadvantage of greatly broadening the concept of the illness, thus blurring the borders separating schizophrenia from other disorders. As a result, American psychiatrists have labeled twice as many people schizophrenic as have their British colleagues.

This unsatisfactory state of affairs obviously needed correction. So two decades ago, a third attempt was made to define this disorder using new criteria. The new model is based neither on an ominous prognosis, as was Kraepelin's original idea of the illness, nor on the dissociative disorder of Bleuler's ego-structure model. It is based only on a set of symptoms that must be present over a certain amount of time.

The introduction of this symptom oriented diagnosis arose hand in hand with the previously described shift of psychiatric focus. In the transition from a subject oriented psychodynamic psychiatry to an object oriented biological view, there was a search for a system that would make individual symptoms easily objectified and formulated. During the endeavor, the symptoms that were preferable were those that were the most noticeable and distinctive. These kinds of symptoms had been described earlier by Kurt Schneider, but they could not gain a footing as long as Bleuler's concept of schizophrenia prevailed.

During the time of National Socialism, Kurt Schneider identified a group of symptoms that were exceptionally bizarre, hard to follow, and tended to occur especially frequently in schizophrenic patients; he described them as primary symptoms. They involved such phenomena as thoughts becoming audible ("I can hear my thoughts in my head"), the feeling of thoughts being withdrawn ("my thoughts are being taken by something outside me"), hearing "commanding" or "interpreting voices," and experiences of the body being influenced ("my movements are guided by a foreign power). Newer research, however, indicates that these symptoms are not unusually specific for schizophrenia.

Nevertheless, the symptoms mentioned above affect the diagnostic conclusions of the World Health Organization (ICD 10). While they have resulted in general agreement between evaluating psychiatrists, they effectively exclude the experiences of affected patients, as well as their histories and actual life situations. It is not only what patients experience during their psychotic episodes that is foreign and unreal for them. Many have difficulty dealing with a diagnosis that turns their subjective experience into a thing and does not consider the deep-reaching involvement of their entire being. Only a small percentage of patients suffering from schizophrenia interpret their psychotic experience as being simply the expression of a physical disorder or a disruption of the central nervous system. In this regard, they differ from those who experience a psychotic episode as a result of alcohol or drug abuse. For most schizophrenic patients, the psychotic experience has far more the character of a dream or hypnotic condition than an event that is entirely separate from them as a person. This may be one of the reasons that schizophrenic patients are not too satisfied with the psychiatric model of their illness. In my experience, many patients feel that model does not conform to the essential aspects of their experience, nor does it take seriously the individual features of their experiences.

*Medical Science of the Brain (Encephaliatry) instead of Medical Science of the Soul (Psychiatry)?*

This chapter ends with a few thoughts related to the challenging question of whether psychiatry continues to do justice to its name as a medical science of the soul, or whether it already sees itself as an applied science of the brain.

In the introduction to the Diagnostic Statistical Manual (DSM IV) of the American Psychiatric Association, there is a suggestion of regret that psychiatric disorders are still referred to as "mental disorders," and that unfortunately, a better designation has not been found, as the term "mental" (spiritual) reflects a reductionist anachronism of body-mind dualism. It was also pointed out (in parentheses) that "mental disorders" (German: geistige Störungen) are called "psychische Störungen" (psychological disorders) in German psychiatry, which certainly indicates how culturally embedded those disease concepts are.

The terms "mental" and "psychological" disorders must be offensive to professionals who no longer believe in the existence of a "spirit" or a "soul." However, one must seriously ask whether doing away with the terms soul and spirit might not have significant consequences for the use of the term "body." (This issue will be discussed at another point in this book).

This new matter-of-fact diagnostic attitude goes hand in hand with the attitude that no longer attributes any significant meaning to the subjective experience of the person who is affected. As a result, the earlier separation of body and soul threatens to encourage a purely materialistic understanding of the person. So far, in modern diagnostic procedures, there has not been a stronger merging of personal and impersonal statements as a result of renouncing a paired approach. The leading representatives of American psychiatry are far more inclined to imagine a psychiatry which focuses primarily on the neurons.[1]

Prominent American psychiatrists Jeffrey Lieberman and John Rush demand, in the name of "A new definition of the role of psychiatry in medicine," that the rationale for psychiatry's primary beliefs must be transferred to the neurological sciences. They state: "The theoretical model of the spirit-brain dichotomy is no longer valid. Psychiatry focuses on an organ (the brain, for example) and on those parts of the brain that are most important for mental functioning (e.g., those that enable perceptions, cognition, affect and behavior)." According to Liebermann and Rush's thinking, the brain plays such a central role that the patients are significant as individuals only because it promotes a humane attitude in medicine to see them that way.[2]

This way of seeing reminds us of solutions attempted during the nineteenth century, when the natural sciences delegated spiritual and ethical questions to the social and humanistic sciences and theology, so they could be free to pursue their own interests. Looking at things that way frees psychiatry from all questions about meaning, seeing it instead as a natural science related exclusively to the brain. At the same time, however, it is presumed that these psychiatrists will form an internal ethic that causes them to act in a humane way.

Nancy Andreasen, the editor of the American Journal of Psychiatry, defines psychiatry as a scientific discipline that aims to identify the biological factors that determine psychiatric illness. This research, she states, must include all aspects of the neurological sciences. Regarding the treatment of the

---

1. (Translator:) The author's point is strongly validated by Nobel laureate Francis Crick's book *The Astonishing Hypothesis: The Scientific Search for the Soul* (Charles Scribner, New York, 1995), which suggests that what we tend to segregate as subjective experiences are nothing but the intricate processes of the brain that we are gradually identifying.

2. J. Lieberman and J. Rush 1996, p. 1391

illnesses, she writes: "In the treatment of these disorders, the somatic therapies are predominant. The term 'somatic therapies' refers to a series of varied approaches whose common trait consists in their being of physical nature. The somatic therapies that are used most frequently are medications and electro-convulsive therapy. Since a biological origin is postulated for these illnesses, these therapies are viewed as something that corrects the underlying biological imbalance. Yet a biologically oriented psychiatrist, just like any good family physician, will note that psychological illnesses have effects upon social and economic developments, and thus will lend his or her attention to such problems. Therefore, for example, marital problems can develop in a depressed patient who has no longer any sexual desire."[1]

> Nancy Andreasen is of the opinion that in future, biological psychiatry will radically change the practice of both consultation and treatment. Instead of the forty-five minute session that tries to carefully explore the events in the patients life, "It could be that the physician, after taking a careful history of the symptoms for one or two hours, will draw out his prescription pad, briefly put down his diagnosis and the reasons for prescribing, mention the side effects of the medications, give instruction in regard to dosages and then ask his patients to return in one or two weeks. Then, when the patients return, it is likely that the physician will spend only fifteen to thirty minutes ascertaining whether they are or are not improving and assessing how their symptoms have influenced their work, their family and their social life."[2]

Andreasen's books have such titles as *The Broken Brain*, *The Creative Brain: The Science of Genius*, and *From Mind to Molecule*. Such titles represent agendas. However, she does not meet the challenge to include in her materialistic hypothesis the element of subjectivity: what the soul is able

1. N. Andreasen 1990, p. 54
2. Ibid. p. 55. (At a later point, N. Andreasen took a less radical position.)

to experience inwardly. Where questions arise pertaining to the interpersonal consequences of biological disorders, she changes course towards psychosocial disciplines.

Florian Holsboer, Director of the Max Planck Institute for Psychiatry in Munich, avoiding compromise even more radically, defines psychiatry as an applied natural science (in the narrow sense of an object oriented science of the brain) and rejects the consideration of any other aspect in the physician-patient relationship.[1] Such a pronouncement is clear and firm. It can also be examined as to its consequences in everyday life. For example, it raises a question about how that kind of psychiatry would deal with those who can be treated only against their will. "Deciding" and "will" are ideas related to a person. They presuppose a subject. Deciding and will are terms borrowed from a language related to an ego, a language that cannot be transferred, sight unseen, into a language that is related to objects. Is it then the case that a psychiatrist who restricts him- or herself exclusively to applied neuroscience must still fall back on the social and spiritual sciences? Can a psychiatrist who represents a significant variation of neuroscience assume the right to treat human beings simply as objects who have no personal will? Does he view or undergo his own personal experience and decisions as if they are objects? Do psychiatric diagnosis and treatment exist for him as something that happens from object to object guided by physicochemical laws? If so, what laws?

Many more questions could be raised, but must wait for answers because so many questions cannot yet be answered. The question of how consciousness and subjectivity come into existence remains open. There is so much that cannot be decided by natural science. Because of this, psychiatrists who prefer a narrow (exclusive) materialism nevertheless find

1. F. Holsboer 1996

themselves forced to accept in their practices the everyday, common, subject oriented language.

Furthermore, their way of thinking has for some time been confronted with the argument that the idea of sickness has no legitimate place in a discipline that is based on and exclusively developed by natural science. The term "sickness" as such is not an unequivocal scientific concept.[1] It depends on assessments regarding what is desirable and what is not desirable, but such assessments differ considerably from one culture to the next and from one human being to another. They are not dependent only on natural scientific insights.

## Methodological Limits of Human Self-Knowledge

In addition to the preceding comments, there are many methodological considerations that argue against the notion that subjective experience and personal consciousness can be reduced to a completely physicochemical picture. If so, physical analysis would presumably resolve a problem adequately. Yet even now, as we try to find a satisfactory formula for consciousness, we run into the most serious difficulties. Consciousness does not just mean being related to oneself. In its broadest sense, consciousness corresponds to one's entire potential for experience. Our language is based to such an extent on expressions that are shaped by experience that an all-inclusive formula for all possible experiences seems impossible.

The difficulty of finding a formula for consciousness continues even when the term is defined more narrowly and restricted to the perception of itself and the world around us. How are we to include "capacity to experience" or "intention-

---

1. W. Wieland 1975, p. 112. C. Scharfetter (1996) also insists that the pair of ideas "healthy" and "sick" presuppose a point of reference for specific action.

ality" in a formula? When we are called upon to characterize consciousness, and especially "person" and "self," as existing in a structured region of the human brain, then every attempt to include them in a formula will raise the possibility that we just want to prove a lack of inner contradiction so that we won't get caught in the trap we set for ourselves.

> In this regard, Alfred Grierer, molecular biologist and Director of the Max Plank Institute for Developmental Biology in Tübingen, writes the following: "In our memories, apprehensions, hopes, wishes and plans we appear the way we are or believe that we are, or the way we would like to be seen by others, the way we are becoming or would not like to become, the way we see our past and our possibilities for the future. Such 'images of the self' contribute to our attitudes, though the term 'images' obviously does not imply concrete, specific things, but rather abstract representations of the person in his own brain. Pictures of the self are frequently contradictory and can never be complete, for no real, physical structure can contain a complete image of itself. Images change in time and alternate in consciousness. They mutually influence each other and, in doing so, have a reflective influence on themselves. Such 'multiple self-images' may belong among those aspects of consciousness that cannot be fully deduced from the physical state of the brain."[1]

A further argument against a complete solution of the soul-body problem is presented from an exclusively physical standpoint: there is a limit to functional procedures that makes the analysis of even simple human ways of deciding impossible. According to Gierer, even a simple behavioral decision such as "If the winter turns out to be very cold, I shall travel to the South" turns out to be impossible to solve mathematically on the basis of fundamental physical manifestations.

---

1. A. Gierer 1998, p. 44

In his book *"Die gedachte Natur"* (tr. *Nature As It Is Perceived*), Gierer points to the so-called "finite cognition theory" that supposedly limits one's ability to decide problems. He begins by stating, "Essential aspects of the body-soul relationship cannot be 'decoded' in the finite number of steps that cognitive theory allows, just as, for example, a secret code can be locked in such a sophisticated way that it cannot be deciphered with realistically limited means."[1]

I believe there are adequate indications that it is easier to decipher the organic preconditions of consciousness, of feelings and of thinking, than the contents of our ego-experiences.

Molecular biologist Müller-Hill is sharply critical when discussing natural scientists who blindly extend their biological findings to psychological and social processes: "Human beings are not just biological objects of exceptional complexity that must elude such calculations. Being gifted with memory and the ability to learn, they have created their own history with language, symbols, etc. It seems self-evident that knowledge of the DNA (genetic code) of all the New Yorkers could not vaguely predict any details of Manhattan, not even a small object such as the Manhattan Bank. It is just as unlikely that the knowledge of Mozart's DNA could be used to reconstruct a lost string-quartet. The material and spiritual worlds created by human beings cannot be derived from human DNA. After the physical history of the very first moment of the cosmos, and after biological history, a third one began, namely human history."[2] "If one considers the enormous development of European thought during the past thousand years, it becomes clear that this development (of mathematics, the natural sciences, the arts) does not have anything to do with biological evolution. Biological evolution does not move that quickly."[3]

---

1. Ibid. p.43
2. B. Müller-Hill 1981, p. 166
3. Ibid. p. 208

As a matter of fact, the biological view of evolution demands a joint effort of brain and environment. As an isolated apparatus, a brain not couched in a surrounding world and history would make no sense. To view an isolated brain as the sole locus for deciding what happens would reproduce an image of inwardness similar to the one Descartes created. It makes little sense to create pictures of the world in one's head when there is no surrounding world in which that information matters.

Natural science is unable to function without language, yet each language is based on an interpersonal dynamism, a language game. Natural science is therefore a specific cultural method shared by natural scientists, or, as Carl Friedrich von Weizsäcker eloquently expressed it: Natural science is ultimately a science of culture.

It is obvious that research in the natural sciences requires contact with nature. It is based on experiments and takes the body seriously. It does not depend on speech alone. Yet without speech, without interpersonal communications, there would be no possibility of a science of nature, because scientific knowledge presupposes common, shared information. Furthermore, one must consider what von Weizsäcker pithily formulated: "A correspondence can exist only between similar things, thus a thought or sentence cannot be used to represent the concrete facts of a case – only an 'eidos' can correspond to another 'eidos'" (eidos as in Plato's term for idea).[1]

*Summary*

That which is designated as illness depends on cultural circumstances. Criteria for health and illness have changed radically not only over lengthy spans of time, but also in

---

1. C. F. von Weizsäcker 1984, p. 98

the course of the last century. As portrayed in Table 2, at least three different ideas can be identified that, step by step, shaped psychiatry during the twentieth century.

The criterion of orderly structure, a remnant of the nineteenth century, was dominant at first: whatever was seen to be at odds with spiritual or physiological order was viewed as illness. Therefore, psychologically ill patients had either to be induced to reason correctly, or the equilibrium of their metabolism had to be reestablished.

| *Table 2: Changes in the Ways Sickness and Health were understood in Psychiatry* | |
|---|---|
| Nineteenth to early Twentieth century | Health derives from inner (physiological or psychological) order. Psychological illness indicates internal turmoil (a result of a disorder in the brain, or a disorder of reason). |
| Middle of Twentieth century | Health derives from the ability to adjust to one's surroundings (Umwelt). Psychological illness is revealed by an impaired ability to adjust (example: the inability to love or to work). |
| Late Twentieth century | Health corresponds to feeling well. Psychological illness is (or causes) suffering. |

Under the influences of Darwinism and psychoanalysis, the need for order was increasingly understood in functional terms. Health was equated with adaptability, illness was viewed as a functional disability. With this, the idea of neurotic difficulties in adjustment became prominent. Classical behavior theory went a step farther, equating psychological disorder with a deficient attitude toward one's environment.

Another distinctive feature became significant toward the end of the twentieth century. In keeping with the World Health Organization's actual definition, a human being is sick when his or her sense of well-being is altered. In this way, how people experience their condition takes precedence over the criteria of order and adaptability. Thus, for example, homosexuality, as a potentially pleasurable behavior, loses the stigma of a psychiatric disorder, while previously it was viewed as dysfunctional behavior that interfered with order (regarding procreation), and as such, an illness. On the other hand, certain disruptions in women's well-being that had previously been viewed as normal, such as depressive premenstrual moods, acquired the meaning and value of illness.

This sort of revision regarding what is considered an illness can be understood only in relation to profound, basic change in society and culture. The more post-modern humans are influenced by technology and science, the more they will be instinctively moved by an elevated sense of themselves to oppose the impersonal values of order and function.

Becoming more individualized in modern life does not exclude, however, the possibility that psychiatric concepts of illnesses could be determined by social conventions, and that they might also play an important role in social and commercial politics.

Modern psychiatric diagnoses are brief descriptions. They piece together individual symptoms in their sequential order and are useful for communication between specialists. They can offer statistical guidelines about which treatment approach, compared to other treatments in similar conditions, is likely to be superior in the short term as well as a longer period. Another advantage of modern diagnostic methods lies in the fact that, in contrast to earlier attempts at classification, they contain no unproven hypotheses related to the causes of the illness, nor to their prognoses.

However, this advantage of implied modesty and simplicity shifts to a heavy disadvantage when these concepts of modern illness are expected to provide information that they are unable to furnish. They are also unsuitable for understanding the singular problems of the individual. Their objectivity is gained at the cost of overlooking all that truly makes one an individual, disregarding how people deal with afflictions, knowing what patients see as positive or negative, the extent they are able to tolerate suffering, and how appropriate they feel their diagnoses and proposed treatments are.

In regard to the observations presented in this chapter, observations based on the history of psychiatry, we see some specific risks. Any uncritical application of modern theories of illness carries the risk of submitting patients to new and less carefully scrutinized systems. Even the criteria of illness that focus primarily on disorders of well-being may leave patients subject to political regulations (of departments of health, for example) that have far-reaching consequences. True, this new system's statistical establishment of norms for degrees of psychological abnormality may no longer serve the goals of political control, which was the case at the time of the foundation of psychiatry, but it does have a financial function politically. The new (so-called non-theoretical) criteria for diagnosis, which pretend to characterize the presence of the psychologically ill in the population in an objective way, may be used to seek out a range of suffering. My concern is not that this will result in pressure to separate and hospitalize patients, but that the push for treatment and regulation might deal with some problems by forcing people to either submit to socially sanctioned methods of treatment, or miss out on financial support.

This is an important argument for the need to remain aware that descriptions of illnesses always include conventions, and that assigning the label of an illness to a certain person can never encompass the totality of that individual.

*Part II:*

*The Unfolding of the Concept*

I am. But I do not have myself.
For this reason we are only becoming.

— Ernst Bloch

# Chapter 4.
# The Body of the Soul is Emotional —
# A Personal Concept of the Soul

*A Difficult Inheritance*

The history of Western thought has given rise to the sense that the individual has both a body and a soul. Today there is an attempt to overcome this duality. Even the recent separation of the world into a subject that perceives and an object that can be perceived is now contested.

The overcoming of a dualistic view presupposes, however, that the two opposing poles are apprehended in a new way before being joined in a comprehensive theory, and the understanding of body and soul, object and subject needs to change. It is not enough to simply take one leg of the old dualism — whether body or object — and make it into the lone support of the human being.

In the field of modern medicine, questioning of the soul's existence and the devaluing of subjectivity that is linked to it probably have not presented as great a problem in most disciplines as they have in psychiatry. To eliminate the subjective side and leave only the objective side turns the human being into a thing. Furthermore, the demise of subjectivity, or the soul, is inconsistent with a daily life that is shaped by experiences such as suffering, fear, sadness, disgust and pleasure. It is just such subjective and emotive ways of perceiving that are the meat of psychiatry. They cannot be surveyed and made into objects by external observers, but are lived only in the first person. One can, however, try to eliminate these subjective experiences with clever theories. Daniel Dennett, a well known researcher of consciousness, is of the opinion that complaints of fear and sadness need not be taken literally. His explanation is that they do not indicate anything about an inner condition, but merely indicate that one person wants to communicate some conscious viewpoint to another.[1] Dennett thereby excludes all that we know about feelings referring to an inner world of experience.

There have been other attempts to convert subjective experience into objective events, to question, in effect, the truth of what has been lived. In his book *The Rediscovery of the Mind*, John R. Searle attempts to inventory these various attempts critically.[2] He implies derisively that there is absolutely no reason to accept just one basic premise of life such as monism, nor two, such as dualism; rather, that life has diverse sides that do not allow for reconciliation with each other.

> "Goals in football, profits, governments and hardship, all have individual modes of being — in sports, commerce, politics, spirituality, etc. Dualists asked how many kinds of things and traits existed, and they counted to two. Monists considered the question and arrived only at one. The real error, however, lay in the fact that they even started to count."[3]

Searle is convinced that psychological and spiritual phenomena are high level biological properties of neurophysiological systems, e.g., human brains. Yet in his thought-provoking book, he raises many good arguments in vehement opposition to the opinion that subjective experience is irrelevant to

1. D. Dennett 1993
2. J. R. Searle 1996. Searle adds to this, among other things, eliminative materialism, functionalism, and an extreme variant of artificial intelligence.
3. Ibid. p. 40

knowledge of human reality, and the idea that human reality is to be studied only by observing patterns of behavior.

## The Help of Language

In what follows I would like to depend on our everyday language that speaks of a first, second and third person. I shall begin by assuming that we are not able to transcend our everyday language, and that we are forced to begin with the usual utterances and meanings of words to express what we experience, our feelings and our actions.

It is obvious that in everyday language we use the first person to voice an intention ("I want to leave"), or a sensation ("I feel pain"), or a feeling ("I feel sad"), or an action ("I looked around myself"), but in everyday conversation we do not speak of an "ego" as an object or noun; we leave expressions such as egoism or "the nature of ego" to be dealt with by the mental or spiritual sciences. Perhaps we should follow the suggestions of linguistic philosophers and not try to introduce into the sciences a private language of the ego, but simply view the ego as a starting point of experience or action and leave it at that.

In what follows I would like to focus primarily on the position of the ego — the perspective of the first person — and the position of the he/she, the perspective of the third person. It is this position of the third person that is assumed by the "science of experience," or so-called empiricism. When empiricism is used in psychology and psychiatry it implies the viewpoint of a third person, even when it involves an indication of the first person, such as, "He hears what I say," or "She sees what I am doing." Everything that can be described in this manner can also be grasped empirically. Yet that which cannot be observed externally is overlooked by this approach.

In the first person I am able to produce thoughts about my feelings and actions (how I feel and at what time I shall get up in the morning). I do not express my experience in a self-created private language, but am dependent on the language that my culture provides, thinking and talking about myself in the language of my fellow human beings. Yet I can only speak about myself in this common language when I assume the point of view of others and consider myself as if from outside, the way others see me. The point is that I, as a mature person, am no longer aware that I, thinking about myself, am assuming the perspective of the third person. I assume I am an individual and think for myself. This I also do, but I do it in a language and from a vantage point that I have learned from others during my early socialization. Therefore, my thinking uses a kind of "generalized third" (G. H. Mead[1]), an idea that has formed itself in the culture and has shaped me.

> This is not meant simply in the sense of an identification, such as when I transfer the convictions of my mother, my father, or a teacher into myself. It means, rather, that my thinking is tied into linguistic representations, and they alone make it possible to assess my situation from a general point of view. I carry this general point of view with me as the generalized sense of other viewpoints in order to examine whether my thinking is logical or not, right or wrong. In this sense, reflecting about the self represents the acceptance of a viewpoint indicating how one might see me from the outside.

---

1. G. H. Mead 1962. According to Mead, thinking is a kind of internal convention in which the 'generalized third' (which contains our culture's vocabulary of reasons and emotions) represents the tool with which we are able to articulate what we feel. The first person experience finds a way to language only when the culturally communicated inheritance of a 'generalized third' is applied to it.
I call the perspective of the first person "first person perspective." It corresponds to what I can experience and feel in myself first hand. The view from outside, namely the perspective of third persons I label "third person perspective," and I label the internalized perspective of the generalized third that is required for reflecting one's own experience "generalized third person perspective."

Historical and neurophysiological data both speak in favor of this view. As I demonstrated in the chapter "Short History of the Soul," it is likely that the subjective mode of thinking — reflecting on oneself — was preceded by a stage of hearing voices, which therefore was a conscious perception of the generalized third person perspective.

Yet I am able not only to reflect about myself. I also experience physical pain, and feel anxiety, anger and happiness. Or to be more accurate, I do not feel such concepts as anxiety and happiness, but I fear, enjoy, hate, etc. Our common language is so heavily shaped by the third-person viewpoint of people perceiving each other that objectified terms such as fear, rage, pleasure have crept in. Instead of expressing our personal feeling and sensing exclusively with verbs (I resent, I enjoy, etc.), thus identifying feeling and perceiving quite correctly as actions, we often use nouns to communicate our feeling, saying, for example, "I feel anger" or "I feel happiness."

*Approaching the First Person*

As I attempt to anchor human perception, feeling and action in my body, I begin with the assumption that these acts are not simply the ideas of a subject (as assumed by subjectivism),[1] nor are they simply reproduced in the body (as reductive objectivism claims).[2] I picture to myself that these acts are in the nature of a living body.[3] This body (*Leib*),

1. Subjectivism believes that those entities we recognize and want are created or constructed by the subject.
2. Objectivism starts from the idea that cognition is dependent not on the subject, but rather, the object of cognition. M. Pauen (2001) wrote an excellent introduction: "Grundprobleme der Phiolosophie des Geisters" (tr. *The Basic Problems of the Philosophy of the [Human] Spirit*; Th. Metzinger (1996) edited a philosophical manual about consciousness.
3. Here again the translator is faced with the problem that the German language makes a clear distinction between *Leib*, representing the wholeness of a body with a soul, and *Körper*, referring to the physical body, while the English term

however, cannot be seen as merely an object, but must be viewed as an acting, experiencing, and feeling organism.

The first person perspective begins with physical experiencing, feeling and acting. But how is it possible for the body to experience its own self and to develop its own perspective? I shall deal with this question in greater detail in the second part of this chapter. At this point I shall limit myself to pointing out that experiencing and feeling can be seen as pre-linguistic expressions of bodily activity. Such self-expression presupposes a complex nervous system. In addition, there is need of a system of symbol formation that, like language, is able to picture something and, while picturing it, simultaneously create something new.

> The question of how a non-linguistic system of symbol formation and human language developed is as yet unanswered. One thing, however, seems sure: symbol formation presupposes interchanges and comparisons. Symbol formation points to something without being absorbed by it. In the special case of speech, this means the following: language uses significant elements (syllables, words and sentences) to help designate significant things (objects and observations) rather than simply making mere pictorial copies.

Yet this also means that something can only become the designated concept if there is another who designates it. For this reason, feeling cannot designate itself; there must be an observer who witnesses what is felt, or more precisely, there must be a framework to which that which is felt is related. While this is a plausible conclusion, it is not clear that observer and observed are subject and object in the sense of Descartes' conclusions.

---

body must do for both, though far more focused on the physical body. In this case, living body (*Leib*) is always meant to convey the whole of the soulish body.

I have drawn attention (above) to another solution of the problem: there are clear indications that a feeling person will assume the perspective of a "general third" (in a given framework) and then apply to him or herself the socially arranged, external viewpoint that is provided to the small child by his or her caregivers.

### One's Picture of the Ego Requires the "Other"

In other words: from the perspective of the first person, one's experience and feelings find their way to language only when taken from a generalized third person perspective, an external viewpoint. From the experience of bodily existence, of that simple "being-ness" that cannot be described, proceeds some essence that is established externally. As a result, the perspective shifts from the bodily to the linguistic. Suddenly there is a symbolic space in which one's personal experience can be located in relation to others'. It is just this symbolizing process that enables the attribution of sensations or feelings to the "ego" we recognize as the symbolized first person.

I do not believe that the riddle of the ego experience can be resolved fully with this visual explanation, but the explanation I have chosen remains very close to our everyday experience. Each person sees in the other one who is able to experience him or herself bodily. It is only the phenomenon of being anchored in the body, this preconditioned first person perspective that makes one a fellow human being that I face.

Is it inconceivable that it is only the image of an ego perspective in another person that establishes the quality of humanness? Is it the fact that we see the face of another person whose eyes tell us, "I am like you and am part of that general third." Is there anything that contradicts the hypothesis that

the other elicits the indispensable first person perspective that
makes a personal relationship possible?

Having been influenced by the idea of being a subject, one
naturally assumes that one's own ego was there first, and that
others derive from this ego, just as in the story that Adam was
created first and Eve was then placed at his side. However, isn't
there a lot that speaks for another way of viewing this? In the
development of human speech, the naming and description of
the third person precedes that of the first person. Children at
first call themselves by the names they hear others use; rather
than saying, "I eat," they say, "Johnny eats," "Anita eats," etc.
Identifying with a name does not mean that children have
arrived by coincidence between that designation and a first
person perspective. For this to happen, they must not only
have learned to apply designations by others (third persons)
to themselves, they must also have experienced themselves
as actively functioning beings and made the leap from that
internal experience to being named by third persons.

To achieve the experience of themselves as "I," children
must go from being "John" and "Anita" — their third person
designations — to viewing themselves both as "other" (from
the perspective of the generalized third person) and as "I"
("myself") in the first person perspective. This development,
fraught with tension, is linked to their social context. Children
require a caring environment and appreciation, as well a certain amount of freedom in play, as well as in learning to walk
and speak. At the same time, preconditions of the central
nervous system have to be satisfied so that the child can learn
to speak of her- or himself as an "I" (in the language of the
others). It also seems necessary that internal bodily sensations
become linked to external, verbal designations.

Of course, in this process some mistakes cannot be avoided.
It is not possible for the child to understand everything the

way others mean it. Also, others will not always understand everything the way the child means it, being unable to always grasp the child's bodily sensations and feelings the way she/he experiences them. As a result, a child learns that there is a personal level, a perspective that is not available to others. This personal level is part of "I," "me," admittedly also defined by society. Yet how I am and experience myself eludes social definition; they are my sensations and feelings.

My living experience of the "I" (or ego), as seen from this angle, is not just a social achievement, because I am also that which I can withdraw from the view and intrusion of the others. Though the development of an "I" presupposes a symbolic space that I share with others, there nevertheless remains that which is experienced by the ego in its own body, hidden to the eyes of the others.

Putting it in different words: The "I," or ego experience, is a locus not only in the social community, but also in the interpersonal world to which others have no access. The ego-perspective or soul that can be turned into a tangible entity does not exist.

Understood in this way, the ego perspective will necessarily withdraw itself from any external view and thus also from all science; the living experience of the ego is always where it cannot be discerned from the outside. The first person perspective turns out to be that which escapes notice from the outside and yet is necessary for an understanding of the whole.

While the ego perspective is not fixed, it nonetheless forms the basis of relationships in human life. Whatever I sense or feel in the ego perspective is just as real as any object that I see, whether a table or a rose. It is simply that such experience is subjective and cannot be made into an object. If in spite of this, if I try to talk about it, I am forced to fashion my living experience with words. Yet with that, my immediate experience is necessarily transformed into something that happened to me. I am not able to communicate my experience directly with language. What, for me, is present and immediate becomes for others a narrated event, a "fact" (from the Latin for "made," or "happened") in the form of a perfect participle. A communication or reflection about a personal experience or action always requires that something precedes what is communicated. In that sense, the first person experience corresponds to a first period, and the reflection or communication to a second period that is always supplementary and contains a piece of the past.

> If I wish to try and present my experience not simply as a fact, but as something that happened, I must be inventive. First I might try to find some analogies to build a bridge to the experiences of the person with whom I'm speaking in order to convey my personal experience. Then I might employ images and parables to provide a frame for what cannot be communicated directly. (A simple example would be, "I am so downhearted, I feel a hundred pound weight on my shoulders.") Third, I could illustrate my experience from new angles in an attempt to separate myself from concrete statements and point to what lies between the lines. I could also try to communicate my feelings with richer expression using poetry or representative art such as verse and stories, or with dance, music or theater. As a religious or myth-oriented individual, I might draw upon paradox or contradictory statements in order to include what could not be said in ordinary terms.

### The Represented and the Other Ego: an Example from Literature

In what follows, I would like to illustrate my theoretical description of the complex relationship of first person perspective and third person perspective by using the example of a writer. George Arthur Goldschmidt not only wrote fascinating stories, he also knew how to interpret his poetically shaped autobiography theoretically.[1]

> Goldschmidt artistically shaped the descriptions of his childhood and adolescence — "Die Absonderung" (tr. *The Separation*), "Der unterbrochene Wald" (tr. *The Interrupted Forest*), "Ein Garten in Deutschland" (tr. *A Garden in Germany*) and "Die Aussetzung" (tr. *Being Expelled*) — using a language that his translator, Peter Handke, characterized as a "Testimony of sleepwalking." Goldschmidt's growing up was full of terror and awe.

The son of a Jewish family in Hamburg, in 1938 Goldschmidt, at ten, was placed in a French home for children in the Alps of Savoy, where the staff treated him as a freeloader. He was continually under the threat of being discovered by the German occupiers. Beaten by both teachers and schoolmates, he developed a masochistic lust associated with the pain he suffered. In his theoretical essay "Narcissus punished," Goldschmidt interpreted his earlier history sociologically and psychologically. He observes how an inner "security of rebellion," with which the abused child opposes his "I am" to the entire world, can develop within the bounds of suffering. He experienced his body as a central essence, a place in which nobody could take away his feelings. Accordingly, punishment changes into lust and becomes the source of erotic self-discovery. Goldschmidt also realized that as a child he was able to discover something that no other human being could have taught him: a place devoid of social contact, a blind point that endured all the punishments. While the abusive teachers were able to hurt and shame him, they could not prevent him from recognizing in the midst of

---

1. G. A. Goldschmidt: "Der bestrafte Narziss" (tr. *Narcissus Punished*), Ammann, Zürich 1994. The quotations are identified with page references.

their punishment that no one could really touch him from the outside, that their power over him was limited. He further stated that in part, he was able to withdraw himself from his abusers and their control by transforming their punishment into a kind of self-mortification. From this experience of self-protection Goldschmidt developed a "negative consciousness," writing, "As if the 'I', in order to be the 'I', would have to tilt over necessarily into what it is not" (p. 19); "I am the one who is different, who is difficult to define"(p. 50); and "I'm nothing of all that one says of me... No description of any kind fits me" (p. 146).

Goldschmidt uses the image of a mirror to show that there is a crack between his external likeness and his inward experience: "I see myself in a mirror, but do not perceive in it the one who is looking (in terms of space, the mirror image is not where I stand, is not at my place). And just as little can this picture that I see of myself be me. In the mirror I do not see what I feel, I do not see me being myself. I see only the features of my face or the form of my body, just as another person who looked with me into the mirror would see them. To be sure, the mirror does show me, but it does not say anything about the glimpse that sees me." (p. 19)

"I recognize myself in the mirror only because I see myself there as being identical with everything else that appears simultaneously with me; I see myself the way I have been affirmed by others. 'It is he,' they say when they see me. The same thing is shown me by the mirror; it shows me the way I appear to others — but not the way I am 'me' in my insides." (p. 20)

"What is strange, however, is the following: this knowledge of myself that I am unable to convey to anyone else, this most intimate thing I have that cannot be put into words, it is, at the same time, the intimacy of the other. Just like the other,

I too find myself outside the range of language. And that through which I elude language brings me closer to the other: she/he and I have something in common. The things we are not able to say are the same, and it is with this that language really starts." (p. 27)

Frequently, though, signs can deceive. During his childhood, Goldschmidt not only experienced the liberating voice of literature, but also the impotence of everyday language. He was forced to accept being unfairly accused, as well as the injustice of his affirmations of innocence being denied and then punished severely. The plight of being an unfairly punished child lead him to doubt the potency of words. He asked himself, "Why turn the signs against me? How does it come about that language works so well for the rest of the world and so badly for me? How is it that language does not say anything about its truth? Thus develops the first crack, the vertigo, as everything threatens to drown..." (p. 32)

Goldschmidt refers to the German poet Karl Philipp Moritz, who mentioned the "negative consciousness" of children in the eighteenth century. Moritz labelled the despair of unfairly punished children "paralysis of the soul," the soul being relegated to a hole in its center. "The soul is prevented from seeing itself in relation to others, and is allowed only to be itself."

This "being oneself" has no real language. All signs can be deceptive, even the non-lingual ones. The child "...knows now of the failure of the signs, knows of their betrayal: The child's body talks, the cheeks redden, the lips tremble, tears flow over the face; everything that expresses my innocence seems to show my guilt. His or her own confusion accuses that child."(p. 35) "Confusion is viewed as a confession: you blush, therefore you are guilty. The language of the body has been taken away by the outside world. Your confusion betrays you, they say." (p. 37)

"Every human being is likely to experience on occasion such moments of emptiness within which all the words dissolve and the inappropriateness of language becomes apparent; these are also moments in which being oneself is exposed to the nudity of the self's mute existence."(p. 58) And summarizing: "Self-consciousness is empty and contains only itself." (p. 147) "Ego has no face, and allows itself to be recognized among thousands." (p. 92)

Beginning from this point, Goldschmidt saw a connection between bodily sensation and being a self. Grief and suffering can cause people to sense that they still exist beyond the pain ("This 'continuing-to-be-beyond-all-the-suffering.'" p. 92) For this reason, there is also the possibility of masochistic triumph: "As you punish me, you also prove to me my existence... 'I shall continue to be!,' a voice silently screams in the crying child." (p. 92) Thus suffering, in the sense of being a quiet rebellion, can strengthen one's awareness of oneself. Greed and lust also allows the individual to sense the "I am" or, more accurately, "I am not that which I desire, I am my desire." (p. 65) Goldschmidt's final conclusion: "There is but a soul that has grown out of the desire."

Such a sentence presupposes that all prior external images of the soul had withered. Goldschmidt is consistent in turning against all the materialistic characterizations of the soul.

The ego is not what he is told.

The ego, indeed, cannot be characterized from the outside, it cannot be "named." It is always where the other is not and cannot be.

What becomes of a psychiatrically diagnosed ego disturbance when we adopt this viewpoint? Where no picture exists, there can be no faulty image. Goldschmidt interpreted his serious, masochistic, self-punishing childhood actions as a reversal of sign language. He deprived his torturers of their power over him by turning the punishment against himself. The external pain turned into his own, partly sweet, suffering.

With this, Goldschmidt pointed indirectly to the fact that it was not just pain and suffering that led to the development of his ego. Pain can also destroy. When unsolicited suffering is made to contribute to the experience of the ego, it is not the suffering as such that causes the ego experience; it is an occasion for the person involved to limit the influence of the external world within language's symbolic space. Then the following experience can introduce itself: there is available to me a range of experience that cannot be duplicated by others, and cannot be objectified. My relationship to my body is highly personal. Others may mistreat my body, but they do not have the power to experience my body with me (the way I do).

> In the borderline situation of suffering, an ego perspective can be revealed that I'm barely aware of when in a good mood. Joyful feelings induce me to focus on the outside: I'm in a good mood, strong and hopeful. Because of this, I'm opening myself to the world, I become part of it. Yet at the same time, it narrows the access to my being "different," to the separateness of the "first person" in me. Only when what is joyous and lustful connect with the awareness of suffering — in a condition of nostalgia, or of a sweet world-weariness, or of yearning expectation — only then am I oriented toward myself by the experience of pain. Then the relatively painful experience confers upon the joy its melancholy attractiveness.

*The Cultural Struggle for the First Person Perspective*

The first person perspective is special because it cannot be understood from the outside. When it finds access to language, it puts itself in the spaces between and at the margins of speech patterns. This obscure feature is also expressed in Goldschmidt's presentation, in spite of — or maybe just because of — his efforts to use language precisely.

In spite of the elusive nature of the "first person," as recipients we are generally able to discern the content of what was expressed by comparing what was voiced in the language of the generalized third to our own experience. This complicated process is natural for us. We are able to establish relationships in this way, and to understand each other intersubjectively. If we denied others their first person perspective, we would have to deal with them the way we deal with a machine or robot.

We would also be unable to appreciate novels or plays. All these art forms come to life because of the first person perspective their characters assume, without which whatever is presented would be senseless (and without which any identification with the protagonists would be impossible). Admittedly, the less theoretical talk about the ego perspective there is in such works of art, and the more the ego experiences of the characters comes alive through the events in the stories, the more we feel personally addressed. In actuality, true art seems to reside in its ability to suggest connections that reach beyond the spoken word. It would leave us cold if the authors of books and plays presented their heroes simply as bearers of certain roles designed to routinely satisfy a function. It is only the implicitly assumed first person perspective of the figures we meet that transforms them from fictitious characters into human beings.

In fact, there is an hypothesis that the focus on the individual in short stories and novels (including even crime novels) began to find a wider audience in the nineteenth century because the increasing spread of the natural sciences and artistry contributed to a compensatory emphasis on the magnitude of personal responsibilities.

In our time, a different cultural trend is apparent: a tendency to return more and more to the experience of the first person. In this connection, I'm reminded of the varied forms of physical exercises and meditative techniques that flourished in compensation for the social overemphasis on commerce and science; those kinds of individual practices strengthen the primary life of the soul and work against the objectification of the human.

Both Eastern and Western techniques of meditation use sensations of the body to magnify meditators' awareness of their experiences. One of the prevailing Eastern techniques of meditation consists of conscious breathing, the so-called mindfulness exercise. Breathing slowly and deeply, the meditator is able to experience the body especially keenly, simultaneously becoming conscious of a relationship with life-giving air.

> Thich Nhat Hanh, an internationally known Zen master, teaches: "You must know how to maintain your attention with your breath, for breathing is a natural and very effective tool to help us avoid absent-mindedness. Breathing is the bridge between life and consciousness, uniting body and thought. Whenever your spirit becomes absentminded, you must recover it with breathing. Breathe lightly, thoroughly and profoundly, and remain conscious of breathing deeply. Then expel all the air from your lungs, remaining conscious the whole time you are exhaling."[1]

---

1. Thich Nhat Hanh 1998, p. 38

Along with concentrating on breathing, one can also seek to
become aware of whatever one happens to be doing – even the
most ordinary activity. Hanh recommends, for example, being
fully intentional in every thought or action during the prepara-
tion of tea, the washing of the dishes, or housecleaning, as if it
were the most important thing in the world. Everyday occupa-
tions can also be used this way as meditative exercises.

In addition to other meditation forms, practices that focus
on bodily experience without pursuing any contemplative
goal are spreading rapidly. Old ritual practices such as sauna
and dance are experiencing, in new forms, a renaissance in
the western world. Athletic exercises are used in many – and
increasingly extreme – ways. Physical practices of Eastern
origin such as Yoga, Qi-Gong and Tai Chi are spreading in
almost epidemic form. What these popular techniques of the
leisure culture have in common is the attempt to deliberately
increase the experience of one's body. In the last few years,
a "wellness industry" has also developed, deliberately intensifying, by means of baths, massages and special diets, the
experience of one's live body.

> The goal of applying these very different procedures is no longer
> the old style of self-realization, i.e., an emphasis on one's self
> image; it is instead a return to remembering and affirming the
> body. It is a trend that clearly emphasizes the first person per-
> spective that has been repressed by science and technique, yet it
> practices that perspective in ways that pull the individual out of
> his or her personal life connection.

### Objective Examination of Subjectivity: A Contradiction

Science, and especially the natural sciences, follow another
path. Hoping eventually to be able to scientifically describe

even the conditions that produce experience, they constantly seek to widen the range of what can be explained.

History allows us to identify several phases of cognition. In a first phase, during the seventeenth and eighteenth centuries, the natural sciences limited their investigations to lifeless matter. In the main, physics and chemistry developed in this way. In the second phase, the natural sciences applied their newly won findings to the examination of living entities. Accordingly, the premises of physics and chemistry expanded to include the biophysical and biochemical as life sciences (biology). Then, for a number of years, the natural sciences were intent on explaining emotional, cognitive, and spiritual processes. As a result, we see the "physicochemical" — or biological — sciences change anew and form a new field· neuroscience. Because without additional hypotheses that reach beyond the isolated elements of a lower level of organization, it is impossible to explain complex cognitive or "spiritual-soulish" phenomena. New understanding of the interactions of the underlaying elements is required in order to understand their higher performance.

People who had to submit to brain surgery (because of epilepsy, for example) were of special interest to modern neuroscience researchers. In such cases, it is possible to use tests to examine the performance of the brain before and after surgery, so a connection can be established between reduced brain function and those areas of the brain that were ruled out as a result of the operation. With time, it is even possible to redirect the electrical activity of a limited area of the brain, or to stimulate certain groups of brain cells and examine how that affects the patient.

The basic assumption in these neuropsychological examinations is that cognitive brain function is based on the physiological organization of the brain. A localized disorder in brain organization should therefore elicit a predictable change in perception or ideation.

Another modern path of neuroscientific research studies the responses of healthy and sick people exposed to specific stimulus situations. In one study, those to be examined were put in a specific mood through the use of either chemical stimuli or psychological means. They were, for example, shown depressive pictures, or were given hallucinogenic substances. Then the activities of different regions of the subjects' brains were measured by a variety of procedures: functional magnetic resonance imaging (fMRI), positron emission tomography (PET scan), or electroencephalogram (EEG).

Another method, developed by Robert Pasqual-Marqui in my former research program at the Psychiatric University Clinic of Zürich, made it possible to receive three-dimensional images of the brain's electric activity for short periods of time. This procedure, called the LORETTA method, has a real advantage in studying the brain's performance because it picks up only the electrical fields of the body, involving hardly any stress on the person being examined, LORETTA is also capable of recording very rapid changes (in the range of milliseconds), so the researcher can more accurately observe the brain's activity during the processes of thinking and feeling.

Even so, is it possible for this methodical approach to indeed picture what is being experienced? If we distinguish between sensation (How does it feel?) and emotion (What did I feel?), that is, between the original experience and the description of this experience, it appears that this method is not capable of catching the immediate experience. As mentioned earlier, verbal expression of feelings is always something secondary; it follows or interprets the immediate feeling in the first person perspective, and deliberately or not, alters it.

Also, inasmuch as experience is always known in the first person perspective, it is impossible to sort it out in rational discussion. It is not like what people communicate verbally, or what they show in their facial expressions, their gestures and the way they act. Those messages and expressions can be objectified. Different observers can agree about noticing one behavior or another, or if they heard a specific remark by the subject. In these cases, it is not particularly important whether a conscious experience was the source of the messages, or the messages came about without a conscious experience.

It follows that neuroscience is well suited to the study of various behaviors (including communication). If a certain behavior is no longer possible after an injury to a specific area of the brain, then the neural basis of that particular mode of behavior is impaired. When stimulating a certain area of the brain inevitably produces a certain behavior, one may conclude that part of the brain is involved in organizing that behavior. It is possible to understand the organizational structure of the brain by observing a large number of such connections.

Modern neuropsychology is already in the position of tracing important behavioral deficits back to certain disorders of specific cerebral organizing components. (It must, however, be acknowledged that behavioral deficits usually cannot be traced to a single region of the brain, as usually several interrelated regions are involved). There is a wide gap between the scientific knowledge bearing on critical brain functions (such as memory and speech) and knowledge of the neural bases of mental and spiritual abilities (such as consciousness and self-awareness). This gap is largely a normal consequence in the history of a science that starts with what can be easily manipulated (such as physical appearance) before going on to what is more complex (such as neurobiology). In succeeding years, further progress may bring us closer to the goal of understanding the foundations of consciousness and our thought processes. We can already foresee developments that will help us understand better the neural ground of emotion. (see: page 188f)

*Aside: Disregard of the First Person Perspective, and its Consequences*

At first I wish to point to the scientific problems that result when the first person perspective is overlooked. It is clear that the failure to recognize the first person perspective, an omission that for years was part and parcel of the natural sciences, had to do with the history of dualism. Accepting Descartes' way of understanding the soul has made scientific medical and psychiatric investigation of subjective experience difficult to this day, and research's neglect of the first person perspective has not been without consequences.

I would like to illustrate the problem that results from insufficient consideration of the first person perspective in the natural sciences, using the example of one of the most frequently cited experiments of the past few years. The experiment is based on experiments conducted in nineteen sixty-five by two German researchers, Kornhuber and Deecke.[1] In those experiments they discovered that electrical activity (a so-called readiness potential) becomes evident in that area of the brain that is responsible for guiding a movement about half a second before the movement of the corresponding group of muscles. If I tell myself that I am about to lift my finger, the area of the brain responsible for this movement is already activated before I lift it. This occurs even if I'm told that I will soon have to move the finger.

1. H. Kornhuber/L. Deecke 1965

These observations, done in the sixties, caused little surprise and seemed compatible with the idea of a guiding center in the brain. Yet about twenty years ago, Benjamin Libet conducted experiments showing that the temporal relationships actually progressed in the opposite way, and that the decision to act was observed only when the readiness potential in the corresponding area of the brain had appeared for a relatively long span of time (between one half and one full second). The way Libet proceeded in his experiments is quite complicated, and a number of critical questions regarding his method were provoked. His instructions were the following: "The persons to be tested were instructed to decide spontaneously to bend, within a given time span (one to three seconds), one of the fingers of the right hand or the entire hand. At the same time, they watched an oscilloscope on which a point was circling. At the very moment the subjects decided to make the movement, they were to note the point's position as if it were on the face of a clock. In another set of experiments, it was enough for the subjects to know whether the decision to make the movement occurred before or after the rotating point had stopped, which was considerably easier for them. The reaction times of all subjects was measured during the experiment by using an electroencephalogram."[1]

The results showed that in none of the tests had the spontaneous decision to move one of the fingers or the hand preceded, or even coincided with, the readiness potential in the corresponding part of the brain. Each time, any indication of initiating a movement followed the readiness potential by a span of, on average, half a second. From this, Libet and others drew the electrifying conclusion that the triggering of movement occurred independently of any personal decision

---

1. G. Roth 1997, p. 307

(ego experience), and that we are misled by the impression that the decision is willed.

Psychologist Gerald Wassermann questioned that conclusion based on his understanding of the experiment's methods. He maintained that the subjects' reports concerning the point on the rotating "time-disc" when the spontaneous decision to move a finger or hand occurred required time to decide, and that this explained in part the temporal sequence of the results observed.[1]

However, an objection claiming that the Libet findings portray a "reversed world" only if one begins with an internal observer who controls or guides the events, seemed far more basic. If one assumes a first person perspective based on bodily feelings, Libet's results are not very surprising. Every action, sensation and feeling is then a first hand experience that only secondarily becomes a fact. The transition from first person perspective to a measured fact requires a further reworking of bodily feeling and action. The neural events' timing is not congruent with the chronological impression we have at the end of the process.

Therefore, it seems to me absurd to conclude, based on Libet's experiments, that ego experience is unimportant, or may even represent a deception. Our way of thinking is based far more on making the elements of experience into a coherent, meaningful story by relating them to a "generalized third." The kind of ego that results from this is not an object-like self that can be physically localized and that, like a helmsman, can guide the living ship of our organism. Nor is there a spectator inside me who sits on a throne watching what is happening in his realm. Nevertheless, I perceive from a first person perspective. This perspective is not invalidated by the cause and effect thinking on which Libet's studies are

1. G. S. Wassermann 1985

based. I can only think that even Libet and the people who interpret him are aware of the first person perspective from their personal experiences, and thus do not consider them trivial in their daily lives. If, as Klaus Grawe, a well known researcher of psychotherapy, says, "Our experience of the ego has a quality that is not unlike the taste of lemonade,"[1] something elicited by some brain activity, then I imagine that even for Grawe, it must be different if he is involved in his routine experience of his ego life, or if he is concerned with the taste of lemonade.

## The Soul that Is, Is Not

Ego experience is not objective. In a certain sense, it is far more real than any reflections about it. Thought would be abstract and endless without the living experience of the self. The living experience of our "first person" keeps us rooted in our bodies. Body and experience are endlessly interwoven. In a short phrase such as "I see you," the subject "I" and the verb "see" belong together, forming an inseparable unit. There is not a primary "I" who then "sees." In the experience of the "I", verb and subject are one; there is no "I' without perception, feeling or action. The ego cannot be separated from bodily experience. Even neuroscience has quite correctly declared its opposition to the idea of ego *qua* object.

When we "feel" ourselves, we do not experience ourselves as an object that is being observed by a subject. This separation occurs only when we reflect about ourselves, or when we are engaged in scientific pursuits. As long as we experience ourselves directly, in the first person perspective, we do not observe our self as an object that introduces itself, or one to which something is happening. Rather, it simply happens or

---

1. K. Grawe 1998, p. 331

behaves that way. In this primary experience, the medium in which something happens or presents itself is not an object-like world reflected by us, but an energy field with a center of gravity. If one wishes to approach this first person perspective rather than focus on circumstances in which things can be observed in sequence, then one is called upon to explain this field of centripetal forces.

Experiencing dental pain is entirely different from know-ing that my tooth is hurting. The former experience alerts me and draws my attention to the pain; the latter treats my pain as an object and explores its cause. While it is the latter event that will motivate me to have the tooth treated, it is the former that is responsible for the fact that I am aware at all. What do I mean by that?

It is obvious that my toothache is not the cause of my existence; in fact, I feel considerably better without the tooth-ache. However, I experience myself only because of sensations coming from all the organs in my body (including my teeth). The sensations in the organs form the basis of my ego experi-ence.

Whatever I see, hear, smell, taste and touch belongs to me, in the sense that these experiences cannot be shared by anyone else. By contrast, anything that is an interpretation or description of what I see, hear, smell, touch or taste is no longer my private affair. As soon as I share the interpretation and representation of my perceptions with those of others, the greater world becomes a reality shared by my fellows.

An acquaintance and I could observe a mountain, a football game, or anything else from a more or less similar perspec-tive, and we could agree about what we see. Yet the sensation of my toothache cannot be shared by any other human being. Even though, as the saying has it "Shared suffering is only half suffering," no one can take my place. A specialist can examine the painful tooth to see whether there is decay or inflammation of the tissues, but this external observation is something entirely different from what is happening to my self. This difference applies especially to personal experience contrasted with observing the brain. The way the brain works can be explained better and better — at least tentatively. Yet this has in no way explained the perception of a feeling in terms of a first person perspective.

> I think the preconditions for ego experience are becoming clearer step by step. Initial progress has been made through research in the neurophysiology of sleep and wakefulness, as well as the study of memory disorders. Additional explanations can be expected regarding the neurophysiological bases of the recognition of one's body (the *Schema* of one's body), the way we recognize objects, the way we become aware of time and so forth.

Progress in neurobiology promises to get us to a level at which ego experience is no longer interpreted in the natural sciences as a secondary phenomenon (an epiphenomenon), or as the product of a fantasy of subjectivism (a pseudo-phenomenon), but where it is accepted as a significant, if not decisive, element of human reality. For, in the words of physicist Werner Heisenberg, "Nature precedes the human being, but the human being precedes natural science."[1]

Our understanding of what is human can be based only on the human being and his or her primary experience. As Heisenberg remarked, "We must remember that what we observe is not nature itself, but nature that is exposed to our way of questioning."[2]

The way a question is formulated is decisive for psychiatry and its understanding of psychological disorders as well.

---

1. W. Heisenberg 1994, p. 58
2. Ibid. p. 60

Therefore, based on what has been stated above I offer the following preliminary conclusions:

1) Scientific analysis is based on third person perspectives, and as such is impersonal. Alone, isolated scientists experience themselves as "first persons." It is only personal awareness of themselves that renders them capable of doing justice to the first person perspective. Yet for many scientists, acceptance of a first person perspective has been made difficult because they perceive it to be a descendant of the Cartesian "subject."

2) Although both psychiatry and psychology, as objective sciences, are not yet able to embrace the first person perspective, it is impossible to exclude it from any therapeutic application. Whenever therapists do not take this perspective into account they will fail to understand their patients who are not objects but human subjects. It is especially those who have been traumatized who depend on being able to experience an internal "being at home." So far, only psychoanalysis and related depth-psychotherapies have taken this inner experience seriously. Even a psychiatry that is biologically based cannot renounce forever the inclusion and exchange of "inner" knowing.

3) One of the greatest challenges for psychology and psychiatry consists of further differentiation of the third person perspective without ignoring the first person perspective of those who are suffering. For even the best analysis will miss what is essential in the person if the first person perspective is not taken into account. Such an analysis would risk overlooking, being scientifically blind to, the significance that personal experience has for life's momentous qualities.

## To be Somebody instead of Something

It seems to me that there is yet another reason that the first person perspective is of extreme importance for psychiatry and the understanding of psychiatric disorders: it enables one to develop an understanding of self that is separate from others'. A being who experiences and protests is no longer a passive object in the flow of the history of evolution. A body that feels is the starting point of a personal history, both dependent on and protesting against its surrounding world.

When G. A. Goldschmidt reflected on how a person could maintain an indestructible ego in spite of the most adverse conditions, he did not believe that the solution rested in the social or neuronal realm. Instead, he recognized that his painful physical experience was a starting point that allowed him to exist apart from others. His "I," or "ego," existed only in the experience of his body and his craving. "The only ego reality is the body which feels... For here appears what is most paradoxical:...What had been intended to cause his suffering, his denigration... is his very highest affirmation: this is truly me." (p. 89f.)

In a news-paper interview, Goldschmidt stated: "One may say that I had been a masochist ... but this term does not fit at present because of the distance in time ... which was possibly the reason for writing my stuff, in order to show this: you can try as hard as possible to define me, and it still will not be correct ... I'm not what someone else makes of me." Also, "Writing has gradually brought me proof that I'm an entirely normal, average, French citizen, and I find that wonderful. I savor the anonymity of my ego ... I would say that I have been psychologically autistic, and that I learned to speak by writing. This is the reason one writes. Namely in order not to go round and round like beer in brewing oneself. This is the opening: one must get out of one's head, and that is simple."[1]

Before he began to write, it was reading that helped Goldschmidt. He kept seeking, and in books found witness for his experience; in Rimbaud and Kafka, but most especially in Rousseau, whose "Les Confessions" *(The Confessions)* allegedly saved him as a child: "What masochistic insanity: there is not a word in the *Confessions* of Rousseau that is not about the protest of the body, not a single world."[2]

For Goldschmidt, masochistic behavior, reading books and writing go together on one line. For him, they are a mix of attempts to save himself that began with his personal experience and drove that experience beyond the corporeal.

Reading and writing, like his masochistic lust from pain, have a lonely, undefinable, personal connotation. It is just this loneliness that contributes to the fact that they do not dissolve in passive receptivity or external determination. "It only seems that the masochistic ego is being suffocated. How much scorn, how much humor, how much unconquerable resistance or triumph is hidden by the ego that portrays itself as weak?"[3] Even reading only seems passive; it is also affirmation of one's personal ego experience. It is in his writing that Goldschmidt eventually finds his voice, yet he remarks, "I come before speech, and only because of this is there speech. The words exist only because I exist, and it is only because I exist that the 'other' exists."[4]

The powerful defiance in Goldschmidt's words seems to be a requirement if one is not to perish in face of a hostile world or an adverse destiny. Accordingly, Goldschmidt, without a morally raised index finger and entirely against the prevalent morality, points out that self-punishment, retiring the self

---

1. Neue Zürcher Zeitung 18/19 March 1995, p. 68: "Wenn wir alles sagen könnten" (tr. *If we could say everything*)
2. Ibid.
3. G. Deleuze: "Le Froid et Le Cruel" (tr. *The Cold and the Cruel*): Essay about Sacher-Masoch, quoted from G. A. Goldschmidt 1994
4. G. A. Goldschmidt 1994, p. 118

(into a world of books) and discussions with oneself (in writing) can also be important to survival.

Similarly, we must consider to what extent defiantly self-affirming ego experience has a protective function in derailed, pathological reactions. Many modern pictures of psychological disturbance seem to me to make little sense, unless we consider the pathological grip of the ego's bodily experience. Among young people, self-abusive forms of behavior — phenomena such as self-injury (auto-mutilation) or refusal to eat (anorexia) — have increased dramatically during the last decades.[1] We see behavior that, from the outside, appears hard to understand, even absurd, acts that contradict and fight each other. Anorexics' refusal of food is not just a negation of food and of participation in a shared meal, their physical feelings of hunger and other discomfort also evoke a sense of the personal body.

The experience of pain or hunger can be understood as a deprivation, but also as a positive indication of the reality of one's own body. The recalcitrant subject becomes aware of his or her living presence. The stubborn urge to cause personal suffering is sometimes the expression of a deeply moving battle against the impossibility of understanding oneself in the face of another's threatening description, and of inner emptiness or confusion; in other words, this means fighting to change from a "something" into a "somebody."

Social factors may play an additional role in this sort of extreme attempt to assert oneself. We probably should not be surprised that others would try to escape by means of extreme subjective actions from attempts to objectify them, when commerce tries to turn them into objects to be traded,

---

1. At the Psychiatric University Clinic of Zürich, self-injuries have doubled between 1987 and 1995 (Ch. Schmid al. 2000). A good summary concerning the self-injuring human being was written by Norbert Hänsli: "Automutilation: Der sich selbst schädigende Mensch im psychopathologischen Verständnis" (1994)

and when they are treated by science as statistically defined, standard cases.

*Personal Experience as Saving Anchor: an Example*

Fabienne is twenty-four. She is tall, an impressive presence dressed mostly in black, well groomed, intelligent, and linguistically gifted. Fabienne would probably agree with this characterization, but these qualities characterize only her presentation and her scholastic achievements, not her person. Her personality manifests in a different manner.

I have known Fabienne for six years. She was hospitalized with suicidal intentions for the first time at eighteen, after running away from home and when ambulant psychiatric treatment had not been able to reduce her scholastic and personal crises. She then continued intensive treatment with a psychiatrist, but repeatedly returned to our hospital for care. The reasons for these voluntary admissions were: mainly acute disagreements with the parents, acute social crises, but also situations in which she experienced the pressure of excessive demands in her studies.

Fabienne sought help in the hospital because she could no longer tolerate being with her parents, or she fled into the hospital because she could no longer tolerate "it," namely, being with herself. Yet what was this "it"? This is difficult to answer. The parents had great difficulties with her suicidal threats, her tendency to run away and other withdrawal tendencies, and they kept delivering ultimatums to the effect that Fabienne would either have to adjust to the family or renounce the family's support. Fabienne's problems were conditioned only in part by these demands, however. She suffered equally from her withdrawal from others, from teachers and therapists to whom she had tried to relate as friends.

The ostensible situation was this: Fabienne was the older of two children of a successful academician and a vivacious homemaker. The father often traveled professionally in foreign countries; the mother focused her attention on her children, especially Fabienne, whose closeness, kindness and warmth she appreciated. Yet the mother was less and less capable of dealing with the state of affairs after Fabienne and her slightly younger sister became teenagers.

Fabienne remained dependent on her parents for a long time. Though she did work for a few years as an assistant in a medical office, she soon entered an expensive private preparatory school, intending to graduate and then go on to university. Her father paid for both her school and her living expenses. Her relationship to her parents could be described as a case of "either/or"; either there was superficial harmony between Fabienne and her parents — especially her mother — or the relationship switched to the opposite pole, even to loss of contact. Fabienne's crises manifested mostly when her parents threatened to disown her, seemingly hoping to teach Fabienne to come to her senses and change for the better by using such ultimatums.

My therapeutic attempts during family therapy sessions repeatedly failed because of the persistent refusal of the parents, especially the mother, who seemed to cling to the motto, "Fabienne is either for or against us."

Initially, Fabienne related to her parents as a mirror image. She fled into the hospital from her home when she could no longer get along with them, and abruptly ended her hospital stays when she could find a seemingly acceptable solution with them. It was only during her third hospitalization that Fabienne was able to tolerate the painful process of separation from her treatment team long enough to move to an apartment her parents financed. During her fourth and last hospitalization, it all came to a head when Fabienne decided to renounce any of her parents' financial support, even if it meant depending on the welfare department and discontinuing private school for the time being. She then tried to live more independently, in keeping with what she had recognized in therapy.

This brief description of the outward events in her life is intended to serve as background for a few equally abridged remarks concerning her internal conflicts. Fabienne tended to manifest her problems either physically or in interpersonal relationships. During adolescence, she tried to get classmates with suicidal tendencies to become attached to her, and then proceeded to cut herself, or punch herself in the face in situations of great tension. Eventually, her neighbors became alarmed by the bloody wounds underneath her right eye, inflicted on herself with a razor. At eighteen, she developed anorexic symptoms, sustaining herself at times with only extremely low calorie food. Yet she never manifested any pronounced and lasting depressive, anxiety, or compulsive symptoms, nor did she display any psychotic experiences. The magnitude of her self-injuries and refusals of nourishment seemed to depend on feelings of powerlessness and emptiness, conditions that were triggered mostly by impending separations (including from nurses and therapists). While Fabienne occasionally spoke of not being able to "feel" herself, this lack of feeling became a problem only when she feared losing a partner she idealized. Then she would first try to prevent the loss by means of suicidal threats, or if that was ineffective, she would injure herself in an attempt to be able to feel herself.

The lack of feeling was not a condition that she observed in herself independent of any external event. She became aware of it only in relating to other people. Similarly, her biographical self-description was pieced together at first using mostly superficial information. Her inner experience, especially her emotions, remained untouched. Accordingly, her personal history remained strangely mute.

One would not, however, be justified in assuming that Fabienne, with her problems of introspection and identity, was lacking in personal decisiveness. On the contrary, Fabienne could be extraordinarily consistent, even stubborn, and could renounce immediate benefits in favor of a fixed goal. It would be inadequate to describe her simply as incapable of tolerating frustration. She seemed instead to lack an inward "court," or internalized pair of eyes, that would affirm presence (being a self) when she felt alone or abandoned. In her moments of feeling abandoned there was no "family romance," no symbolic imagination available. Her tendency to idealize seemed intended simply to represent the image of a person who would not disappoint her. Yet Fabienne felt all the emptier when those idealized images crumbled. At that point she lacked a vision of the "other" she had pictured to herself, and this brief lack became a moment of intolerable emptiness. In those times she could, to a degree, lessen her tension, or at least physically distract herself from the intolerable emptiness for hours or days with her self-injuries. These self-injuries made sense to her, but they could not replace that other ego that she was missing.

Rimbaud said, "'I' is someone else." In hospitalized patients, this "someone else" can neither be exorcised from the patient, nor can it be replaced by another person. Nevertheless, in Fabienne's case, it became possible for the treatment team to recognize that her recurrent pain over incipient separations was the basis of her suffering, thereby avoiding adding further pathological and reinforcing influences to her attempts to control herself. As had been discussed with her, she was offered very close attention and supervision when she was extremely tense or in danger of injuring herself. Furthermore, in the spirit of helpful behavior modification, she was given the opportunity to turn to a therapeutic coworker when she felt she might endanger herself. The links between the emotions she devalued and her tendencies to injure herself were also emphasized in Fabienne's psychotherapeutic sessions. Whenever it could be done responsibly, her less harmful self-injuries were accepted for what they were, namely, attempts to experience herself when no other person who could affirm her was outwardly or inwardly present. One might view this acceptance of her search for herself, communicated more in her stance than her words, as a therapeutic attempt to offer this indefinite individual — Fabienne — a caring partner who, though unable to remove all distress, could nevertheless be available whenever the distress became excessive.

Over several years, with gradually decreased hospitalizations and with continued psychiatric treatment (mostly outpatient), Fabienne developed the beginnings of a personal history, and with that, a personal identity. Her personal development enabled her to make independent decisions even while socially dependent. She became more conscious of her own body, and started to broaden her inner range of experience. The place of inner emptiness and self-administered physical pain increasingly changed as she was personally affected by sadness and psychological pain.

In that regard, one might ask in what way Georges Arthur Goldschmidt was different from Fabienne?

Goldschmidt affirmed his lust by making use of his own body, even to lust derived from pain, justifying his longing and his pain as something that belonged solely to him. Fabienne experienced some relief by injuring herself and refusing food, but did so without reaching the point of being able to accept herself. Goldschmidt lived on the ground of his origin and history. In unspeakable distress, he created a symbolic world and a counter-world. Fabienne is incorruptible and inexorable in her search for her self, yet the experience of her injured body is not sufficient to help her find an inner space. It is the repeated experience that, though sad and suffering, she is accepted by others, that gives her the courage not to simply fight against the inner emptiness, but also to acknowledge her pain and sadness. Then she can picture something in herself that cannot be defined by a third person: an ego that introduces itself through the feelings and longings of her body. Or, as Fabienne once wrote to me, quoting the poetic words of Saint-Exupéry: "The human being sees clearly only with the heart." Like the Little Prince, human beings require an encounter in order to recognize: the soul as an object does not exist, but we can experience it and imagine it.

*An Attempt at a New Self and Body Idea*

Does emphasis on personal experience imply that one is still paying homage to the kind of subjectivism that was overcome a long time ago? Does emphasis on the first person perspective revive a separate, personal, soulish area distinct from the body? Is the function of an emotion such as the fear that points to danger changed into a soulish content?

This danger exists. Our Western manner of thinking is influenced by body-soul dualism to such an extent that in every discussion of a psychological phenomenon, the image of a detached soul (as seen from the time of Plato to that of Descartes) comes sweeping along. The idea that emotions help us deal with various life situations awakens its counterpart, the rational thinking of Aristotle, another thread that winds through Western history. According to this latter mode of thought, it is the form, or in other words, the purpose that makes an object what it is. Thus a chair becomes a chair only if it has a certain form that serves that purpose. Chairs are for sitting, whatever materials are used to make them. It is the legacy of Aristotle that leads us to equate emotion with function. Emotions are there for survival.

It is, however, quite possible that this idea is more complicated. Maybe one does not have to resolve the disagreement between Plato and Aristotle, even though there are historians who view the history of Western philosophy as nothing but footnotes to the discussions between Plato and Aristotle.

As we try to delineate a model of emotion, it is undoubtedly important to follow Plato and Aristotle, or the two systems of thought they initiated. Yet we also note that human perceptions, feelings and actions are neither immaterial nor simply functional, but are bodily events that encompass both body and soul. This third view is surprisingly close to the Judeo-Christian tradition that has always vigorously shied away from views that divide subject and object, or form and substance.

This book began with the basic thought that it is only the subjective experience of an ego — the first person perspective — together with the third person perspective, i.e., the view of a 'generalized third,' that makes one human. Any attempt to reduce humans to one or the other viewpoint makes them into either robots or spirit beings. Subjective experience eludes definition, because it cannot be made into a thing.

Yet we speak of people's experience, feeling and acting, meaning the intangible beyond which one cannot probe,[1] that which makes human beings Individuals. While their actions characterize individuals' ethics, it is their feelings that estab-

---

1. (Translator:) The term *unhintergehbar* is explained here by the author as referring to the fact that one cannot go beyond the 'first person'. German philosopher, Manfred Frank spoke of the "*Unhintergehbarkeit*" of Individuality.

lish humans' orientation in the world. Perceiving and feeling are the very foundations of any manner of orientation.

There is good reason to place actions, and therefore ethics, in the center of our thinking about human beings, thereby developing a philosophical and religious image of the world similar to the one Jewish philosopher Emmanuel Lévinas formed so impressively.[1] In the way they shape our inner orientation and influence our attitudes toward the external world, perception and feeling are in the foreground of medical and psychiatric questions. Psychiatric problems can develop whenever a person's perceptions and feelings collide with value systems that render one's experience questionable. This will be the subject of the closing section of this book.

*Bodily Landscapes of the 'Soulish' — Comments Pertaining to the Neurobiology of the Foundations of Experience*

First, however, I would like to explore more closely what there is about sensing[2] and feeling, and in how we must understand these terms. Sensing and feeling are verbs that express what is currently taking place. They correspond to an event that is proceeding and cannot be frozen in time. Only when I start thinking about my feeling (active phenomenon), does that feeling (verb) turn into a feeling (noun), i.e., an objective fact. Similarly, feeling (verb) can become an object

1. One of Lévinas' crucial statements concerns becoming oneself by challenging another. He claims that the genuine self does not originate of itself, but rather as the result of an individual not refusing to meet the demands another's suffering places on him. A concise introduction to Lévinas' thought, and especially to his main works, "Totalität und Unendlichkeit" (tr. *Totality and Infinity*) and "Jenseits des Seins..." (tr. *Beyond Being*) is found in Bernhard Taureck 1997.

2. (Translator:) Here I run into another instance of linguistic difference that seems to reflect slightly different cultural experience. My dictionary translates both *fühlen*, and *empfinden* as feeling, although it translates the noun, *Empfindung* not only as feeling but also as sensation; the English language allows the two to overlap. In order to convey the significant difference the author underlines here, I shall use sensing and sensation: for *Empfinden* and *Empfindung*.

when some accompanying physical expression (such as blushing or lowering my gaze) is observed by another. It follows that a feeling is a combination of subjective experience and objective change on the physiological and behavioral level.

It is interesting that the same thing cannot be said of sensing. While one can reflect about a sensation and speak of it, the sensation cannot be observed externally like a lowered gaze or the physiological occurrence of a blush.

What, then, is the difference between feeling and sensing? In German, the *finden* (of finding) in *empfinden* (sensing) refers to discovering, while feeling is related to touching, thus displaying a bodily origin. Linguistically, something can be touched by feeling and thus be discovered and sensed as something special. I point out this linguistic difference between feeling and sensing because it appears in modern scientific insight as the assumption that feelings awaken sensations, but not all sensations go hand in hand with feelings. To explain this, I need to change the perspective and resort to neurobiological findings, calling on the following reflections of Antonio R. Damasio, a leading American neurologist.

The human organism is constantly active. This is reflected in the unceasing action of nerves that parallels the activities of various organs and parts of the body. Normally we are unaware of this varied activity (especially the neurological aspects). We respond mostly to new or increased stimuli, signals that stand out from the normal background. For example, we sense the stomach when there is acid reflux, or the right arm when it keeps hurting after a fall, but as long as nothing unusual happens, we are not aware of the stomach or the arm's ordinary presence. Damasio calls the impression of this ever-present, neuron-influenced activity "background sensation." He writes, "Background sensation is our image of a bodily landscape... The concept of 'mood,' while related to this background-sensation, is, however, not quite accurate. When background sensations remain for hours and days constantly the same, and do not perceptibly change with the ups and downs of our thought contents, then it is probably the overall content of the background sensations that contribute to a good, poor or neutral mood."[1]

When background sensation is suddenly disrupted, when there is a considerable change in the activity, we then become aware of the change in terms of a sensation.

Picture yourself suddenly hearing an unusual noise on an evening stroll. You feel scared, perhaps crouch defensively, your breath comes faster, and you sense the increased activity of your heart. You may not be conscious of these physical reactions, but these changes in the activities of your organs will nevertheless be transmitted to your brain from nerve endings that carry impulses from skin, blood-vessels, intestines, muscles and so forth. It is especially the cortical regions of the frontal and parietal lobes of the brain that will show a change in activity as a result of the information received from the organs. In this regard, one must not assume that the change in activity is static, or localized in a specific area of the brain. Rather, different areas of the brain, connected in a network, will show alternating patterns of activity.

Signals from the organs reach the brain by chemical process, as well as by nerve pathways; when one is frightened, hormones and peptides reach the brain through blood circulation.

The combined neural and hormonal information form a "picture" of the body landscape that changes constantly. This is not a visual, or other kind of representation of that

---

1. A. Damasio 1997, p. 208 (Translator: As far a I am aware, this is one of the most difficult instances of translating a German translation back into English, clearly not always choosing the words that were used in the original.)

landscape, but rather a pattern of variations that essentially corresponds to an electric field.

Up to now I have sought to illustrate what happens in our bodies when we have specific sensations. Usually, when we are awake, thoughts are added to these sensations. When a certain sensation involving a specific body landscape is regularly associated with a similar thought (of impending danger, for example), the sensed body landscape and the thought image join to form a consistent pattern of sensation and image. From Damasio's point of view, it is these patterns of combinations that correspond to a "feeling." The feeling of fear would thus be composed of sensing a body landscape characterized by a rapid pulse, rapid breathing, perspiration, and increased muscle tension and the memory of threat or danger (in our chosen example, a sudden noise). In grief, the experience of suffering a terrible loss combines with a physical shift characterized by rapid pulse, lower skin temperature, a typical change of the facial muscles (a sad expression) and, possibly, weeping.

It is of practical and theoretical significance that the neural connections and the areas of the brain involved with the occurrence of sensations are not identical with the neural patterns of activity (i.e., the areas of the brain) that are required for their presence. It is the different cerebral patterns involved in imaging and sensing that make it possible for patterns of sensation and ideas to join as a feeling. Furthermore, it is the distinction between the neural representations of ideas and sensations that makes it possible to approach emotional problems therapeutically, from either sensations or ideas.

> Exactly how the neural images and the sensations combine with each other remains an open question. In the case of a specific feeling, there is disagreement among researchers of emotion as to the sequence in which idea and sensation appear. While one

side thinks that specific pictured situations (e.g., danger) must be present in order to change the body landscape, others insist that a spontaneous physical change can evoke the appropriate situation or idea. Both views are probably correct. What is certain, however, is that a feeling belongs with a sensed body landscape.

One hundred years ago, William James asked what would be left of our feelings if all of our physical sensations were turned off, writing, "If we picture to ourselves a strong feeling and then attempt to eliminate from consciousness any perception of bodily indications, we will then observe that we retain nothing, no soulish content that would allow us to reconstitute the feeling, and all that is left is a cold and neutral condition of intellectual perception... What would remain of the feeling of fear if I did not have the sensations of an accelerated heartbeat, shallow breathing, trembling, weak knees, goose-flesh and nausea? Lacking them, I could not picture fear using even my strongest will."[1]

Clinical psychologist Paul Ekman, a respected American researcher of the emotions, conducted experiments in which participants were asked to move specific facial muscles.[2] When subjects tensed facial muscles related to the expression of feelings, Ekman noticed the occurrence of more than accidental states of feeling that corresponded to those groups of muscles. The volunteers, however, did not know that their muscle movements had anything to do with feeling. These and other observations prompted the speculation that feelings were linked to sensing a specific condition of the body; for example, with feelings of fear, there was a physical defense reaction against danger. If this is the case, then different feelings must distinguish themselves from each other in relation to the physical mode of activity.

1. Quoted from A. Damasio 1997, p. 180
2. P. Ekman 1992

Language clearly encourages us to separate fear, happiness, distrust, jealousy, etc., as different feelings. Language also points to the connection of feelings with body sensations. Thus fear may be expressed as "almost having a heart attack," "being breathless," "feeling oppressed", "shuddering," or more crudely, as "being scared shitless."

Language and modern science agree, inasmuch as feelings are not seen as occurring only in the head, but as affecting the entire body. They take place in the stomach, in the heart, or they penetrate into the bones. Feelings are related to the head only inasmuch as they find their neural assimilation in the brain.

When I feel, I do not feel an abstract soul; rather, I experience myself bodily. That is the reason for the title of this chapter: "The Body of the Soul is Emotional." But I feel, and that is more than I can expect of a body. How do modern researchers of feelings picture the ability of a body to feel?

## A Model of Emotions

Every emotion presupposes a trigger. Biologists like to picture a dangerous animal, a serpent, or a hungry bear as triggers of emotional reactions. Yet these animals don't play a significant role in our everyday lives. In the zoo they are isolated behind fences and glass, where they evoke far more astonishment and admiration than fear or anxiety, a fine example of the fact that a stimulus does not denote danger in an isolated way, but only in a specific context. In everyday life, other threats have taken the place of dangerous animals: dangers in traffic, disagreements and breakups of important relationships, insecurities in our professions and financial difficulties. These social dangers, while not any less frightening, are more difficult to separate from our overall situation in life than an unexpected encounter with a jungle serpent.

However, most researchers of emotions assume that, basically, the mechanism that triggers an emotion is no different in a social situation than it is in the jungle. A stimulus indicating danger leads to a series of defensive processes that are included under the heading of "emotional reaction patterns." In any case, research with humans must recognize that the triggering of emotion is more heavily dependent on the assessment of danger by the affected person than it is in an animal.[1] It is for this reason that in psychological research with humans, great value is placed on how a certain situation is interpreted or appraised, whereas in research with animals, one simply assumes a direct connection between the stimuli and the way their organisms react. It is, however, not overlooked that some human ways of reacting have developed on the basis of relatively simple conditioned stimuli.

Joseph LeDoux, renowned researcher of the emotions from the University of New York, assumes that there is a direct pathway for the reaction pattern developed by evolution.[2] (*Figure 1, page 191*). In the case of a fear reaction, this direct and fast route of information processing leads from the sense organs that receive the stimuli via nerves and brain pathways to the thalamus in the diencephalon, and from this important switching center to the amygdala in the forebrain. This almond-shaped brain center has a special role in the way humans react, because it releases (by activating other brain centers) the physiological and behavioral changes that occur with fear. The amygdala also causes an activation of circulation (by stimulating the lateral hypothalamus), an increase of stress hormones (by stimulating the paraventricular hypothalamus), or the paralysis of terror (by activating the central

---

1. The link between cognition and emotion, between mental images and feelings has been described very clearly (and amusingly) by Mick Power and Tim Dalgleish (1997).
2. J. LeDoux 1998

gray matter). This fast, direct method of triggering fear takes only a few milliseconds from stimulus to change of behavior. It is probable that specific constellations of stimuli can produce a fear reaction by this fast course without an analysis of the basic stimulus pattern. Damasio starts with the idea that, "We are wired for immediate feeling response when we become aware of specific signs or stimuli in the outside world or in the body, occurring alone or in combination. Examples of such signs are size (such as when we are in the presence of very large animals), extreme wingspans (a hovering eagle), special kinds of movement (like those of reptiles), unusual noises (like snarling and grumbling), or special conditions of the body (like pain during a heart attack)."[1]

Then there is the slower, more indirect path of fear response pattern that includes the cortex of the brain, since there are also signals that are sent from the thalamus to the sensory areas of the cortex (see *Figure 1*). Here the impulses are associated with other neural patterns (for example from memory stores). Following complicated preliminary work in the cortex, messages are then sent to the amygdala, which can again trigger the physiological and behavioral modes of response of the fear model. This indirect means enables the interpretation and assessment (the "appraisal") in cortical areas of the source of the danger, but it takes about twice as much time as the short path does to process the information.

LeDoux sees the meaning of the short, or direct, path as a quicker reaction time: "The direct path enables us to begin to react to potentially dangerous stimuli before we clearly know what these stimuli mean. This can be very helpful in dangerous situations. Yet the advantage of this solution requires that the indirect path via the cortex be in a position to trump the direct path."[2]

1. A. Damasio 1997
2. J. LeDoux 1998, p. 164

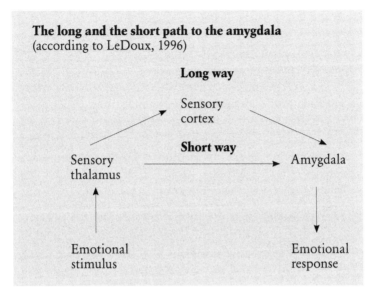

*Figure 1*

*Assessed Basic Feelings*

Reacting with emotions is, however, not the only way for the human organism to respond to a stimulus. Parallel to that kind of emotional event, a perceived stimulus leaves traces in the memory (a part of the just-described emotional system) that are stored in an independent memory cache. Humans thereby have at their disposal memory that retains its stimulus only in its spatial constellation, without exhibiting any emotional coloring. This kind of spatial processing of data occurs in the region of the parietal lobes that cover the so-called hippocampus, while emotional memory traces are stored in other structures of the brain.

However, in time, the initial "double entry" of events — the separation of the implicit emotional traces of the responses, and the explicit memory of the facts — is clarified, whenever necessary, by the "working memory," a sort of short term collection of varied impressions and memories. The linking of emotional and factual memory traces can thereby produce an emotionally colored recollection in long term memory. Yet the initial separation makes it possible for facts and emotions to be remembered independent of each other. If, for example, my factual memory has lost the details of a prior event (such as the fact that a car blew its horn just before I had a car crash), if my emotional memory retains the coupling of the sound of the horn with the crash, then hearing a similar horn, I might react without knowing why I am scared — without recalling the event.

There is plenty of evidence to support the idea that our ability to recall emotions is more reliable than our ability to remember data. This would fit well with the fact that we frequently find it impossible to discover the original cause of conditioned fear responses, because there is no conscious memory of the decisive, triggering moments of the frightening experience.

Information from recent examinations even points to the possibility that the hippocampus, the center that processes factual memory, is damaged by chronic stress, while the amygdala, the center of emotional memory, is energized by stress. If these findings are shown to be correct, we will have learned that we tend to become more forgetful of factual data when under stress, while the same condition promotes the tendency to more emotional reactions.

However, the above description of the body's functional adjustment to the source of danger does not adequately explain the methodology of the emotional response. For even when a fearful response, by taking the short neuronal path, occurs automatically, the source of the danger is usually experienced quite consciously by the affected person.

According to LeDoux, conscious perception of the fear response presupposes that the physical changes and the external triggering stimuli are connected. This process is most complicated. In LeDoux's model, the short term working memory is charged with transferring the neural pattern of the stimuli into a symbolic figure, thereby causing it to become conscious. Yet LeDoux does not tell us *how* this transfer of electrochemical processes of personal experiences to brain mechanisms to mental actions, must proceed.

In his analysis of the fear response, primarily based on animal experiments, LeDoux rightly limits himself to this sequence: (A) external stimulus − (B) bodily (mainly neural) readjustment − (C) organism's response to stimulus. In this regard, the middle link (B) of his line of reasoning is distinguished from the beginning and ending conditions of a potential danger that must be overcome. The organism must survive. The bodily readjustment (B) becomes a contingent function that follows the stimulus (A) and its management (C). This way of thinking does not view the organism or body as the starting point of a process, but instead sees it as the middle link in a sequence that is determined by its beginning and its end.

The first person perspective does not invalidate this basic idea. Yet because fear is experienced consciously, its experience can become the starting point of a new dynamic. The person involved can evaluate the experience intellectually or emotionally, as, for example, shameful. The experience can be put into words and discussed with other people independent of its bodily expression. In this context, the experience is no longer the result of a process, but rather the starting point of a personal dynamic based on physical sensations, but no longer restricted to bodily sensations. Experience in terms of the first person perspective, quite independent of the idea that humans have a capacity for introspection, achieves an autonomy that puts the body at the center, no longer treating it as merely functional (in the sense of serving a stimulus-response pattern).

> This is also demonstrated in literature, representational art, religion and philosophy. Anxiety plays a significant role in all of these. As a matter of fact, twentieth century philosophy made anxiety the focal point of its inquiries. In contrast to its role in the evolution of biology, the experience of anxiety became the starting point for an interpretation of the world. No longer considered a bodily experience and an unconscious consequence of the fight for survival, anxiety became the fundamental condition, the existential basis of life, whose challenge must be accepted. The conscious experience of anxiety became a cultural phenomenon that in turn reflected upon the individual.

Let us, however, stay with the individual and consider how a situation evaluated as being dangerous is processed intrapsychically. In this case, we will disregard abstract existential threats and, following the long tradition of cognitive psychotherapists, think of some simple examples.

Over the long term, the estimation of dangerous situations seems to occur in two radically different ways. On one hand, thoughts may contain sharply defined content such as, "That approaching car could hit me," or "My wife might leave me." These limited thoughts refer to specific dangers without indicating a comprehensive attitude of life. They are but the cognitive estimates of defined danger, called "propositions," because they represent factual descriptions.

On the other hand, these kinds of ideas may convey an overall attitude. Such implications (from the Latin *implicatio,* meaning infolding) do not contain defined, concrete facts but are, like parables, pregnant with adaptive content. Examples are, "I'm an absolute zero," or "I don't have a chance," broad statements that usually represent attitudes that are far more comprehensive than propositional, and thus have a much stronger influence on what happens emotionally.

Different propositions may often join under a single implicative schema. The implicative schema, "I'd not have a chance," may encompass the limited thought, "My wife will abandon me," as well as, "I have no money for rent." When isolated thoughts (propositions) are placed in a larger, implicative context like, "I'm a complete mess," they may achieve far greater and broader effectiveness than when they are not related to such an implicative schema.

Unfortunately, this rather complex link between proposition and implication commonly results in well-meaning advice to anxious patients which reinforce, rather than alleviate, their fears. A reassuring propositional statement such as, "You judge the danger wrongly, it is not as bad as you think," can reinforce the implicative assumption, "I must be incapable and without hope, since others think I'm not even able to correctly evaluate my situation." This broad estimate of one's powerlessness spurs the anxiety more than a concrete estimate of a specific condition.

Up to this point, we have followed the sequence from a stimulus to the assessment of danger and on to the pattern of reaction, using the example of fear. I have indicated that in this sequence the reaction to fear is in no way clearly defined. This is because my thoughts, associations and attitudes regarding the situation are decisive in forming an estimate of the actual danger. Indeed, a dangerous incident might cause me to feel so insecure that I'd begin to smell danger everywhere, and I would constantly check each of my wife's moves out of fear that she might leave me.

Another possibility is a situation during which feelings of fear release a swarm of other feelings. It has been well established that persistent, long-lasting fear often leads to anger and rage. One must also bear in mind that I can find words to express thoughts about my feelings and behavior better than I can convey my immediate experiences and feelings. This is because our language is based on observation, and no intelligible (first person perspective) private speech exists for sensations, feelings and actions. After first encountering fear, I am more prone to reflect and offer an interpretation of what I have felt and the way I have acted. I don't seem to be able to recall the experience of fear I suffered without evaluating it. My feelings thereby become embedded in a world of thoughts that increasingly overlays the original experience. If inclined toward self-criticism, for example, I may reproach myself for having risked the dangerous situation (such as heavy traffic that contributed to the accident). On the other hand, if I'm a person of faith, I may thank God for my good fortune in the unlucky situation. I might return to the routine of the day, or I might continue to ask myself anxiously what other kind of incident could happen next. I could blame others for not having warned me, or even for being responsible for my having gotten into this dangerous situation.

The innumerable possibilities in evaluating the event show clearly that the experience of fear soon is covered up with thoughts and worries that initially could not have had any influence on the appearance of the fear. These thoughts and worries are based on earlier experiences that are unrelated to the actual experience of the threat. Nonetheless, those thoughts and traces of remembered feelings merged into a complex that can no longer be unraveled. As a result, the naked feelings are charged with cognitive evaluations and images with which they have basically nothing to do. Research in psychology and psychiatry has shown unequivocally that it is not the initial feeling of fear that provokes a disorder, but it generally is the *interpretation* of the feelings of fear that leads to severe anxiety disorders (more on this in the next chapter). It is not the underlying feeling that is pathological, but the cognitive and socially embedded complex about what happened that may lead to disorders. To use the expression I have employed earlier, it is not the first person perspective of the experience that is active in the anxiety disorder, but rather the objectified depiction of the fear that threatens the ego, causing it to be in a state of alarm as if that were a real external danger.

The emotional model that has been presented, along with its therapeutic consequences, has been thoroughly scrutinized in regard to the feeling of fear. There are, however, good reasons to believe this model could also be usefully adapted for the study of problems related to other emotions. I therefore intend to develop, in the next chapter, a theory of illness that assumes the first person perspective as given, and brings the sphere of emotional problems into correlation with the appreciation of feelings.

> I will confront the task of bringing the most prevalent psychiatric disorders into relationship with the most important basic feelings. Our psychiatric problems must not be separated from our experiences; at the same time, they must not be shifted exclusively to the third person perspective and thus become objectified. On the contrary, I would like to show that it is precisely a certain kind of objectification of sensing and feeling that contributes to our psychological quandaries. I shall investigate the basic emotions of anxiety, sadness and disgust, attempting to describe how defending against them and devaluing them contributes to psychiatric problems.

To this effect, I will summarize here the ideas that have been presented up to this point.[1]

---

1. I have been urged from several sides to also contemplate a second person perspective. I can, in fact, with a "thou" — a "person" — establish a different kind of relationship than with an "it," or a "somebody." I believe, however, that the I-thou relationship presupposes that not only I, myself, have a first person per-

*Summary*

Sensation and emotion are, from the first person perspective, physical experience. Judgements (as well as other attitudes apart from experience) are cognitive processes that develop through innate disposition and life experiences. In other words, cognitive attitudes are informal processes, namely patterns of the brain's neural activity. Admittedly, sensation and feeling also presuppose patterns of neural activity, but they reflect processes of the entire body, presupposing changes in organs such as the heart, the lungs, skeletal muscles, skin and so forth. In this sense, the popular idea that the soul lives in the organs is unmistakable. Saint-Exupéry's words in *Le Petit Prince*, "We see well only with the heart," is not only true in a metaphorical sense, it also contains a proven, if poetically expressed, insight. Perhaps I'm only completely myself when I sense and feel all this with my entire body.

As the old saying goes, *"De gustibus non est disputandum"* (there is no arguing taste). Sensations and feelings, too, are so deeply individual that they cannot be generalized. Yet we generally begin with the assumption that others are able to empathize at least partially with how we feel. They cannot, however, do that based on general knowledge, but only on the basis of what they themselves have experienced. What I feel, i.e., what I experience "first hand," is the first person perspective. This kind of experience is a necessary precondition of my ability to empathize with what others experience. It's unique quality is that it cannot be objectified and turned into something pathological. We, however, thanks to memory, are able to turn what we have experienced into an object of

---

spective, but that the other, my "thou," also has one, i.e., the I-thou connection is characterized by an interpersonal mutuality of two "first persons." That makes the addition of a second person perspective questionable, even unnecessary, in a theory of cognition.

our observations and assessments. As soon as we do that, we have distanced ourselves from the experience. As presented schematically by Table 3, the experience has now turned, on a line indicating the passage of time, into something we experienced (that is, what has already happened).

| Table 3: From Immediate Feeling to Subsequently Evaluated Feeling | |
|---|---|
| Chronological Order | Occurrence |
| Present (present process) | Feeling (verb) (I feel) |
| Past (fact) | Feeling (noun) (I have felt) |
| Past reviewed in the present | An evaluated feeling (I accept, disregard, judge what I have felt) |

The experience of a feeling thus becomes a re-collected feeling; feeling (verb) sad, for example, becomes a feeling (noun) of sadness. As a further step, we are able to judge that object-like feeling and assess it as negative, and therefore undesirable. Once feelings are objectified and assessed, I can also try to hide them as if they were things, or publicly expose them. Feelings such as sadness can also elicit other feelings, like when I become disgruntled because I'm sad. I may also try to hide from others what I felt, or to disregard it. In these situations I view my feelings from the position of a third person who can observe the repercussions of my feelings on my body or on my words. Then I am not only sensing and feeling, but setting myself apart from my feelings and dealing with them from the perspective of a third person. With that, I have internalized the subject-object split; I no longer experience myself as a unity, but have become at one and the same time both subject and object, observer and observed.

In the first approach to the issue of emotions, I begin with the notion that my sensations and feelings can elude my attempts to clearly fix them. Yet I am in the position of being able to submit my sensing and feeling to judgment from the perspective of a generalized third (in myself). The judgment may be appropriate or inappropriate. It can create problems or solve problems. But it cannot question my sensations and feelings.

In my relationships with other human beings I have found that in the long run, it is of little help to act as if I was someone I'm not. It is not helpful to be quiet and friendly when in fact I'm angry and when I am concerned … It is of no help to act as if I felt entirely safe, when in fact I am fearful and unsure.

– Carl R. Rogers

## Chapter 5. Overwhelming Self-Assessment – An Attempt to reach a New Understanding of a Feeling Person's Illness

*Assessed Basic Feelings and their Consequences*

The predominant model of psychiatric illness is still heavily influenced by an older, mechanistic view that has proven itself useful for explaining various diseases. Kidney disease, for example, can be traced to organic disorder due to a tumor or an inflammation. In psychological disorders, however, that model is inadequate. Psychological suffering is associated with functional changes in the brain, but usually cannot be traced back to demonstrable damage in some physical organ.[1]

In this chapter I shall try to group in a different framework the disorders that are characterized much more by psychological distress than by a distinct physical disorder. I interpret these disorders as expressing an abnormal change of the human organism in unusual situations. Such alterations usually

---

1. (Translator:) Admittedly, there is an exception: that model proved applicable in research on Alzheimer's disease, an illness defined from the beginning as pathological, structural damage to the brain. While Alzheimer's, in its course, manifests a variety of clinical symptoms, no similar structural disorders of the brain have yet been found in all cases of anxiety and affective disorders.

go hand in hand with a devaluation of basic physiological feeling.

As was pointed out in the preceding chapter, whether one experiences and feels "immediately," or the feelings are received secondarily as knowledge (as in reflection or evaluation), there is a fundamental difference. In the first case, the person is one with the lived experience; in the second, she/he relates to the experienced emotions as to something that happens to him or her. Depending on how they evaluate the latter possibility, they may assess the emotions as an enrichment or as an encumbrance.

The second group of disorders involves the possibility that one can suffer not only from organic disorders, but also from an idea, such as the image one has of oneself. What is experienced then is no longer unquestionably one's own plight; it can be a personally or socially undesirable fact. It is evident that this more complex form of suffering is also accompanied by temporary changes in the activity and metabolism of the central nervous system. The basic problem, however, is not an injury to the nervous system; it is based on the self-disparaging judgement of a perceived emotion. Thus it can neither be understood nor resolved by observation of the physiological processes in the brain alone; attention must also be paid to the primary subjective experience, and to the patient's assessment of this experience.

To do full justice to this dynamic, one needs a view of illness that is both personal and focused on the patient's experience. By this I intend an understanding of illness that sees the mode of emotional experiences and its assessment as central. Rather than beginning with behavioral disorders, this attempt seeks to define problematic emotional groups.

In order to differentiate between the problematic groups, I will focus on the five fundamental feelings of fear, anger, sadness, disgust and joy, as well as a few composite feelings such as shame and guilt. It is possible, by dealing with and appraising these basic emotions, to touch upon different groups of problems and describe them in their classic forms. In everyday life one runs into various overlapping groups, but a clear description of dissimilar groups of problems is helpful in developing distinctions in understanding the varying forms of psychic suffering, and for developing differentiated therapeutic approaches.

Currently, it is the problematic field of anxiety that has been most explored, so to illustrate our approach, we shall consider it first. Then, because it would be impossible to deal systematically with all the groups of problems within the space of this book, the problem groups of sadness and disgust will be examined in place of all the others. Sadness, and especially disgust, are feelings that have a greatly under-rated role in human life. Greater knowledge of them will contribute to the understanding of many other forms of psychological suffering.

## The Problem-Group of Anxiety

"Life," as poet Martin Amis wrote, "is made of anxiety." Anxiety appears to be ever-present, widely diverse in its forms, and as necessary for life as pain.

No one can avoid anxiety. Søren Kierkegaard, considered the founder of existentialism, saw anxiety as the basic emotional experience of modern times. He presented the idea that, "Everyone must learn to experience anxiety, otherwise he will perish because he never feared or because he drowns in anxiety. Yet he who has learned to experience anxiety in the right way, has learned the highest."[1] Overwhelming, primal fear was recognized by the turn of the nineteenth century in psychology and psychiatry as the dominant factor in numerous illnesses. Emil Kraepelin, a Munich psychiatrist who founded the modem doctrine of psychiatry early in the twentieth century, firmly stated in his textbook, "By far the most powerful emotions we observe in our patients are those of anxiety."[2]

In fact, the psychotherapeutic schools of the twentieth century developed largely as a result of the confrontation with and discussion of anxiety, giving it central importance in both psychoanalysis and behavioral therapy. Sigmund Freud's first papers are dedicated to anxiety neuroses. At first, Freud interpreted the occurrence of anxiety as an expression of the blocked energy of drives (the impaired release of sexual tension). In an article published in 1895, he described anxiety as the result of interrupted coitus.[3] He also considered "Neurasthenia (a kind of nerve weakness) drenched with anxiety" to be a result of masturbation. Thirty years later, however, he saw anxiety far less as a result, and more as the cause, of psychiatric disorders. He pointed to anxiety as the source and crucial aspect of various defense mechanisms, and viewed it as a threat of danger to the ego because of intrapsychic conflicts.[4]

Behavioral therapy, too, initially began with the treatment of anxiety states, and continues to this day to show the best

---

1. S. Kierkegaard 1844 (1960)
2. Quoted from P. Pichot 1989, p. 238
3. In his paper "Über die Berechtigung von der Neurasthenie einen bestimmten Symptomenkomplex als 'Angstneurose' abzutrennen" (tr. *About the Justification of Separating from Neurasthenia a Special Complex of Symptoms as 'Anxiety Neurosis'*) Freud described this "first theory of anxiety," also named "toxic theory."
4. In "Hemmung, Symptom und Angst" (*The Problem of Anxiety*) Freud presented his second theory of anxiety, which became the defining theory for psychoanalysis. Here the ego sets in motion mechanisms of defense in order to overcome the danger to which the anxiety points; these mechanisms then result in the neurotic symptoms.

results in this area.[1] In existential philosophy and its therapeutic applications, anxiety turned into the foundation stone
of the living world. In the somewhat stilted language of this
therapeutic orientation, it became the fundamental mode of
*Dasein*, or existence; the concept of existential anxiety that
resulted became the watchword for an entire age, largely because it reflected the basic emotions of so many during the
twentieth century.

It would, however, be erroneous to link anxiety exclusively
with modern times. Many much earlier thinkers tried to
understand anxiety. Whereas anxiety was, for the Greek philosopher Plato, an affair within the soul that had nothing to
do with the body, Aristotle interpreted anxiety as a necessary
bodily function. In keeping with this view, Aristotle saw human courage in the fact that people confronted unavoidable
fear, while Plato urged that in misfortune one should harness
the power of reason and remain as logical and relaxed as
possible, not allowing anxiety to appear.

These different positions can be observed and followed
throughout the history of the West to the present day. On one
side, we find anxiety viewed as a negative and inferior soulish
quality that one must try to avoid and control. On the other
side, anxiety is seen as a meaningful element in life that may
contain an important message.

It is possible, however, that these two perspectives represent
not only different views, but that they also speak of different
emotions. Many languages distinguish between anxiety and
fear. Those who are afraid know of a specific danger and view
their fear as a normal warning. Yet most of those who are
anxious are often unable to understand the reason for their
anxiety. While fear goes hand in hand with the clearly defined

---

1. I. Marks, a most experienced practitioner, published a paper in 1993 titled,
"Living with Fear: Understanding and Coping with Anxiety," offering a readable
review of applications in Behavior Modification Therapy.

trigger of a recognized danger and has a clear-cut function, we find that anxiety has no clear direction. The difference between anxiety and fear that Kierkegaard first formulated was expressed in 1913 by Karl Jaspers with equally simple and concise words: "Fear is oriented toward something, anxiety has no object."[1]

Should anxiety be associated with soulish experience – that is, with a mode of existence – and fear with apprehension, something frightening? Does fear, then, emphasize the warning character of this realm of feeling, and anxiety emphasize inner experience? When I feel fear, my attention is oriented toward an object, and I prepare to flee. When I am anxious, I sense an inward bodily tension, recognizing myself as a subject. Anxiety shows me how I am attuned, and has no outward object. Anxiety refers me to myself, fear points beyond me. Fear prompts me to protect myself against external or physical danger.

This differentiation of anxiety and fear is not without contradiction. Those who represent function-oriented views find it difficult to accept feelings of anxiety that lack an external cause. As a result, they define anxiety as fear, but fear that cannot be avoided, meaning that no goal-oriented behavior is possible. On the other hand, some who represent views regarding the soulish essence of anxiety have attempted to portray fear as, ultimately, existential anxiety. So, for example, they link fear of wide open spaces or dizzying heights to deep-seated existential anxiety.

The wisdom of language does not, however, allow itself to be subdued by such subtle reflections. In all Western languages, terms for anxiety derive from a group of Latin words (e.g., *angor*, *augustus*, *anxiosus*), that allude to "narrow" or "being constricted." It is the experience of limitation that is at the

---

1. K. Jaspers 1973

root of anxiety. Physical constriction can be experienced in the neck or the chest (as indicated by the medical terms "angina" and "angina pectoris." The experience of constriction can also be related to an external narrowing, the experience of narrowness going hand in hand with physical restlessness.

Thus anxiety is experienced as a threatening narrowness (in French, *angoisse*, in German, *Beklemmung*) that is also physical. Anxiety is then linked to restlessness, trembling, sweating, palpitations, dry mouth, increased pulse rate and rapid breathing.

If one not only experiences anxiety but also fears a specific danger, then the experience of anxiety is given an external reason. People who are afraid know what triggers their anxiety. They will try to avoid the source of the danger, whether by careful withdrawal or precipitous flight. Therefore, fear usually goes hand in hand with a certain behavioral tendency: the so-called avoidance behavior. To resist this behavior, counter-force is required, such as holding firm to an inner conviction, or strong persistence in spite of external pressures.

In principle, one can distinguish four different levels on which anxiety/fear experiences occur.

- The experiential level: soulish experience of anxiety
- the physiological level: bodily changes during the state of anxiety
- the cognitive level: the appraisal of a situation as dangerous to one's goals or to oneself, engendering fear
- the behavioral level: attitudes about fear that lead to avoiding situations that are sensed as threatening.

While the first two levels are present in every kind of anxiety, we can observe that the next two levels require a certain interpretative framework, except in the case of genetically determined fear reactions that are like reflexes, e.g., being

startled upon suddenly seeing a serpent (see LeDoux: The
Direct Way; *Figure 1*, Chapter 4).

The frame of reference can differ considerably from one
person to another, especially since one's assessment of a
situation's degree of danger depends largely on biographical
experience and personal value judgments. Those once bitten
by a dog are likely to avoid such animals. Conversely, one
who grew up with a dog as a playmate will exhibit affection
for dogs later. Those whose lives have been very insecure and
thus are in need of being accepted by others will fear criticism
much more than those who grew up under favorable conditions and have developed autonomy and confidence.

Also, the first experience of anxiety will determine how one
subsequently deals with anxiety. Those who were ridiculed
whenever they experienced anxiety during childhood will be
inclined to view anxiety as a sign of weakness, or even of
shame. They will try to systematically avoid the experience of
anxiety, or will feel extremely insecure when anxiety occurs.
On the other hand, those whose initial experiences of anxiety
were taken seriously by supportive parents and friends will
be able to accept anxiety far better, and will develop more
confidence in regard to it. Examples of adverse early history
have shown that the experience of anxiety, if considered negative, can become a source of additional fear in itself. "Anxiety
about anxiety" is basically a fear of anxiety. Since the results
of anxiety are considered dangerous and are feared, a devil-
ishly vicious circle of anxiety and fear of anxiety develops,
further amplifying the anxiety. People who have had painful
experiences in collective situations – not being able to concentrate during an examination, for example – are likely to
fear that comparable anxiety will cripple them in later exams;
during examinations, the anticipation itself may trigger an
anxiety attack.

Distinguishing between anxiety and fear is helpful, because personal anxiety is an unquestionable experience, whereas an object of fear can be analyzed. So it is possible to question one's fantasy about or interpretation of a circumstance one fears, thereby reducing, or even neutralizing, the anticipatory anxiety (the apprehension). While the experience of anxiety can be acknowledged and tolerated, it cannot be manipulated mentally. Since fear depends on intellectual assessments, illogical conclusions or deceptions are possible. Thus it is feasible that our apprehensions may be unfounded, but that we are, in truth, still afraid of ghosts. If the cognitive assessment of a situation turned out to be irrelevant, then even ghosts could not scare us. In this regard, we find that the German language is very articulate; we fear ghosts, but we are free of anxiety as long as we remain fearless.

> In the Grimm's tale "About one who went off to learn to fear," we are told of a youngster who was concerned because he could not experience "shuddering." He remains undisturbed even when he is exposed to the kind of ghostly situations which fill others with dread when they merely hear stories about them. He deals successfully with ghosts in the towers of the castle and with the spirits of the dead; he does not lose his coolness even in face of some horrendous, black cats. While others fear for their lives because they believe in ghosts, he remains fearless and meets the spooky nightly events as if they were ordinary, daily occurrences. His recipe is as successful as it is simple: he is not concerned because he's a rather dull character, and lacks the kind of fantastic imaginations that could evoke fear in him. He *gruselt*, that is, he shudders only at the end, when the maid suggests that one should wake him by pouring over him cold water full of little fishes. In this case, he is not confronted by fantastic imaginations. It is the vision of little fishes wiggling between his legs that finally evokes the shuddering anxiety he had previously missed so much.

Why are fearless human beings rather rare, while a large seg-
ment of the population is afraid, if not of ghosts, then of even
trivial things and dangers that have no rational basis? One
possible reason is that irrational, exaggerated apprehensions
succeed in distracting us, at least for a while, from existential
fears about death, meaninglessness and isolation, helping us
to ignore these real dangers. They enable us to fixate on the
fears that pesters us most, thus interfering less with our ability
to deal with our ordinary, day to day tasks. They distract us
from the basic questions of human existence and make it
easier to avoid the vertigo of mounting existential anxieties.[1]

At the same time, these imaginary images of dangers make
it possible to experience a kind of "anxiety high," allowing us
to be in the position of experiencing anxiety without being
nakedly exposed to the vulnerability of anxiety. As a result of
properly calibrated "shuddering" – such as on roller coaster
rides or in horror movies – we experience the desired phenomenon of anxiously experiencing our own selves, namely
the hair-raising sensations of bodily anxiety. We stimulate
our ability to experience this without being disturbed by apprehensions over which we have no control. This makes it
possible to approximate an experience of anxiety that would
otherwise be blocked by negative assessments about anxiety.
Ordinarily, we do not seem to welcome anxiety. We do not
like to characterize ourselves as being full of anxiety, and so
are inclined to whitewash even the confrontations with our
own abyss in order to feel less severely the thorn of anxiety.

If people deny the experience of anxiety any access, they
are in danger of not being able to feel themselves adequately.
When anxiety is denied, repressed, split off from conscious-

---

1. "Anxiety can be compared to vertigo. He whose eye looks suddenly into a yawn-
ing abyss experiences vertigo. Yet what is the cause for this? It is just as much his
eye as the abyss; for how would it be if he had not looked down? Thus anxiety is
the vertigo of freedom." (S. Kierkegaard 1960, p. 57)

ness, or projected upon others, one's relationship to reality and one's fellow humans suffers a change: the world can no longer be accepted as it is. The causes of anxiety are covered up, and terror is reshaped to appear as everyday life. To play on the words of Roland Laing, "In place of the experience of negation (frightening emptiness) enters the negation of experience."[1] (Sigmund Freud had earlier commented that the splitting off of our feelings alienates us from ourselves.)

This alienation from oneself and reality is found, for example, in people who project outward what they fear will happen to them in an attempt to avoid working through their anxiety over losing someone close, or their sense of existential nothingness. It is a truism that people and communities whose identities feel threatened are inclined to create scapegoats, examples of which include Jews, witches and Communists. In fighting off existential anxieties and transferring them as external apprehensions to foreign groups of people, it is not only gnawing self-doubt – such as the experience of negation – that can be kept at bay. It is also possible to develop a goal-directed, mostly destructive campaign against those scapegoats and thus avoid one's own tension. These harmful, externally directed actions can be prevented by the acceptance of existential anxiety.

It appears especially important to place anxiety in a broader context so as not to fall prey to the opinion that anxiety is merely a physiological event or an isolated behavioral problem. We find that anxiety always has several levels, even in a single individual. Finding the most suitable way to deal with anxiety is a crucial issue, since fear goes hand in hand with anxiety and anxiety can be increased or limited by specific apprehensions.

---

1. In his book *The Politics of Experience* (1967), Laing drew a distinction between "the experience of negation" and "the negation of experience."

While it is not anxiety that causes illness, anxiety can go hand in hand with ideas and apprehensions that lead to illness or impairment. Anxiety growing into a fear of anxiety can escalate so rapidly that it may eventually be perceived by the subject as something foreign. This anxiety, rather being experienced as something belonging to the subject, becomes an intruder who threatens to destroy what is experienced as one's own. Rather than being anxious, one is now intimidated, an imposed tyranny that swiftly produces a suffering whose intensity is comparable only to the severe pain of a bodily injury. Help is of great importance. This special condition of "anxiety disorder" can be understood by comparing it with the normal condition of anxiety. There is evidence to support the opinion that helping patients with anxiety presupposes their acceptance of the anxiety.

> Example: Karen R. suffers from agoraphobia, the intense and irrational fear (phobia) of wide and high spaces (Gr. *agora* = market place). She suffers from an apprehension that if she walks in the city, she might fall and be hit by a car. Crossing a bridge is a nightmare for her, because she envisions being drawn down into the depths it spans. These and other similar apprehensions force Karin R. to drastically restrict her life.
>
> In spite of being impaired by her apprehensions, she does not locate the source of her problem in the agoraphobia, but in experiencing anxiety. She takes anxiolytic medications to gain control over her fear. She becomes aware only in the course of cognitive behavior modification therapy that it is not the anxiety but her apprehensions that cause her incapacitation. She then learns step by step to face and experience a certain amount of anxiety. Then she is motivated to go – first only in fantasy, then in reality – into the places she fears and which trigger anxiety due to her apprehensions. By exposing herself deliberately to her anxiety, she no longer experiences herself as a passive object

that is being frightened, but as a subject, one who is able to experience anxiety.

## Disorders that are Linked to Anxiety

The World Health Organization (WHO) makes a distinction between three basic types of anxiety disorders.[1] They differ mainly in their symptomatology and course.

*Phobias*, the most numerous of the three, are characterized by the fact that special locations (wide spaces, narrow rooms, great heights), specific items (pointed objects, dead animals) or animals (spiders, mice) are avoided because they trigger intense fear. The triggering situations themselves are not necessarily dangerous. As bridges, tunnels, elevators, etc., they may be part of one's day-to-day life. When such situations must be avoided, there are restrictions in the individual's life. Fear of open spaces (agoraphobia) can lead to profound invalidism, while a phobia of spiders (arachnophobia) is less compromising.

*Panic Disorders*, the second type of basic anxiety disorder, are defined by the WHO as a series of episodes that are accompanied by anxiety and include shortness of breath, dizziness, and other physical symptoms. In contrast to phobias, panic attacks can occur without external provocation, and usually are of short duration. Those affected most often experience their anxiety as a consequence of sudden physical changes. It is only when these attacks begin to merge with phobic avoidance that there are more serious impairments.

*Generalized Anxiety Disorders*, the third type of basic anxiety disorders, involve neither the physical experience of panic nor the avoidance of outer events. Those affected suffer from con-

---

1. H. Dilling et al.: IDC10 (1991): A concise review of the classification and therapeutic possibilities of anxiety disorders is also found in B. Küchenhoff/D. Hell 1995.

tinuing tension and irritability. They feel exhausted, unable to find rest because of "inner anxiety." They feel the pressure of anticipation even when not faced with an external task nor expected to master a phobic situation. This third type of anxiety disorder offers few biological or social avenues of approach and is inclined to be chronic. It manifests most of all in the way people experience themselves, rarely offering access to objective observations.

The WHO's classification of anxiety disorders is based on the symptoms and the criteria of the course of illness at hand. It can be understood better when the inner dynamics of those affected are considered. In the case of phobic avoidance, one's apprehension is directed towards external objects and situations. It is not one's personal life that is subject to discussion, but rather the evaluation of external observations, so, for example, a fear of heights involves the possibility of falling from a high cliff, or the idea of falling from a high bridge.

During a panic attack, it is common to dread the catastrophic failure of one's body. No outer objects provoke anxiety; instead, there are serious forebodings, mostly concerning the function of the heart, or the circulation of air in the lungs. The sufferer may fear a coronary occlusion, a circulatory failure or suffocation. In their anxiety, people suffering from panic do not truly experience themselves; fears focused on the body fill the foreground entirely. For those with panic disorders, hypochondriacal fear precludes access to the personal experience of fear. By his own estimate, he does not suffer primarily from anxiety, but from the potential failure of a bodily organ. One who suffers from a panic disorder does not seek help from a physician because of fear, but because of physical symptoms such as rapid heart beats and shortness of breath.

The experience of anxiety seems to be found in the foreground only of generalized anxiety disorders. Upon closer inspection, however, we find that the anxiety retreats behind the person's apprehensions and is discounted in various ways. In this case, however, we can see that the cognitive apprehensions are not directed toward external situations, as in phobias, nor toward bodily functions, as in panic disorders; instead, fearing anxiety (anticipatory anxiety), they focus on the appearance of the anxiety itself. As a result, any imagined anxiety becomes, as an object of fear, the trigger of ongoing apprehension. It is difficult to treat generalized anxiety disorders, because their source is an imagined object that does not exist as a concrete reality.

These basic types of anxiety disorders can thus be separated by the fact that clearly different apprehensions are found in them: in a phobia, an external object is seen as dangerous; in a panic attack the peril is a bodily failure; in generalized anxiety disorders, fear is evoked by anxiety itself. With all these differences, anxiety disorders have in common the attempt to ward off and avoid the experience of anxiety. Yet because of that, sufferers cannot achieve victory over their anxiety. It will break through as soon as apprehensions increase, and when the anxiety can no longer be hidden or turned into a thing. The components of this sequence have become known by the somewhat confusing term of "Circle of Anxiety" (see *Figure 2, next page*).

This model of the circle of anxiety dates back to English psychologist David Clark,[1] who assumed that certain bodily feelings and their corresponding apprehensions reinforce each other, acutely raising the experience of anxiety. This sequence has been most closely examined in panic disorders.

1. D. M. Clark 1986. In the area of German language, it was, among others, J. Margraf and S. Schneider who acquainted others with a clear description of the "Circle of Anxiety" in their book "Panik" (tr. *Panic* 1989)

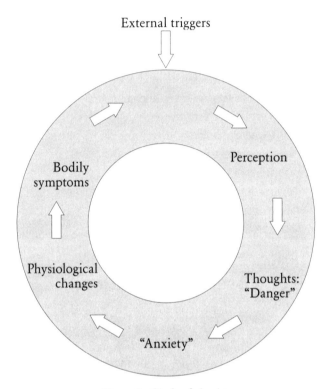

*Figure 2: Circle of Anxiety*

In typical panic attacks, an increased heart rate or more rapid breathing go hand in hand with the patients' apprehensions, because they believe they are suffering from dangerous heart or lung disease. The apprehension engenders fear that results, through the release of noradrenaline, in an increased heart rate and frequency of breathing. Once sufferers become aware of this acceleration – extra systoles and shortness of breath – they feel their apprehensions are proven correct, and may react as if fearing impending death. Thus the anxiety can build in minutes into a genuine condition of panic.

Today, at the suggestion of American psychiatrist D. F. Klein (1962), acute incidents of anxiety are called panic attacks. This does not, however, refer to a new kind of illness. In his paper "Studien über Hysterie" (*Studies on Hysteria*) published in 1895, Freud described the complaints of Katharina, an eighteen-year-old woman, that correspond exactly to the disease pictured above.[1]

Freud described his dialogue with the young woman:

"What are your complaints?"
"I have terrible shortness of breath. Not always, but sometimes it takes hold of me so hard that I think I'm choking."

This, initially, did not sound neurotic, but at the same time it began to seem to me likely that what she said could be only a substitute description for a condition of anxiety. Out of the complex of feelings of anxiety, it was the moments of her shortness of breath that she emphasized excessively.

"Sit down, please. Describe for me this condition of 'shortness of breath.'"
"It just comes over me, then lays itself like a pressure on my eyes, my head becomes heavy, and there is an unbearable humming. I'm so dizzy that I think I'll fall, and then it squeezes my chest so that I can't catch my breath."
"And you don't feel anything in your neck?"
"My neck gets very tight, as if I was going to choke!"
"And is there anything else with your head?"
"Yes, there is hammering as if it was going to split."
"Yes, and does this not scare you?"
"I always think that I must die, and otherwise I have courage. I go everywhere, in the cellar or across the entire mountain, but on the days when I have this, I don't dare to go anywhere. I always feel that someone is standing behind me and will suddenly grab me."

While Freud interpreted what happened with this young woman mostly in psychodynamic terms, using the psycho-

1. Quoted from S. Freud 1972, p. 185f.

physiological model of the circle of anxiety, the origin of her suffering would be viewed today as a combination of neurobiological changes and psychological issues. (It is possible to experimentally demonstrate the interactions between physical changes and physical apprehensions.)

It is especially useful to apply the circle of anxiety in therapeutic situations with patients suffering from panic disorders. With the patient's prior consent, it is possible for the therapist to provoke faster breathing or a faster pulse rate using simple bodily exercises.

When patients focus on the bodily experience of increased respiratory and pulse rates, they tend to react with negative feelings. As the heart and pulse rates increase further, they notice unpleasant thoughts going through their heads. Typically, they wonder if the heart will really be able to tolerate the increased demand, and if they are getting enough oxygen. Such thoughts are usually followed by additional apprehensions, leading to picturing a truly catastrophic scene. Most often this spiraling anxiety leads to a fear of dying, due to anticipating heart failure, choking, or collapse (from fainting).

During a psychotherapeutic session, this anxiety progression can be interrupted by helping the patient think of other things. A patient with panic disorder will calm down when it is made clear that the heart, quite in keeping with cardiac physiology, is beating faster because of physical exertion. As far as breathing is concerned, the patient can be asked to concentrate on abdominal respiration. This exercise not only distracts the patient from fearful thoughts, it may also oblige the patient to breath more slowly. Most of the time, these measures make it possible to break the diabolical cycle of physical sensations and frightening interpretations. The procedure has an additional advantage: patients with panic disorders increasingly recognize the connection between their symptoms and their apprehensions, giving them an instrument of self-help.

I concede that when people are very "uptight," it is difficult for them to let go of those apprehensions that have become ingrained and be open to a factual interpretation of what is taking place in their bodies. When there is considerable anxiety, we find first a tendency to avoid the experience and focus on certain ideas, or some tangible object. Thinking of death is the extreme version of the tendency to link rising anxiety with specific dangers, and to explore the surroundings and one's own body for possible causes of the anxiety,

In this way, fears become ever more comprehensive, eventually involving one's whole life. Yet it is just because of this mechanism that therapy may succeed in turning all-consuming apprehensions into specific, approachable apprehensions. Progress can be made therapeutically if, in psychotherapy, one succeeds in untangling death fears or other puzzling anxieties into separate, identifiable fears. This principle is especially successful in the treatment of panic disorders and complex phobias.

According to current behavior therapy theory, human anxiety spontaneously diminishes when the situation that triggers the fear is no longer avoided, and when the process of habituation has begun. Therefore, behavior modifying therapies place considerable importance on exposing patients to their triggering situations. This implies that those who suffer from anxiety disorders are exposed step by step, either gradually or rapidly, to the situations or objects they fear the most. However, these procedures seem to be permanently effective only if they do not attribute the decrease in anxiety to external influences such as, for example, the effect of prescribed medication. Even to consider the effectiveness of the procedure to be the result of some internal psychological process, such as a cognitive ritual or a special prayer, will sooner or later undo the positive effects of the treatment. For lasting effectiveness, the procedure requires that anxiety is experienced directly and without any suggestion that it is a helpful defense. It is not simply a matter of tolerating a feared situation, but also of purposefully experiencing the anxiety, which presupposes conscious acceptance of the anxiety experience. In terms of the concepts used in this book, that kind of experience corresponds to the first person perspective, while intellectual avoidance maneuvers and opinions that sidestep direct experience, correspond to the third person perspective.

Specific behavior modification therapies that use either gradual or rapid exposures can be successful in people who show no evidence of self-devaluation or a general inclination to be afraid. Reasonably isolated *phobias,* such as the fear of narrow spaces (claustrophobia) or fear of dogs or spiders respond quite favorably to this method. The therapy's goal is for the patient to experience, as a result of being confronted with a situation she fears, that her fear is unfounded. The anxiety endured in the scary situation the person managed to tolerate has, finally, a self-affirming, liberating effect.[1]

The treatment of *general anxiety disorders* by means of such confrontations and reevaluations is far more difficult. When one's own experience becomes the reason for apprehension, then there are limits to the effectiveness of being exposed to the anxiety.

A brief example reveals this problem:

Rosmarie H., age 40, was trained to be a nurse, and worked for a long time as a teacher in a nursing school. She had to leave that job because she was constantly tense, could no longer sleep adequately and had begun to worry if her teaching was doing

---

1. R. Stern/L. Drummond (1991) offer an excellent introduction to the practice of behavior modification and cognitive treatment.

justice to her students. Inclined to be excessively orderly and perfectionistic, she experienced pressure that eventually left her unable to meet her own high demands. Yet in spite of being freed from her job, she continued to suffer from ever-present anxiety; she was concerned lest she buckle under too much pressure and end as a failure among her fellow human beings. In this tense state she constantly worried about herself and her fellow human beings. She was afraid that some mishap would befall her nephew, or that she might be bothered on the street by unknown people. This social fear and her tendency to withdraw became even greater when a shelter for refugees was established in her neighborhood. She was also worried about many ordinary situations of everyday life, such as not being able to fall asleep, receiving surprising telephone calls, being ridiculed because she had gained weight, losing her physician, etc. As a result, Ms. H. found herself in a state of overstimulation, irritability, and a predisposition toward being frightened.

In a general anxiety disorder, the reduction of specific apprehensions is possible only to a limited degree, as the anxiety has various names and can be corralled only so much; both the tendency to think a good deal and anticipatory anxiety about all kinds of everyday things are in the foreground. Even though the pronounced readiness of fear leads the person to judge innumerable things to be dangerous, it is impossible for this free-floating anxiety to attach itself to external objects. Ever new fears provide evidence that the battle over which the fundamental anxiety is fought cannot be won. In this disorder it becomes clear that the distress consists far less of individual, specific apprehensions, than an insecurity that reaches deep existential levels. Often there is insecurity about oneself that contributes to the inability to accept one's experience, so the person must constantly fight for affirmation and self-control.

In keeping with the above observations, it appears that help with this kind of problem must focus primarily on supporting self-respect and promoting the patient's potential in daily life, especially in social competence. With this disorder, the importance of evaluation and affirmation of feelings becomes clear. If these existentially vulnerable persons' experiences of anxiety are not properly appreciated, they end up feeling that their very existence is uncertain. Conversely, full acceptance of their fears opens a door into meaningful discussion of circumstances in life that offers something beyond treatment with psychopharmaca (though they are often required). An accepting, psychodynamic understanding of one's personal development will also contribute to the unburdening. It is obvious that there is also a place for limited success in the overcoming of individual fears, and these successes help strengthen the patient's self-opinion. Yet this anti-phobic help, focused on what is feared, will not take the place of deeper understanding of the fundamental, existential anxiety.

Anxiety states are complicated by compulsions. In these cases, people try to block their apprehensions, such as a fear of being infected by germs, with specific actions, such as ritual washing of the hands (washing compulsion). These compulsive actions can become so time-consuming that they hamper, and in severe cases, make it impossible for the person to cope with everyday tasks. Other examples include compulsions to control or to create order. An individual who suffers from the compulsion to control must repeatedly check, for example, to see if the door to the home is locked, or a burner on the stove has been turned off. Behind these compulsions is the idea that without such control, an accident, such as a fire, will occur. Such apprehensions may be recognized as unreasonable, or even senseless, but it is impossible to stop the ritualistic compulsive actions, because the one affected would otherwise be forced to confront the experience of her or his anxiety.

One major problem with these compulsive controls is that they calm the fears for only a short time. Performing the controlling actions only further reinforces the fears, because the experience of anxiety is not accepted but instead is even further repressed by focusing on the fears and the compulsive actions. It is not the surfacing of anxiety that constitutes the sickness in compulsive disorders, it is defending against anxiety that prolongs the illness.[1]

When persons with compulsive disorders defend against anxiety, it happens in two steps. First, the anxiety that surfaces is cognitively brought into contact with any external dangers that are imagined. This is the origin of what are called obsessive or compulsive thoughts, which are simply object-bound apprehensions. The second step consists of attempting to restrict these apprehensions by using compulsive actions, such as ritualistic hand washing or controlling behavior. In this way, the initial anxiety is removed from personal experience and either becomes the object of controlled fears, or is pushed away like an enemy.

Therapy must locate a path that leads from the compulsive actions back to the fears behind them, from obsessive apprehensions to naked anxiety. In treating compulsive disorders, there seems to be no way to avoid embracing the experience of anxiety. It is true that the symptoms of anxiety can be reduced by anxiolytic and anti-depressive medications, but any lasting reduction of compulsive thoughts and actions requires finding a new, more open attitude toward the experience of anxiety, respecting anxiety not as an enemy, but as an essential element of life. At least partial acceptance of the experience of anxiety is a prerequisite of treatment that exposes patients to their disorder. This treatment has also proven unusually suc-

---

1. J. Rapoport (1993) described the problem of compulsive disorders in an exemplary manner.

cessful with patients suffering from compulsive disorders: the patient is asked to do exactly what she/he most fears without resorting to any counter measure.[1]

This procedure can be presented in the following way:

Therapist: "What happens when you touch something dirty?"

Patient: "I become anxious, even though I cannot explain it to myself."

Therapist: "Then, when you wash your hands, you calm down. I imagine that the hand washing is rewarded by a calming effect, so that in the next confrontation with dirt, the hand washing is even more thorough?"

Patent: "Yes, it has become a habit that I can't break by myself."

Therapist: "The more you wash your hands, the greater the likeliness that you will wash them again. For this reason, during therapy you need to touch something of which you are afraid, and then refrain from washing. In that way, the vicious cycle can be broken, and you will be able to dispense with the reward of a compulsive ritual. This requires that you tolerate the anxiety. Anxiety is, I admit, uncomfortable, but it is not dangerous. It is not the anxiety that hampers you, but rather the obsessive idea that something bad will happen it you experience the anxiety."

We find unusual extremes when dealing with the anxiety of psychotic patients with, for example, schizophrenia. In such cases, defenses against the experience of anxiety are not restricted to irrational obsessions, as is true of those with anxiety and obsessive disorders. The projection of the anxiety experience goes a step farther, because the cause of the anxiety is denied, or reality is misinterpreted and the effect is seen as if it had already happened. In such cases, the fear is replaced by a delusion, which is accepted as a reality and therefore doesn't need to be feared as a future threat. This reversal process also means that the patient's reality that evoked the

---

1. Review in P.M. Salkovskis/J. Kirk 1991

anxiety is changed into a distorted ("ver-rückt", crazy) reality for which the psychotic patient bears no responsibility.

Such a distorted reality can be helpful to explain the lack of emotions that patients with schizophrenia show. It is not unusual for them to talk about horrible stories of pursuit and torture without showing any emotions. As their experiences have changed from the first person perspective to the objective third person perspective, their world has become factual and inanimated. Because of that, the psychotic patients' experiences may seem like science-fiction where they are surrounded by artificial beings with artificial intelligence. The patient may perceive himself/herself as a robot being directed from outside his/her realm of reality.

On one hand, the compelling power of psychotic delusions protects the patient from an overwhelming sense of being threatened, but that also reduces the possibility of engaging with the reality of everyday life, because the anxiety is unchanged. When everything is determined by foreign influences, and even one's body is manipulated from the outside – as also happens in hypnotic trances or one's dreams – no acts of free will are possible.

In addition to decreasing the experience of anxiety by jumping into a delusional state, psychotic patients have demonstrated another method of denying anxiety: remaining apart from everyday reality through avoiding all opportunities for being involved in everyday affairs. This manner of avoiding anxiety and reality is described most impressively in the short story *Bartleby, the Scrivener* by Herman Melville. Bartleby, a law clerk, withdraws from any call to perform some special duty by answering clearly and concisely, "I would prefer not to do so." Even when asked to leave the office, he sticks to his answer, "I would prefer not to do so." By politely refusing to do something without commenting about how he feels about the demand, Bartleby manages to avoid being involved in the possibilities life offers him, and thus does not allow these possibilities to become realities that he has established. He maintains a state of potentiality and thus avoids the anxiety of having to achieve something. Italian philosopher Giorgio Agamben has interpreted Bartleby's behavior as an attempt to annihilate creation, and with it, the anxiety that dominates creation (in this connection, Agamben used the term "Ent-Schöpfung" [dis-creation]).[1]

Yet even psychotic patients are not entirely free from anxiety. Whenever some personal experience breaks through the gaps of their alienation – not unlike the grass that finds space between concrete slabs – they are seized by anxiety and fear. Psychosis can be viewed as an attempt to escape overwhelming experiences of anxiety, but also – when the psychosis wanes – as an anxiety-creating experience. Anxiety thus appears on the way into the psychosis, as well as on the way back out of the psychosis.

In treating people who are ill with a psychosis, one must concede great significance to feelings of anxiety. In general, schizophrenic psychoses are viewed primarily as a disturbance of one's cognitive capacities. Anxiety, however, represents a crucial element in a psychotic development. It is one thing to diminish anxiety with medications, but allowing anxiety to surface, to the extent a patient is able to accept it, is no less important a goal. The greatest challenge lies in linking one approach with the other at the right time and in the right measure. A precondition for all this is that psychotic patients are accompanied over long periods of time (and with suitable closeness) by people who are able to tolerate anxiety well. Then it is possible for them to find islands of a shared reality and mutual experience. It is also very helpful to psychotic patients for their companions to be able, to some extent, to sense the rifts in their own reality.

1. G. Agamben 1998

Søren Kierkegaard, whose life was affected by profound anxiety, believed that there is always a certain amount of longing in anxiety. Thus he writes, "For in anxiety a condition introduces itself from which he longs to emerge, and it speaks up because longing alone is unable to free him... What I say at this point may possibly seem to many people to be an obscure and poor speech, if they admire themselves for never being anxious. I would respond that one should certainly not be anxious with people, with finite things. Yet only those who have lived through the anxiety of possibility have grown to the point where they no longer fear not because they now can escape the frightful things in life, but because those things are always weak in comparison to the fears of possibility. And should a person speak up and imply that it is fine that he never has experienced anxiety, I would happily offer him my explanation: namely that this is so, because he so grievously lacks spirit."[1]

## The Problem-Circle of Sadness

Sadness, like anxiety, is a basic, important feeling, one often equated with grief. Grief, however, tends to be experienced passively – one is "burdened by" grief – whereas sadness (the German term derives from *truren*, to lower one's head is experienced more actively.)

Sadness must be separated from depression. Sad people experience themselves more or less intensely, and they may weep. By contrast, people who are depressed suffer from a loss of feeling, so even the flow of tears is blocked.

While sadness is not something to be desired, it is more tolerable than other negative feelings. Anxiety provokes more defenses than sadness, and goes hand in hand with a greater loss of self-confidence. According to the studies of Bartlett and Izard (1972), sad people report less psychological ten-

---

1. S. Kierkegaard 1960, p. 55f.

sion than those who experience anger, anxiety or disgust. Poets, too, have continually pointed to the positive aspects of sadness. Like Gottfried August Bürger, they have praised the quietness of sadness, singing like Peter Huchel of "die Nacht der Trauer" (tr. *Night of sorrow*), or dreaming like Goethe of the bliss of melancholy:

> Do not dry, do not dry
> the tears of eternal love!
> Oh, how empty, how dead does appear
> the world to the half-dried eye!
> Do not dry, do not dry
> the tears of unhappy love.

("The Bliss of Melancholy," by Johann Wolfgang von Goethe)

In a beautiful little book edited by Reklam, titled "Komm, heilige Melancholie" (tr. *Come, holy Melancholy*),[1] can be found a collection of more than one hundred German poems that praise sorrow, grief, melancholy, sadness and tears.

So why is it that sadness is generally still considered negative? Tomkins, a researcher in emotions, suspects that it is precisely the negative aspect of sadness that is meant to emphasize the meaning and purpose of this feeling. Sadness or sorrow, he points out, awaken sympathy only when they are perceived not as positive, but painful. Furthermore, a situation that causes sadness can be dealt with only when sadness is considered as something one must get rid of.

> Tomkins concludes: "Sorrow is not a toxic, paralyzing affect that necessarily calls for avoidance strategies, but rather, it promotes remedial strategies which turn against the sources of the sorrow. The presence of sorrow indicates the possibility of remedial reactions either by the individuals themselves, or with their assistance. The course of the normal development can be

---

1. L. Völker 1984

assessed by considering the size of the sorrow-spectrum. To the extent that individuals may show many kinds of insensitivity to sorrow, there is some developmental retardation... Any society in which no sorrow is created by illness, injustice, discrepancies between what is possible and what has been achieved, by a lack of excitement and joy, or their anxieties, their humiliations and hostilities, is an underdeveloped society."[1]

Though sadness is at times hard to bear, its positive effects are nevertheless unmistakable. Tears and sadness can have a freeing effect not only for the individual, but also can contribute to the cohesiveness of a group, whether a family, a circle of friends, or a larger community.

"Inasmuch as separation causes grief, it is the avoidance or anticipation of grief that bonds a person to relatives and friends. If we did not miss relatives and friends, one of the important forces that ties us to others would be lacking.

A large group of young people was asked to imagine, and then write down, how it would be to live in a world without grief. Most of them wrote that this would be a world without joy and love, without family and friends. Many among them even questioned whether this would still be a world of human beings."[2]

Different societies and cultures vary in regard to their attitudes towards sadness and the ways they encourage their children to repress or to express sad feelings. In Western cultures, and especially in northern countries, children are raised to show no sadness, and especially no anxiety ("Boys don't cry!"). Both genders are encouraged to observe their feelings critically, and to deal very carefully with them, especially with feelings of sadness that give evidence of being bonded to another person.

---

1. Quoted from C. E. Izard 1981, p. 329
2. C. E. Izard 1981, p. 320

In this connection, we must draw special attention to the attitudes of various cultures toward so-called negative feelings, individualization and any tendency to remain connected. Societies that tend to keep people in a tangle of relationships, making them dependent on family and social structures, deal differently with sadness and other negative feelings than do cultures that emphasize individuality and independence in their people. Sadness is rather favored in cultures committed to relationships and group-cohesiveness, such as in eastern Asia or the Pacific islands, where expressions of anger are rather restrained. On the other hand, in cultures with a strong focus on individualism, one finds that establishing oneself with anger and rage is more valued than expressions of sadness that ask for consolation. It is likely that during the last centuries there has been, in the Western industrialized nations, less repression of the expressions of rage and anger that accompanied the weakening of ties with community and family. What is especially impressive is the increase in feelings of disgust during the period in which industrialization and pushing for better hygiene gained in importance. The emphasis on feelings of disgust that (as we shall explain) helps people set limits, also contributes to individualization tendencies.

Sadness is usually triggered by loss. However, as with anxiety, the loss need not indicate a specific occurrence. The realization or sense that something one considers important is missing is enough to trigger sadness. Even children in their first year of life will respond with sadness. Izard, a noted researcher of emotions, remarked, "The first cause for grief is birth itself, namely the physical separation of infant from mother."[1]

The loss can also be a personal ambition, an intellectual value, or a belief. All that is necessary to trigger sadness is the idea of loss. The loss need not actually have occurred yet; it can be an anticipated event. It can include people, animals,

1. C. E. Izard 1981, p. 322

homes, and other objects. All that is required is the awareness that what was lost had special importance. At times, a simple association to loss can evoke sadness, as when I watch a movie that my late wife especially liked, leading my thoughts back to her.

Physically, sadness produces a facial expression that is the same in people of all continents, so it translates quite well from one culture to another. In expressing grief, the eyebrows are pulled upward and the corners of the mouth downward. Since the muscles of the chin move downward at the same time, the middle of the lower lip moves upwards. This facial expression is often accompanied by bending of the body toward the earth. Crying and moaning are characteristic expressions of sadness, but crying also occurs in moments of great joy (tears of happiness), or intense frustration and rage.

Sadness is accompanied by vegetative changes shown by a rapid heartbeat and lowered skin temperature. However, the physiology of sadness has been studied far less than its psychology, which we have discussed briefly. This is partly because sadness is much more difficult to reproduce in animals than in human beings.

> Sadness must not be identified only with mourning or grief. While sadness represents a feeling, mourning is a process of assimilating (absorbing and integrating) an experience of loss. Thus, ever since Freud, one might speak of mourning work, in which a loss is being worked through. To the process of mourning belong, in addition to cognitive reflections, emotions such as feelings of loneliness and despair, rage and anger.

## Disorders Linked to Sadness

It is interesting that psychology and psychiatry know of conditions of illness in which appropriate sadness is lacking, but no illness in which sadness is expressed with unusual fervor. The feeling of sadness is weak or simply absent in pathological reactions. In depressive disorders, one might speak of terrible dejection, but this refers to the crippling of physical feelings, namely the lack of deeply felt sadness (a more extensive presentation is found in Chapter 7).

One is, in fact, unable to cry or experience profound (and contagious) sadness when faced with a severe depression. Those who have developed depressive disorders find it liberating when they are again able to allow their tears to flow freely.[1] It is a reliable rule that the more one is capable of experiencing sadness, the less severe is the depressive blockage.

Sadness seems to be a problem in our society, even though there is no evidence that it exerts any morbid influence. The problem is related less to the emotion than to a decline in personal contact when sadness is present. Dealing with sadness becomes increasingly difficult for those who have become socially and emotionally isolated, because they are alone with the feeling; where there is no personal contact, the compassion sadness usually elicits in another is lacking. In people who mostly live alone, their sadness tends in the long run to "run on empty," because it remains unresolved.

The conjunction of unresolved sadness and depression does not seem accidental. Does one become depressed because no one has responded to her sadness? Large scale examination of different populations does show that women, as well as men, suffer more frequently from depression when they are alone.

By contrast, married men often suffer less from depression than married women. The latter are overcome by depression when, in addition to being busy with household chores and small chil-

---

1. (Translator:) Goethe's Faust, emerging from a severe depression: "My tears are running, the earth has me back!"

dren, they receive so little support from their partners that they feel emotionally alone.[1]

In my book "Welchen Sinn macht Depression?" (tr. *What Sense Does Depression Make?*), I described depression as sadness that has been denied admission, citing a number of research findings in support of that view. At this point, I'd like to summarize the results showing that people who become ill with depression often have histories of losses after which they were left alone or lacked adequate support. Many depressives react with unexpected pain to new situations of loss that evoke sadness. Though depressed people experience little or no sadness during the illness, one can demonstrate by the analysis of mimicry and gesture, aided by videos, that their facial features clearly display characteristics of sadness. Based on various clinical examples, I was able to show that "being sad" is rejected and repressed by patients, because they consider that feeling strongly negative.

In *Cognition and Emotion* (1977), Power and Dalgleish point out that physical sadness can be triggered by association, on the basis of conditioned responses. In other words, it is possible to be sad without knowing the cause, and without being able to initiate grieving in order to deal with the loss effectively. I base this on the observation that unexplained sadness causes anger and vexation in a very special way, especially when the affected person, being emotionally or socially isolated, has to depend entirely on himself, receives no support from "third persons," and so must experience in solitude the physical constriction and the enervation of being sad.

The *complex* or *abnormal grief reaction* is somewhat similar to the depressive state. However, according to the criteria of the World Health Organization, it is differentiated from depression because self-blame, psychomotor retardation, apathetic

---

1. G. W. Brown/ T. Harris 1978; see also D. Hell 2002

inhibition and other important symptoms of depressive blockage are often absent. On the contrary, after a loss, typical grief
reactions like searching for the deceased, disbelief pertaining
to the death and a persistent cognitive preoccupation with the
deceased person are very noticeably present.

> The life of Queen Victoria offers an example of that sort of
> complicated grief reaction. When she was forty-four, she lost
> her beloved husband Prince Albert. She completely shut herself
> off from the world, refusing to carry the crown and insisting on
> wearing black dresses most of the time. Before her death, forty
> years later, she ordered that, among other things, a plaster cast of
> the hand of her deceased husband be buried with her.

> Even less extreme grief reactions can have far reaching conse-
> quences. Survivors sometimes insist that the bedroom of the
> deceased remain unchanged for decades. Grief reactions can
> even lead to imagining the deceased being living in another
> person, or in an animal.

How does such a complicated, abnormal grief reaction
come about? Most researchers of grief[1] start from the assumption that those affected are so shaken by the death of
a partner or relative that they are quite unable to face the
loss. Consequently, they want to keep the deceased person
alive in their thoughts, and try to avoid every thought of
his or her passing. While they are able thereby to reduce
the intensity of their grief, they pay for this suppression of
reality with a diminished capacity to deal with the reality
of their loss. The result of this abnormal grief-process is a
delayed or prolonged grief reaction that occasionally leads to
depression, even suicide. After examining eighty-two widows
and widowers, Prigerson and his coworkers were able to show
that complicated grief reactions result, in the long run, in

---

1. The scientific literature about grief is summarized in English in J. Littlewood
   1992 and in German in H. Goldbrunner 1996.

a definite decline in function, in sleep disturbances and in depressive disorders.[1]

In treating people who are in danger of grieving in a complicated or abnormal way, it seems particularly important to mitigate their experience of sadness. This calls for genuine sympathy from those who care for the bereaved. It can also help to point out that feelings of sadness, rage and disgust are a normal part of grieving. Sadness is not seen as being damaging to the treatment process, but rather as a prerequisite for accepting the situation that has arisen, and learning to reorient oneself.

Beyond this rather pragmatic way of looking at the situation, we find that being sad provides survivors with a feeling of personal identity in a time of feeling that everything familiar might dissolve. This viewpoint is easily overlooked by researchers in the field of emotions, who are inclined to interpret feelings primarily as adaptive functions. Richard Lazarus[2] argues that sadness leads only to resignation and is therefore not suited to the struggle for survival. He writes, "There appears to be no clear tendency for action in sadness – there is but inactivity and retreat into oneself– which contradicts the concept of feelings."[3]

Is sadness not a feeling just because it does not show an inclination to act? Even if one ignores the fact that sadness is a very clear message to others, one must realize that an exclusively functional interpretation of behavior overlooks the fact that emotional expressions that can be objectified are ultimately based on primary experience. This kind of feeling, accessible only to the first person perspective, allows people to experience themselves, especially when loss has placed them in question.

1. H. G. Prigerson et al. 1995
2. R. Lazarus 1991
3. Ibid. p. 251

Every language contains – with good reason – innumer-able expressions for sadness that reflect this personal feature of bodily experience. Thus in German there are expressions such as *Herzeleid* (heart-suffering), *Herzweh* (heart-pain), *Bekümmernis* (worry) and *Kummer* (sorrow), as well as *Jammer* (misery). The old German word *truren* is probably related to *drusian* (old English – sinking, to become sluggish, losing one's strength). Its proper meaning would be something like "hanging one's head," or "lowering one's eyes," both typical of human grief.

The degree to which a physical expression of sadness arouses empathy in others can be illustrated by the fact that tears, in contrast to all other bodily fluids (saliva, blood and urine) do not elicit disgust. On the contrary, tears appear to be "pure." We are instinctively attracted by tears; they evoke a protective reflex and the instinct to console those who weep. Tears, if we accept them, are also able to cause us to be gentler with ourselves. It is only when sadness and crying have become unacceptable through so-cially conditioned disapproval that we become hardened against ourselves.

## The Problem-Circle of Disgust

Feelings of disgust are only rarely studied. Research has overlooked them for a long time, barely considering them. Feelings of disgust occur very early in humans. Even small infants show, in certain situations, evidence of disgust by their facial expressions. As we move through life, feelings of disgust and dislike accompany us wherever we go. They not only influence food intake, but also make obvious the people we literally cannot stomach, those we detest. They also distract us from images that correspond to poor taste, which might pervert us.

While sadness is a social, and anxiety an existential feeling, we might say that disgust corresponds best to some sort of feeling about oneself. Does this surprise you? If so, it should be pointed out that disgust calls us to shrink back from what does not belong to us. Disgust erects a barrier between myself, my body and my surroundings; it builds a wall around the ego. Our saliva is not disgusting as long as it stays in our own mouths, but we would experience feelings of disgust if we had to drink our saliva out of a glass into which we had spat it. In starker ways, we could make the same observation about bodily eliminations: urine, feces, or sweat. It seems that what is ours becomes foreign and suspect once it has left our bodies; what once was part of us is something to be avoided. This is not always so: small children like to play with their feces. It is only when they are taught to feel disgust that they let go of this delightful game. When parents declare something to be offensive and disgusting, it becomes dirty and must not be touched. As soon as something becomes disgusting, it no longer belongs to us. The experience of disgust ensures in a fundamental way that there is a process of separation and limitation, something that could not be accomplished as spontaneously and thoroughly by indoctrination.

There is plenty of evidence to show that feelings of disgust serve not only physical distinctions between what is ours and what is foreign, but that they also can create borders in our world of thought. As a result, there are ideas that spontaneously evoke distaste, while other ideas appear to us as friendly and prized.

At a certain age we have finished building a net of thoughts and ideas that constitute our world view. At the same time, we have excluded other ideas and thoughts and react aversely when confronted with them. This is the case not only with religious and political convictions about what is valuable, convictions that can motivate local, national and international strife; the same principle applies to our aesthetic convictions, our fondness for sports, and everyday behaviors that may be either attractive or offensive.

The connection between cognitive ideas and disgust is most easily demonstrated in religious value systems. Many religions link attitudes of inner worth to external commandments about purity; many forbid the consumption of certain kinds of meat, or the enjoyment of alcoholic beverages. Thus the Muslim may not eat pork or drink alcohol, while Jews are clearly instructed in Leviticus (11) regarding all they are allowed to eat and all the foods they must avoid. The prohibition against eating reptiles is pronounced in Leviticus with these expressive words;

> "You are not to eat any creature that moves about on the ground, whether it moves on its belly or walks on all fours or on many feet; it is detestable.
> Don't defile yourself by any of these creatures.
> Don't make yourself unclean by means of them or be made unclean by them."[1]

The history of religion allows us to follow the development of the outward rules of cleanliness found in the Torah as they evolved into religious obligations in regard to personal purity. Thus the Jewish Christ preaches, "What goes into a man's mouth does not make him unclean, but what comes out of his mouth, that is what makes him unclean."[2] Paul, also a Jew, interprets Jesus' saying to mean that it is not eating or drinking that are important to the kingdom of God, but rather fair and peaceful action.[3]

Thus disgust and aversion increasingly involve a person's character traits and are not restricted to external things one must avoid as part of a communion of faith. In the Psalms[4]

---

1. Leviticus 11. 41-43 (International Bible Society)
2. Math. 14.11 (International Bible Society)
3. Romans 14.14
4. Psalms 5. 7

we find that it is the liars, the forgers, the bloodthirsty that are an abomination, while Christ shudders, seeing people's arrogance.[1]

For the individual, feelings of disgust are first directed toward foods that we should not put into our bodies. Thus in German (and English), disgust means, "It makes me vomit," but over time it is not just foods that evoke feelings of disgust, but also certain behaviors, and eventually certain attitudes and thoughts. Now not only spoiled foods are disgusting, but also repellent people and prohibited ideas.

Even if feelings of disgust are less and less restricted to foods in the course of one's life, it is notable that the expression of disgust in the human face remains that of aversion and abhorrence with anything they find disgusting, as if they had to ingest the sickening item. Disgusted people give the impression of choking, or imitate spitting out something. The upper lip is lifted and the nose turned up. Stiff upper lips and snootiness (an elevated nose) are already clear indications of someone's undesirability, posture that, for showing dislike, makes choking no longer necessary.

Feelings of disgust and nausea go hand in hand with increased salivation, slowed pulse-rate and elevated galvanic skin reflexes. It is probable that psychological dislike is based on the kind of bodily sensations that are aroused by contact with an object that cannot be digested (or with indigestible thoughts).

In terms of its historical evolution, disgust can be traced back to nausea, to a gag reflex that serves to get rid of potentially toxic material. Frequently, a bad taste is also involved, entering the mouth and resulting in nausea in the stomach. At the same time, facial expressions indicate an attempt not

---

1. Luke 16. 15

to allow any ugly smell to enter the body, leading to the expression, "I can't stand a certain person or substance."

It is especially the rhinencephalon (the area of the brain involved in smelling) that developed into an important organ for processing and evaluating stimuli, as if there were a connection between the development of the human ego and the ability to set themselves apart by means of disgust. Rozin is one of the few researchers of emotions who has primarily analyzed feelings of disgust.[1] His opinion is that the cultural evolution of the feeling of disgust is what led us to finally become human: "Our analysis suggests the cultural evolution of disgust brings it to the heart of what it means to be human."[2]

Feelings of disgust can contribute to distancing us from objects, persons, opinions, events and situations. I feel disgust at the thought of eating grasshoppers or snails, which are highly regarded by gourmets, but I can also experience distaste when I'm displeased with the behavior or the "smell" of a person. Finally, some movie scenes, or the bodily punishment of children, may evoke in me distaste, aversion and even a desire to vomit. In Schiller's play "Die Räuber" (*The Robbers*), Karl Moor expresses his disgust for an entire epoch: "I feel disgust in face of this century of bureaucratic clerks," and true to his disgust, he tries to withdraw from the whole of that social misery.

The most difficult situation to deal with occurs when one experiences a kind of existential disgust and wants to withdraw from existence. French philosopher Emmanuel Lévinas has examined the existential wish to "get out" from the perspective of philosophy. His book "De l'Evasion" was published three years before Sartre's first famous book, "La Nausée"

---

1. P. Rozin et al. 1993. Somewhat later, William Jan Miller wrote *The Anatomy of Disgust* (1997). The first comprehensive description of disgust from the standpoint of cultural science was published by Winfried Menninghaus (1999).
2. P. Rozin et al. 1993, p. 390.

(*Nausea*).[1] Lévinas shows the connection between disgust (*nausée*) and the revolt of the person himself. The feelings of disgust that serve to warn the body against foreign materials and other external phenomena can eventually turn against the person himself. "Though disgust makes it impossible to be what one is, one is at the same time glued to oneself, closed in within a circle that chokes… it is the experience of pure being." (p. 116) "The nature of the disgust is nothing but his existence, nothing but his incapacity to escape from this existence." (p. 119) Lévinas thus sees consciousness as developing from this basic feeling of disgust. The ego is not only shielded from without by feelings of disgust, it also becomes conscious of itself – as a result of individually experienced disgust (inner-directed) – without being able to escape its existential presence. According to Lévinas, it is only by turning toward and relating to other people that the self consciousness characterized by disgust can be transcended.

## Disorders Connected with Disgust

In Lévinas' writings there is a melancholy undertone that characterizes the experience of the depressed. However, they are rarely able to convey this disgust, and even less often can they accept their sense of self disgust without immediately condemning it. As a result, disgust takes hold of their existence, and they can neither affirm it nor find a way out. Now they are not only disgusted with the world, they are disgusted with themselves.

Unacknowledged disgust makes it almost impossible to understand why one has withdrawn from the world. Disgust with oneself also leads to self-devaluation, unless the feeling

---

1. E. Lévinas: "De l'Evasion" (1982). The quotations are taken from the pages indicated.

is recognized as the potential, or even the precondition, for relinquishing the attachment to oneself by using the energy of the disgust.

Disgust for oneself does not diminish one's experience, but it does prevent one from deriving narcissistic pleasure from experiencing oneself. Thus, where there are hidden, unaccepted feelings of disgust, people are in danger, like many depressive persons, of becoming sick of themselves with no way to use those feelings for creative, contemplative, or altruistic changes.

> Hans Saner described "cognitively melancholy persons" as those who are disgusted with themselves, but who create a contradictory world by no longer caring about the protective removal of their narcissistic disgust. "Maybe the reason that so many artists and philosophers are melancholy is because many of them are more skilled in managing themselves in non-protective, contradictory worlds than in the protective world. Their creations, if successful, combine what at first seems irreconcilable: gazing into the abyss of life has left them without illusions; they are authentic in sensing what is human, but joyful in their calmness and feel light in the freedom of the moment."[1]

Is it possible that our idea of ourselves and our western culture is so firmly based on seeing disgust as something it is normal to reject that we have been led to overlook this important source of self awareness? In any case, the problematic cycle of disgust has, so far, largely been neglected in psychology and psychiatry. The feeling of disgust as aversion and abhorrence still needs to be recognized and added to the understanding of psychiatric problems. These feelings are likely to play a significant role not only in depressive disorders, but also in phobic and compulsive disorders (concerning their devaluations and defenses).

---

1. H. Saner 1998, p. 235

Power and Dalgleish deserve great praise for having evaluated those disorders by considering the feeling of disgust and its analysis.[1] Based on considerable research, they share the conviction that some phobias have less to do with anxiety than with feelings of disgust. Many people who recoil from mice, flies, or even pets like dogs and cats, do not anticipate being attacked by these creatures. Instead, they experience disgust in their presence, and do not want to touch them. Shrinking from contact with blood (hemophobia) is typically echoed by physiological changes seen with disgust (slowed pulse and lowered blood pressure), which do not fit the physiological reaction typical of anxiety (increased heart rate).

Many compulsive disorders express themselves as well-defined thoughts that provoke disgust The idea of getting dirty through harmless contact with the hands or clothes of another person can provoke feelings of filth and disgust. In other situations, fear of contracting an illness is linked to a disgusting sense of getting dirty. In such cases it is not so much the fear of catching an illness that triggers a compulsion to wash, but rather the disgust brought on by contact with something unclean.

One could conclude that some *compulsive disorders*, like certain blood and animal phobias, are not really anxiety disorders, as prevailing diagnostic procedures assert, but rather represent "disgust disorders." Additionally, disorders such as social phobias may have more to do with being shamed and with lowered self-esteem (disgust with oneself) than with anxiety. We may also find that hopelessness, the primary motive for many suicides, is related to the problem of dealing with self-disgust. The final word has not yet been spoken, but as we learn to understand the unfavorable circumstances

---

1. H. Power/T. Dalgleish 1997

of depressive disorders, the theory of illness will be forced to deal with this significant basic feeling.

> Those who are prone to become disgusted more easily or more often are inclined to keep their immediate surroundings especially clean and orderly. When they are depressed, feelings of disgust take on extreme proportions, and when it becomes impossible for them to keep their surroundings clean and orderly, their dissatisfaction and anger are intensified. This development feeds a diabolically vicious circle of contradictory feelings and judgements, leading to impotence and incapacitation.

*Summary*

The concept of "anxiety disorder," like the expression "abnormal grief-reaction," might lead one to see anxiety and grief as the source of disorder and illness, but it is not anxiety, sadness, or other basic emotions that make people sick. The experience of great anxiety or sadness is not, in itself, "sickness." It is only the intimidation that takes hold when fears assail us that leads to disorder and impairment of life.

When seized by panic, we are driven by catastrophic fears, which have to do with anxiety. They distract us from our inner experience by drawing our attention to imagined dangers. Those suffering from panic attacks rarely mention anxiety; instead, they complain about heart palpitations or shortness of breath. They do not judge themselves to be "sick" with anxiety, but fear they are physically ill.

Similarly, we find that phobics avoid situations such as crowds of people, high bridges, tunnels and elevators, seeing those situations as excessively dangerous. It is not the anxiety that causes them to be phobic, but the cognitive assessment of those situations. Even those with "generalized anxiety disorders" are not sick because of their anxiety, but because they fear the anxiety.

According to the findings of behavior therapy, one should not treat anxiety, but rather the cognitive fears that hinder accepting the experience of anxiety. In the same way, in abnormal grief reactions it is not grief, but the refusal of sadness on which treatment must focus. Also, in phobias or compulsions that go hand in hand with feelings of disgust, one must not doubt the disgust; the goal of treatment is to recognize the obsessive ideas and compulsive actions that contend with the feelings of disgust. The therapeutic aim is, therefore, to strengthen experience and perception from the first person perspective, and to question the patient's opinion of those alleged problems that are seen from the third person perspective. Only those who can accept what they themselves sense and feel can withstand their cognitive fears.

*Part III:*

*Practical Application*

When a person does not sense that she/he is loved
and accepted, no amount of wisdom will serve to
make him or her happy.

– Barbara Herzog

# Chapter 6.
# A Basic Therapeutic Problem – The Shamed Shame

*Meaningful Suffering, or Sick because of Shame?*

The ideas I have presented that aim to relate psychological problems to devalued experience have practical consequences, which will be discussed in this third part. With
this, the circle will be closed. In the first part of the book, I
attempted to follow the historical preconditions of currently
prevailing concepts of *psyche* and disease. In the second part,
I attempted to develop methods based on the latest biological
and sociological views of illness for finding direct access to
the understanding of the soul and illness. In the third part,
I will attempt to apply the previously mentioned concepts to
their importance in everyday life.

As I started to write this book, I was interested from the
very beginning in giving substantial space to presentation of
the subjective experience of both sick and healthy people. So,
in the preceding chapters, I introduced several examples from
my clinical experience. From these one may infer a therapeutic attitude characterized by paying attention not only to the
behavior, but also (and mainly) to the patients' experience, as
well as their evaluation of themselves. In the therapy, I do not,
however, bring their experience into the foreground in order
analyze it; rather, I try to promote patients' awareness of their

personal experience. I am not as interested in establishing an objective, socially adequate assessment of the experience – as happens in cognitive psychotherapy[1] – as I am in reinforcing the individual's first person perspective, compared to critical analysis of the experience.

The view expressed here does not locate psychological illness in primary experience and feeling, nor in unpleasant sensations. Psychological illness is instead related to underrated sensations and emotions that have gone through a process of self condemnation. Any suffering that has been trivialized as merely a feeling, a meaningless "thing," may become a meaningless disorder for the affected individual. It then assumes the aspect of a disease, thought it is important that one make a clear distinction between illness, suffering (German: *Leiden*), and disease (German: *Krankheit*).

The term *Leiden* (in old high German *lidan,* related to traveling, driving) is, like experience, a phenomenon of the first person perspective, and is brought on by an intolerable physical or social condition, as in suffering bodily pain or a distressing social situation. The suffering is clearly not identical with what caused it, nor does it, as such, constitute a disorder.

The situation is different with disease. "Being diseased" is socially defined and equates to judgment from a third person perspective. For this reason, characterizing a state of suffering as disease is always a rather complex process that includes social value judgments. What the "first person" suffers, however, differs from the concept of sickness. Sickness exists only when it is reflected in the patient's own judgement; it is a matter of feeling.

---

1. Cognitive Psychotherapy has adapted the basic concept of Behaviorism (inclusive the stimulus- organism-response-model) as its therapy goal is also an adequate adaptation of the organism to its environment. That is why it also differentiates between functional ("right") and dysfunctional ("wrong") thoughts. (see A. T. Beck 1976)

Stating it more precisely, one could say that illness as a psychological disorder does not consist of painful perceptions or unpleasant feelings. To a larger extent, being psychologically ill signifies a condition of suffering in which patients experience themselves as demeaned, trivialized or separated from self – in other words, viewed by others as pathologically altered.

The distinction between suffering and illness, between unpleasant feelings and disorder, is not a word game. It is deeply important to therapeutic approaches in psychology and psychiatry. This will be clarified in what follows. To this end, we will focus on two problematic issues that affect everyday psychiatry with unusual force: suffering from shame and suffering from depressive blockage.

Using the example of shame that can lead to social-phobic impairment, in this chapter we shall attempt to show how unavoidable feelings of shame can become an enormous burden. This can happen when shame is seen as a defect, especially when the human capacity for experiencing shame is itself used to stigmatize and shame others. In the next chapter, I would like to explain how the inability to experience feelings, especially the devaluing of negative feelings, can turn into a problem that provokes a sickness. While shame represents the very nature of a concealed feeling, one can see that depression leads to what appears to be emotional emptiness; however, on closer scrutiny, one can recognize negative feelings, which show up like "islands of melancholy."

From a therapeutic standpoint, it is important in both of these conditions that one offer latitude and acceptance to muted or hidden feelings. The personal experience of shame must be expressed and freed from the destructive cocoon engendered by others' attempts to implant shame, and oppressive feelings must be lifted and separated from the depressive sense of being worthless. Similar principles apply to other conditions, as when anxiety must be differentiated from intimidation, or disgust from the inflicting of nausea. In all these instances, it is necessary to protect basic, immediate feeling (the "first person" perspective), and to oppose any forced, external determination of feeling (through the "third person").

Shame is still seen as something that must be avoided at all cost, while the significance of anxiety has always been recognized, and the experience of anxiety has been an integral part of the treatment of anxiety disorders. For this reason, it is especially appropriate to look into the presence of shame feelings, and to separate from that internal experience the "shaming" that comes from outside.

### Shame and Shaming

As I pointed out in the beginning of this book, psychological disorders are often aggravated, if not provoked, by shaming. Many psychiatric patients suffer just as much from the stigma of having a "shameful" problem as from the psychiatric disorder itself. The example of Ruth X. shows how intensely one can suffer from the shame of having a stigmatizing disorder.

Ruth X. was admitted to a general hospital after falling downstairs. The nature of the fall and her behavior caused the attending physicians to suspect that she was suffering from a depression, and may have thrown herself down the stairs intending suicide. A psychiatric consultation yielded the following information: for several weeks, Ruth had experienced herself as increasingly blocked; she also experienced the demands of her small household and her teaching position as excessive. However, she did not throw herself down the stairs to kill herself; for that, the cellar staircase would have been too short. She intended only to break a leg, or sustain some other injury that would free her of her obligations. In her deep distress, she could not think of another way to unburden herself. In any case, she could not possibly imagine asking for a leave of absence due to suffering from a psychological disorder, as she felt that the label of psychiatric illness would be too shameful to bear.

One might see this medical history excerpt as extraordinary. It is extraordinary only because as this patient acted on a fantasy that many others share. How many others have wished for a broken arm simply to have a generally accepted reason for time off and for being given (as physically ill) authorized and understanding care?

Is the shame eliminated by transforming a psychological problem into a physical disorder? That was not the case for Ruth X.; she continued to suffer the feeling of shame even while being treated as a person with a physical injury. Filled with shame, she couldn't escape the discrepancy between her inner, hidden experience and her outer behavior. Indeed, she felt even more ashamed for having played a role that was inappropriate for her. The shame became increasingly acute as she suffered from that contradiction, and her mood declined further.

### Shame as Guardian of the Door to Oneself

What are feelings of shame? The above example suggests that shame is primarily evaluated negatively. Most scientific attempts to define of shame describe it as a negative, indeed destructive, emotion. In his pioneering book *The Mask of Shame*, Leon Wurmser emphasizes that, "The threefold blemish of weakness, defectiveness and dirtiness constitute the nucleus of the subjective pole [of the subjective feeling]of shame."[1] Tomkins, another prominent researcher of shame, describes those who experience shame as people who, "Feel as if they are naked, beaten, alienated and lacking in worth and dignity."[2] Even Helen Block Lewis, the third researcher who has contributed in the past few decades to shame receiving the attention it deserves, considers shame an uncanny and self-destructive feeling.[3]

Shame appears to accompany a devaluation of oneself. There are also attempts to derive shame from basic feelings of disgust, to see in the shame a form of disgust with oneself. Yet disgust with oneself is probably more a rejection of self than it is shame. Shame also contains features that are not found in contempt for oneself. Shame does not necessarily lead to rejection of oneself, but when it is experienced consciously, it always goes with the feeling of being naked, exposed. This feeling of exposure might be the result of something the person did, or it could be provoked by a third person. Those who are ashamed are preoccupied with criticizing themselves; they try to hide. They would prefer to crawl into a hole, to be swallowed by the earth, or to "die from shame." Shame concerns not only the behavior of the person, but her very self, quite in contrast to guilt, which goes hand in hand with criticism of one's actions. Shame represents a threat to one's very self, questioning and deeply shaking it.

The German word *Scham* (shame) probably derives from the Indogermanic term *skem*, which signifies something like disguise, or hiding oneself.[4] Whoever is ashamed wishes to protect himself, hoping to protect his insides from being hurt

---

1. L. Wurmser 1990, p. 60
2. S. Tomkins 1963, p. 118
3. H.B. Lewis 1987
4. The author remarks that in German, *Scham* (shame), *Hülle* (wrap) and *Haut* (skin) are probably derived from the same root. It is interesting that shame has to do with the border between outside and inside. (B. Pfau 1998)

worse. Thus he is careful, not wanting to reveal his secrets to the outside world. Blushing may give him away, but it may also indicate that those who are ashamed have more than enough to do with themselves. Blushing can be understood as an interpersonal signal, a plea for others to desist from further shaming, because they turn red, indicating that they already feel humiliated. Shame can also come from the realization that one is seen by others as one does not wish to be seen, or that one's prestige or attractiveness is failing within one's community. In this sense, shame is a socially communicated feeling.

However, shame presupposes self-appraisal; it is not enough to be negatively appraised by others. In order to experience the shame, I must take on a negative evaluation when I communicate my self-worth. Even when provoked by something outside of oneself, shame also requires the activation of an inner process. Furthermore, shame does not require an external trigger. I can feel it by myself because, for example, though others didn't notice, I failed to do something and was able to quietly hide the fact. I don't seem to need an external relationship in order to feel ashamed. What goes with shame, however, is the critical attitude I have towards myself.

French philosopher Emmanuel Lévinas, analyzes this astutely: "Considering shame, one places the social viewpoint in the foreground, forgetting that in its deepest manifestations it is a highly personal affair. When shame is present, one is unable to hide what one wanted to hide. The need to escape in order to hide is frustrated by the impossibility of flight. Thus, what manifests itself in the shame is precisely the fact that one is related to oneself, and the most radical impossibility is to flee with the idea of hiding from oneself, the unavoidable presence of the ego before itself ("du moi a soi-même"). Therefore it is our intimacy, our presence before ourselves, that is shameful. This presence reveals not our nothingness, but the totality of our existence."[1] It is for this reason that shame does not lose its compromised character in solitude, where it manifests its most unique nature. Shame remains linked to the deep requirement that we must accept the responsibility ourselves.

Shame presupposes an inner relation to oneself. Those who do not sense in themselves a symbolic space, or self, and who, like Narcissus, love themselves only as a mirror image are unable to see themselves as shameful. They do not have an inner counterpart and so are able to see themselves only the way others do, as an external counterpart. People living in a symbiotic union, for example with a parent, can experience shame only in those moments when they are able to separate themselves internally from the parental figure. It is only this internally effected separation that allows the injury to the personal self to be felt. As long as the symbiosis persists, it also protects against the shameful experience of oneself.

At first view these things appear complicated, but they can be seen repeatedly in daily life, and this example will help to clarify the connections:

> Mrs. C. explained these things to me with unusual clarity. She has led an extraordinary life, inasmuch as she never had to make herself independent, but as a fourteen year old, began a relationship with an older man who initially spoiled her. Because of these unusual conditions, her childish attachment to a parent-figure was never dissolved. There was a persistent kind of "twin self" that initially consisted of her and her mother, and later of her and her partner. At the end of her schooling and without any training for a job, she married her older partner and they lived together for the next twenty years. In spite of tensions and some serious abuse, her inner bond to this man persisted. He left her after twenty years of marriage, and though she was forced to live

1. E. Lévinas 1982, p. 112f.

alone, she was incapable of giving up her attachment to him. She continued to feel at one with him, even though she was separated from him. Divorced against her will, she was now forty. The apparent reason for her treatment was the aggravation of a chronic depression that had been treated before in other places.

In our therapeutic discussions, I came to know Mrs. C. as a patient who presented some weighty emotional problems, but who was capable of verbalizing her problems quite precisely. She described the thought of being divorced as intolerable, stating that for her, only a life in a duality was possible. She said she could never accept herself as only half of a destroyed marital unity, and that whenever she was forced to think of her divorce, she experienced it as an annihilating disgrace that caused suicidal impulses. This was why she had not spoken to anyone about the divorce verdict; she lived with the belief that the separation and divorce would one day be reversed.

Mrs. C. tried in these ways to keep alive, against all obstacles, the idea of an inner tie to her divorced husband. Her struggle was all the more moving because she did not escape into a delusional world, but accepted the divorce judgment as a reality.

During her therapy, feelings of shame always emerged when she allowed herself, even for a moment, to accept the idea of an inner detachment from her former husband. Initially, the active, emerging experience of shame was so intense that Mrs. C. would quickly wall herself off from it. To imagine herself alone and completely without her husband released the feeling that she was bleeding to death internally of shame (words which raised in me the image of a bloody operation separating Siamese twins).

It was somewhat easier for Mrs. C. to accept shame that was not linked to her husband. For that reason, I first tried in the course of therapy to focus on and learn about her experiences of separation during everyday hospital life (from other patients or therapists). These were less threatening. Any evidence of shame arising and being exposed could then be discussed and explained as prerequisites for an eventual inner independence.

I chose this example in order to show how the dissolution of an inner fusion – symbolically, the separation of a "Siamese twin-self" – goes hand in hand with shame. Shame has been described as self-feeling, a state of feeling tied to the fact that we deliberately focus on ourselves (M. Lewis 1993, p. 91).

Shame appears to be the premium that must be paid for being driven out of a comprehensive feeling of belonging. One may, like Mrs. C., judge this ejection into solitude as negative. One might also, however, see this ejection from paradise as the prerequisite for one to be able to act responsibly, to be an individual.

The appearance of shame is not a "fall," and certainly it is not an original sin. Instead, it is a witness to a step in development, pointing to an awakening in oneself. A precondition for this step in development is the withdrawal of the "other," the figure who turns into a person against me, a face that expects answers and forces me to be responsible.

## Misused Shame

It is no disgrace to experience shame. The experience, however, clearly shows those affected that they are vulnerable and dependent, finding themselves only through attraction to others. Shame can also be misused. We can be shamed because we have a sense of our vulnerability. Shaming others is appalling. It takes advantage of their vulnerability and wounds in order to push them aside or force them to comply with one's suggestions. Ridicule and scorn are tools of shaming, affecting people who can experience shame like a slap into the face. The shock of such a slap temporarily wipes out the feeling of self, an incomprehensible event that tears apart the personal network of meaning. Using of the other's experience of shame, the shamer degrades the target's feeling of self, a trauma that leaves a hole in the self. Only later, when the shame is reawakened, can what happened find meaning. At that point, the physical experience of shame fights against the cruelty that attempted to force a vulnerable person to give up and to become a tool of society.

Unfortunately, shaming is not just an external event that affects the inside. The scorn of shaming can also scar people in their innermost experience, in the way they picture their selves. Shaming, in this case, attacks from the inside. It changes the sharp feeling of shame that is witness to one's evolving self into something that gives the impression of being harmful in itself. In this situation, the person as a whole is threatened. Shame gives way to a kind of indignity whose destructive effect makes it impossible to live as an independent ego responsible for itself. Now every move toward autonomy that is accompanied by experiences of shame calls into play the humiliation of being shamed. Only a narcissistic life style, devoid of any genuine relation to oneself, or a symbiotic life, now seems livable. As shown in the example of Mrs. C., a person's reluctance to be independent can be related to an overwhelming experience of being shamed as a result of this very individuation. Yet as long as shame is inadmissible, there is no hope for the kind of bodily anchoring of the sense of self that can enable the vulnerable self to survive unavoidable traumas.

Max Scheler, in "Über Scham und Schamgefühle" (tr. *About shame and feelings of shame*) (1913), pointed to the fact that shame, as a protective affect, is basically a positive value. He wrote, "In one sense of the word, an essential feature of shame is its being a way of feeling ourselves. Thus it belongs to the sphere of our self-feelings. Indeed, in all shame an act occurs that I would like to call 'turning back toward the self'."[1] Without this 'turning back toward the self' that is about becoming aware of one's own person as an inner representation, shame seems impossible. This explains why people with narcissistic and symbiotic structures rarely experience shame. Scheler illustrates what he means with many examples. Among them he describes a highly ashamed woman. She is able to undress without shame in front of a physician as long as in this situation, she does not need to present herself as an individual, but can simply play the role of a patient. But as soon as this bashful woman is seen by the physician, maybe with a slight desire, as an individual, she responds with intense shame because she is thrown back on herself (Scheler expresses this as "the turning back toward the self").

> Psychoanalyst Günter H. Seidler describes various levels of the psychological dynamics of shame in a profound, but very complex book, titled "Der Blick des Andern" (tr. *The Glance of the Other*).[2] He starts with the inward differentiation of the experience of self by which shame becomes possible. Shame, he states, reflects the line separating personal expectations and experienced reality: "Shame manifests itself when the subject moves in search of agreement but encounters something foreign, and is forced back to the starting point. Shame by itself differentiates 'foreign' and 'familiar'; it assumes the function of building a border between external and inner worlds."[3] Elsewhere he states: "The external dividing line between the 'intention of the ego' and the 'other' turns into another, internal dividing line, between the ego and the self. It is at this boundary line that the shame becomes manifest."

While the feeling of disgust draws a line between what belongs to the inner organism and that which lies outside the body, we find that the experience of shame draws a line in the

1. Quoted from H. Seidler 1995, p. 32
2. Ibid.
3. Ibid. p. 320

soulish realm between external expectations and the inner space that contains the images or ideas of the self. When a developed image of the self is questioned from the outside, the sense of self is in danger and the feeling of shame draws attention to this threat. It is for this reason that I call shame the " Guardian of the Self."

Evidence from developmental psychology also points out that shame presupposes an inner sense of oneself. Michael Lewis, pediatrician and psychiatrist, has shown in exhaustive studies that small children recognize themselves in a mirror only after their fifteenth month.[1] When a child is put in front of a mirror after being given a smudge on her face, she will begin to touch this mark only after the fifteenth month, while a younger child pays no attention to the smudge. Only between approximately fifteen and eighteen months do children begin imitating the image they see in the mirror by making faces, sticking out their tongues or observing how they disappear and reappear on one side of the mirror. These behaviors seem to point to the development of an objectifying recognition of the self, that is, the recognition of oneself from the viewpoint of another. Shame requires a further step in development and manifests itself only some time later, namely when the idea of a self has become internalized. Darwin observed that blushing begins at about two and a half years of age. At the Institute for the Study of Child Development in New Jersey, Michael Lewis and his team demonstrated that three year old children show evidence of shame when they are unable to solve relatively easy tests (tests they think they can solve). Conversely, these children showed pride when they were able to solve tests that were unusually difficult.[2]

---

1. M. Lewis, 1992
2. Ibid.

Based on these brief comments regarding the development of the self and of shame, one might conclude that shame is a differentiated feeling that requires an objective awareness of oneself and that draws attention to any endangerment of the self. In Genesis we read that shame is related to the differentiated recognition of man and woman, good and evil and self and other. After eating from the tree of knowledge, Adam and Eve first recognize their nakedness, then being naked in front of each other, and third, their nakedness before God. The resulting shame leads, like any shame, to the experience of oneself: I'm ashamed of myself in front of others.

Shame is a fundamental human feeling. It is related to the experience of oneself which excludes a "pre-personal" unitary experience that animals seem to exhibit. Shame points to the possibility of self-reflection, without its being expressed as an exclusively spiritual or intentional act. Instead, in their shame, humans experience themselves as dual natured: on one hand, they experience themselves emotionally, that is soulish-bodily; on the other hand, shame touches on the idea of the self, namely on cognitive aspects. Shame thus presupposes a reflected self, yet integrates this idea of the self within a soulish-bodily experience. In this way, the capacity for shame becomes a logical affective behavior, since recognizing and feeling go together: I recognize myself before myself and before others, and I feel that between my idea of myself and the expectations of the "others" (or even of myself), there is a difference.

While shame represents an emotion within a differentiated experience of oneself, it would be wrong to assess it only negatively. This is different from the act of shaming by stigmatizing others, that is, third persons exploiting the basic human capacity to feel shame in order to make others pliable as their instruments. It is different because shame can help people become aware of their vulnerable and threatened self. For this reason, it is important to distinguish between shame being perceived and accepted by others as a subjective feeling, and being turned into an object that must be rejected as a demeaning, degrading remark. In the latter case, the personal experience of shame transforms itself into a shaming, degrading event. The shame is then assessed as a disgrace, and "inward shaming due to humiliation" arises. In this case, any justification of one's experience of shame is withdrawn. Now one is not just awakened by his own experience of shame; his shaming also results in simultaneously questioning himself in his innermost being.

Persons who feel ridiculed and shamed by the outside world may try to defend themselves. Their resistance is more effective when they can turn the external shaming into their own concern. When being shamed and being ashamed begin to merge and the inner shame becomes an object of the shaming, then the adversary is no longer only external, it has slipped into the target and attacks him from the inside.

As a result, we have not only the possibility that the inner experience of shame will be suppressed by a shaming judgement, but also that the shame and shaming judgement will reinforce each other in a vicious cycle as the devaluation of the shame evokes new shame. The cycle is destructive because it undermines any positive sense of self and simultaneously destroys the person's inner feeling of self love. I believe that shaming, the lowered esteem, is far more destructive than the experience of shame as such.

The writer Saint-Exupéry may have had something similar in mind in his masterpiece *The Little Prince* when he portrayed in poetic words a vicious cycle of shame and being shamed. In the story, the little prince runs into a tippler:

"What are you doing here?" he asked the tippler, who sat in silence before two rows of both empty and full bottles.

"I drink," replied the tippler somberly.

"Why do you drink?" asked the little prince.

"In order to forget," the tippler answered.

"To forget what?" inquired the little prince, already feeling sorry for him.

"In order to forget that I feel ashamed," the tippler admitted, lowering his head.

"Why do you feel ashamed?" asked the little prince, hoping to help him.

"Because I drink!" said the tippler, wrapping himself in total silence.

And the little prince, dismayed, went on his way.[1]

The tippler is ashamed of his abuse of alcohol and tries to get rid of his shame by drinking more. Just as in this story, a vicious cycle begins to develop when an additional link – such as alcoholism – is formed between the experiences of shame and being shamed; it then becomes the basis for shaming oneself. The shaming now consists of the person's own socially condemned actions. With that, those who are ashamed and those who shame them become one. Shame and shaming, their physical sensations and their belittling remarks, occur in the same person. Shaming reflects values adopted from one's social environment, while the feeling of shame is experienced directly. The first person perspective and the opinion of a generalized "third" are intertwined in the same person, resulting in the destructive vicious cycle. Here, in contrast to the narcissistic and symbiotic problems mentioned above, the experience of shame is not eliminated, but continues as a painful sense of self. It is just this acute perception of shame that can provide resistance to the cheap defense of fending off the shame with a drug.

1. A. Saint-Exupéry, "Le Petit Prince"

At the beginning of the vicious cycle of shaming and shame there is often, in the person's life history, a deep psychological trauma that has had so serious a shaming effect that it has torn the person out of his or her context of meaning. Where the symbolic network that forms the person's history is torn as a result of an intense or a long-lasting trauma,[1] there is a danger that the subject will deal with the shame by using drugs to cover them up and/or cause euphoria. Yet as long as one's sense of self continues in its wounded and vulnerable state, shame over the process that threatens to destroy the self will persist.

Drug dependence is almost always associated with problems of shame, because the inability to stop using the substance is experienced as added shame. The same principle applies to compulsive eating and starving, which are always accompanied by expressions of shame. Other psychological disorders (of sexual function, social phobias, personality disorders – especially of the borderline type – depressions and psychoses) also trigger shame and are thus related by their historical development.

Based on clinical experience, I must conclude that being ashamed and dealing with shame can be counted among the most important of daily psychiatric problems. These problems are often overlooked, probably because they rarely show up openly; they tend to be expressed indirectly, in, for example, being humiliated, in defensive outbursts of anger, but also in feelings of guilt behind which shame is hidden. A trusting therapeutic relationship is needed before the evidence of the shameful experiences can be found.

---

1. In *Stigma and Mental Illness* (1991), P. Fink and A. Tasman showed the historical background and social assumptions that make psychiatric patients' experiences of being shamed daily occurrences. P. Gilbert (1997) sees a person's loss of social attraction as the primary reason for the phenomenon of being shamed.

Experiences of sexual abuse are extraordinarily traumatizing and shaming, wounding their victims in both physical and soulish integrity. The events are so extremely invasive that at first they may elicit more feelings of powerlessness than of shame. As a result, the abused person, to some extent, loses access to her own world of feeling and must feel insecure within herself.

In view of the resulting sense of danger and uncertainty, the abused person will try to regain her feeling of self and control by varying means. She may, for example, make herself responsible for the incident that victimized her. In fact, when people are severely traumatized, it is very often observed that they look for evidence that they somehow caused or facilitated the traumatic event. Victims of sexual crimes often blame themselves for having walked in a dark street, for not having screamed enough during the assault, or for not having exercised more caution when encountering the aggressor.

By making themselves the perpetrators, victims manage, at the price of self-blame, to retain a bit of autonomy and independence. This self-blame and thought of being guilty usually does not indicate any preexisting, pathological personality trait. Making themselves (in fantasy) partly responsible for the assault, they manage – paradoxical as it may seem – to experience feeling less shamed, even though they bear more shame and guilt. These feelings lend meaning to the meaninglessness that erupted so forcefully, and allows the victim to find a sense of self in the midst of the unimaginable.[1]

Thus it is all the more important to make a clear distinction between destructive shaming and the protective experience of shame when working with those who have been abused or traumatized. Differentiation of the two is somewhat difficult in both the German and English languages. While the difference between humility and humiliation is quite obvious, it is

---

1. The fact that many publications deal with the theme of rape and incest does not invalidate the fact that a complex feeling situation has barely been studied, and certainly has not been understood. It is particularly difficult to investigate the relationship of shuddering to agitation (see: G. H. Seidler 1995).

difficult to distinguish between shaming (which one suffers passively) and shame (an emotion experienced actively). Yet it is the traumatized persons who suffer, because their shame – in the word's physical sense of intimacy – was misused. Often they can find a way back to themselves only when they are allowed to express their rage over the shaming they experienced without having to discount their inner experience.

What, ultimately, will help victims get over a severely traumatizing event without damage to the soul or symptoms that persist? Is it not only the experience of the vulnerability of one's soul, but also the ability to feel vulnerable even against one's will? Is it the experience of not being just a soulless machine, not being pure consciousness, but of being able, as the victim, to sense and feel bodily? The unwillingly borne shame may not be about capitulation in the face of being overpowered as much as it is an expression of a feeling of self that was wounded but not destroyed. It is regained shame that manages to turn around the situation, if the one who is ashamed can confront the cruelty of the one who shamed.

### An Example: Internalized Shaming and Required, Protective Shame

Marianne M. is a single, forty year old pharmacist who, in the course of a fairly long psychiatric treatment, has taught me a lot about shame and shaming, even though she entered treatment for an entirely different set of symptoms. Her psychiatric history will be mentioned in the following only insofar as it sheds light upon the dynamics of her shame.

At the age of 9, Marianne was repeatedly abused sexually by an elderly neighbor. He threatened to kill her if she ever gave away "their" secret. When the abuse became known in spite of this, people spoke about her, but not with her. Her world treated her as if she were a person with a contagious illness. She was no longer allowed to play with other children during leisure time, but was asked to stay in the house. She was also referred to "play therapy" because of poor scholastic performance. The traumatic events were not discussed, either at home or in play therapy. Clearly, her parents and her teachers were so overwhelmed by the event that all they could do was protect Marianne against further abuse.

Marianne felt greatly shamed, partly because of her powerlessness during the sexual abuse and partly because she was excluded from participating in some areas of her everyday life. She could not talk with anybody about her feelings, and had the impression that her parents treated her as a "bad child." There was no one she could turn to, no trustworthy person with whom she could discuss and analyze her traumatic experience and her feelings of its shame, so she tried to conceal her shame and hide her soulish wound from herself. She felt that she had become unclean, but warded off this sense with her "honorary code of the warrior." As a young girl she stood out as being willful and stubbornly courageous. She would not allow herself to be easily put down. But though she maintained her warrior-like attitude after the traumatic event, her battle was mainly with herself and the internalized shaming. In contrast to the way she had been before, she no longer dared to protest stubbornly; instead, she tried to win the acceptance of her parents, teachers and supervisors through superior performance and outward conformity. Her compensatory approach was successful, inasmuch as she distinguished herself again and again in her preparatory school. She graduated with the highest grade average in her class, and then completed her studies, with the highest distinction, as a pharmacist. She did not, however, attain what she had hoped her performance would accomplish; the scholastic and professional honors had not washed away her internalized shaming. On the contrary, she found that even small failures deepened the wound of her shame, forcing her to exert even more self control, fighting against her self-deprecation by seeking external successes.

Then, when her ability to perform reached its limits and began to decline after years of excessive effort, Marianne's self-worth crumbled completely. Now twenty-five, she was severely depressed. Initially, the depressive process could be controlled with antidepressants, but Marianne could not avoid further depressive periods, which only increased her vulnerability. She believed that she had lost face among her coworkers and, painfully humbled by her depression, she became suicidal. At times she concluded that only death could protect her from the reproachful looks of others, and from her own self-condemnation.

A prolonged psychiatric and psychotherapeutic collaboration was required before Marianne was gradually able to reveal herself in session. When, for the first time in her life, she was able to speak of the sexual abuse she had endured, her hesitant report was repeatedly interrupted by her fear that the therapist would not take seriously what she was saying, and might even find her ridiculous. The memory of her severe childhood trauma seemed inextricably tied to a complete discrediting of her entire personhood. Thus, for Marianne it was not only the entire experience, remembered in all its details, that was shameful; the shaming she experienced had spread throughout and could barely be separated from her personal life.

For this reason, even though she did feel that her confession freed her of a painful burden, Marianne was helped only moderately by finally being able to confide the sexual abuse to someone else. The shaming had penetrated deep within her, branching out and forcing her to continually see herself as a failure. Seeing herself this way was so tormenting that Marianne felt the need to protect herself with phobic avoidance maneuvers and compulsive controls.

Her persistent self-condemnation and enormous will to perform drove her to aim for special distinction in her psychotherapy. She believed that she could get the therapist to like her, earning his approval by achieving an exceptional level of recognition. Therapy therefore became a constant source of the danger of being shamed again if she could not attain her expected level of progress, or if she had to accept regressions as part of the bargain.

Only the experience of not being rejected by the therapist when her performance diminished, and of being accepted even as shameful, enabled Marianne to carefully reevaluate her feelings of shame. With surprise and some disbelief, she noticed that talking about her feelings of shame unburdened her, and that the admission of her feelings of shame did not weaken her sense of self, but strengthened it. The more she learned to trust her so-called negative feelings, the more she was also able to be aware of previously rejected bodily feelings. This development allowed her to break through her social armor a little, and to cautiously let go of the social withdrawal on which she had relied. She reestablished contact with some of her prior acquaintances, devoted herself to her nieces and, surprising even me, joined and participated in self-exploration groups and courses in body-oriented meditation. Even though she suffered some frustrating crises, she slowly developed a stronger feeling of her body and her self.

However, it would be a mistake to see therapy at this point as complete, and to consider the wound caused by Marianne's shaming to be healed. Every reminder of the trauma still frightens her as though the abuse was about to occur. Nevertheless, some essential things have changed: she no longer experiences her very existence to be questionable as a result of her unpleasant emotions. Far more than before, she takes her feeling of shame as a personal, physical reaction that counterbalances the shaming she suffered. As a result, she experiences herself less as an object that is actually being shamed, and more as a subject that is bothered by a memory that can elicit shame. An incident of shame thus becomes her personal experience and does not turn into something with unfamiliar features that is imposed on her. As she herself once said, "I now am ashamed as Marianne, and I'm ashamed for what was done to me." Earlier she seemed to assume, "I cannot feel ashamed, or I will turn into an object that will be shamed; the damage I suffered consigns me to contempt, making me a slave without rights who must always yield." The injustice of Marianne's shaming is not repaired (atoned), but it no longer is able to blind her feelings of shame so that they drown in the misery of shaming.

As I was treating Marianne M., I experienced empathically and impressively how very freeing it was for her to open up to her feelings of shame and accept the experience of shame. For psychotherapist Helen Block Lewis, an analogous therapeutic experience became so central an aspect that she made the discussion of feelings of shame the pivotal point of her treatment of patients.[1] Her experiences convinced her that many psychiatric disorders persist because of hidden shame. According to her, many psychiatric treatments do not progress because they overlook the hidden problem of shame. She therefore considers many resistances in psychotherapy to be conditioned by shame. She writes, "In the last few years I have become convinced that 'resistance' is a misnomer for 'shame' and 'guilt'."[2] She sees working through the hidden

1. H. B. Lewis 1987
2. Ibid. p. 24

shame to be a central task in any psychiatric treatment, and believes this particular focus to be more important than reconstructing repressed memories. "The traumatic past as cause of neuroses must admittedly not be underestimated, but its power is related to unresolved conditions of shame and guilt that were engendered by traumatic events or continuing mistreatment during childhood."[1]

To allow shame its rightful place during psychotherapy, it is important to know that shame can be triggered by the treatment itself. In fact, many patients feel it is shameful to be obliged to admit that they needed treatment. It is especially during the first psychotherapeutic sessions that feelings of shame emerge. These can be important, as they may, for example, mitigate against blurting out all at once so many problems that the patient is emotionally overwhelmed by them.

The patient's feeling in subsequent therapeutic sessions that the therapist is able to look through him, or is (or wants to be) independent of him, can also be experienced as shameful. The structuring of a therapy for which one must pay can trigger feelings of shame as well, and even worse, it can evoke the shaming impression that one is trying to deceive oneself, or is being deceived.

In being aware of possible shame when dealing with patients, it is important to recognize that shame can influence interpersonal relationships, too. Shame is irritating. When shame is hidden or repressed, it is important to recognize that the therapist can become contaminated by the patient's feeling of shame, raising the potential for developing mutual tendencies of shaming. Mutual defensiveness may appear at times of emotional openness, because both members of the

1. Ibid. p. 25

therapeutic dyad may experience themselves as directly or indirectly shamed by the other.

In that situation, even therapeutic advice may seem threatening if the person asking for help gets the impression that she is being appraised critically. Defensive statements by a therapist such as, "You must reach your own decision in this matter" can be perceived by the patient as shaming in reference to her indecisiveness or dependence.

Dealing with the shame of psychiatric patients presupposes a kind of "shame strength" in their therapists. By this I mean that their partners in psychotherapy must not be hesitant in regard to their own shame, but must be in the position to feel ashamed within the range of what is possible. The goal of therapy is not freedom from shame, but rather a conscious acceptance of the feelings of shame, and the ability to avoid shaming attempts.

## Shame and Stigma

Up to this point, I have pursued the difference between "shame" and "being shamed" on an individual plane. Shaming, however, also has a social dimension that concerns the psychiatric patient.[1] Psychological disorders are second-rate illnesses, often branding their carriers with the label 'not completely reliable.'

To work against this stigma, many affected by this shaming view of psychiatric disorders have gotten together in self-help groups and associations of those who have had experience with psychiatric treatment. Their relatives have created orga-

---

1. Shaming involves an affront to a norm, which is why the feeling of shame is also linked with being seen and observed. When shamed, one wants to disappear from others' sight. This connection, investigated all the way from Aristotle to Sartre, has some religious roots, as was shown by Christina von Braun in "Versuch über den Schwindel" (tr. *Exploration of Vertigo*) (2001).

nizations that stand up for the rights of psychiatric patients. Also, specialists in psychiatry have defended psychiatric patients against this biased view. All these people are united by the hope that in successfully fighting the shaming judgements of psychiatric patients, they can reduce the stigma. As the stain and stigma of psychiatric disorders diminish, we expect that patients will suffer less from shame. How are shame and stigma related? I see this question as decisive to the success of efforts to stop the stigmatizing.

The word stigmatize is derived from the Greek *stigma,* which means something like "marking," or "providing with a sign." In ancient Greece, *stigma* did not have an exclusively negative meaning. Tattoos with decorative or religious purposes were given this term, just as it also designated the warrior mark given to a hero who had distinguished himself in battle. Thus Christ's wounds were described as *stigmata* in Paul's letter to the Galatians. It was only late in the Roman era that the term stigma began to acquire the implication of a defect, when it became equated with the markings of criminals and slaves and thus became a sign of disgrace.[1]

In our time, stigma is known mostly in its negative sense. As used by sociology, it refers to an unwelcome deviation from the norm, something that is tarnished socially. Yet deviation from the norm is not always a stigma. Citizen groups have repeatedly succeeded in changing a stigmatizing concept from negative to positive. In this regard, the acceptance by the homosexual community of demeaning words such as "queer" and "gay" is impressive. Words that were meant to shame became acceptable labels when their negative assessments were rejected. Similarly, in movements for the emancipation of homosexual women, some terms used to degrade them

---

1. The history of the term "stigma" was investigated by B. Simon in P. Fink and
   A. Tasman (1991)

were adopted and affirmed, their shaming connotation now confronted with a pride that was desensitized to shame.

In the case of psychological disorders, these conversions are possible only in a very limited way. They presuppose that a behavior judged by the majority as sick or disordered is now accepted as positive rather than negative (as the Heidelberg group in Germany and Laing and Cooper in England attempted to do, with little persistent success). One major problem of such attempts is that psychological problems are not caused only by processes of stigmatization. Apart from the social reasons, there are many other causes for them.

Furthermore, most people suffering from psychiatric disorders are motivated not only by the desire to escape the stigma, but also the desire to become healthy. However, health is more often defined today as the absence of suffering. Even the World Health Organization largely equates health with well-being today. Since the psychiatrically ill usually suffer considerably, and because they cannot be assessed as healthy, their only alternative lies in having, at best, a respectable disorder. As mentioned at the beginning of this chapter, there are good reasons for not equating suffering with disease, but instead to see in suffering (*passion*, as in compassion) the experience of persons from the "first person stance." Yet with the separation of suffering from illness, it is also necessary to define health differently than is commonly done today.

Such an attempt would need to prevail against the polar thinking in today's Western world that speaks of painless health and painful illness. Health (in the sense of well-being) is used mainly as a word of reassurance, while sickness is used mostly as an ominous term. Sick people are not shown respect for their condition, though they gain recognition for their will to recover, to regain function, and to accept treatment.

As sick persons they are, one might say, on a leave of absence; as healthy persons they are reinstated.[1]

Considering this state of affairs, it is quite understandable that mainstream psychiatry tries to free the psychiatrically ill person of his blemish, or stigma, by portraying the disorder as treatable, equating it with an organic disorder. Today the equality of psychological and organic disorders is no longer confined exclusively to the demand for equal legal and social treatment. Instead, the equality is meant literally, i.e., that psychiatric illnesses are organic disorders. As such, they are to be treated in the same way, just as all sick people have the right to the same treatment.

This process of undoing the stigmatizing contains at least two problems. First, psychiatric problems are not simply an expression of physical problems; there is a clear difference between a diseased organ and a problem of the psyche. Equating brain and psyche does not work for those who have psychological problems and experience themselves as having their own memories, ideas and plans. When a memory or an idea causes them pain, it is something entirely different from having a headache. In cases involving psychological problems, those affected feel responsible for their experiences in quite different ways than they would in the function of an organ. The latter happens to them unconditionally, while the former involves a personal history that has developed into a web of symbolic connections to a self. It is the possibility of suffering as a result of social stigma that reveals not only the power of cultural influence, but also the unavoidable assumption that the affected individuals have a position in regard to the interpersonal happening.

---

1. This thought is further elaborated by H. L. Goldschmidt (1976, p. 161f.). C. F. von Weizsäcker (1984, p. 320f.) tackles the question of health and illness with a similar, fundamental approach. In suffering, for example, a person's resistance against injustice and brutality may find expression.

The consequences of equalizing psychological suffering and organic disorders reveal the problem of this attempt: it deprives people of the first person perspective and views them exclusively as objects seen from the third person perspective. Psychological suffering, at least according to our current understanding of matter, threatens thereby to become a determinable thing. This sequence, however, is rarely stated quite as openly. Rather, there are attempts to find a way to reduce the human problem to a thing, disabling the individual human self in a less obvious way.

*Gentle Materialization (turning former no-things into things)*

These days the media are campaigning to remove stigmas that contrast healthy and sick feelings, that, in other words, distinguish steady forms of emotional expression from erratic. As a medical concept, it generally suggests that strongly negative feelings are bodily disorders, but does not relate moderate and positively viewed feelings to their physiological base. In general, this humane form of characterizing feelings has been very successful. Because psychological suffering is now attributed to a physical change, it enables those who formerly considered themselves to be questionable to free themselves from guilt. Since at the same time they receive the benefit of society's agreement that their illness is a physical disorder, it is easier for them to accept their temporary impairments.

The identification of depression with a brain disorder, for example, can relieve patients significantly during the acute phase of their illness. The view that their suffering is due to a somatic phenomenon makes it easier to accept their diminished ability to work or relate to other people; they also feel less compelled to fight against the depressive blockade. If the depressive mood is explained as a dysfunction of some part of the brain, one is less obliged to feel guilty. The biological explanation may also contribute to relatives and acquaintances understanding and accepting their situation. One might even assume that the previously mentioned Mrs. X. would not have felt the need to throw herself down a flight of stairs to achieve the respectable status of a "genuine, sick person."

Nevertheless, it seems to me that generally equating *psyche* with *soma* does not come out correctly. The somatization of functional psychiatric disorders has been successful mainly due to its psychosocial influence. It lightens burdens that spread widely because of a misunderstood psychological view of depression and other disorders. For example, the cognitive and emotional blocking of depressed persons has often been underrated where concepts of depth psychology have been applied. Severely depressed persons were often expected to deal with tasks they were clearly not able to master. In addition, it was commonly not noticed that psychodynamic interpretations of severe, depressive forms of suffering could be taken by patients as reproaches that implied they were responsible for their own suffering.

The current somatization of depressive suffering can thus be seen as correcting a misunderstood psychological view of the depressive experience. It allows the patient to shift a negative assessment from the ego experience to the condition of the body, thus seeing the physical condition as negative rather than herself.

Admittedly, there is danger in this. The reduction of disagreeable occurrences exclusively to physical processes identifies a person with her bodily functions. In such a view, the psychologically ill seem to be nothing but malfunctioning brains. This kind of diagnosis causes the loss of one's place in history and culture; in a certain sense, sick people drop out of the matrix of their biography and their uniqueness.

This reductionist view enhances the risk that people will no longer trust their own feelings. Instead of living with their feelings, they may start seeing themselves *as* being against them. It is true that they could thereby be relieved of personal responsibility for negative feelings and guilt, but they also would lose some of their emotional rootedness in beginning to question the evidence of their emotions.

I see much more of this loss in people who were diagnosed as suffering from a depressive disorder and whose illness has run an unfavorable course. These persons seem no longer to trust certain feelings such as sadness and anger, and increasingly are inclined to control their feelings. In doing so, they lose spontaneous confidence. In spite of the initially positive therapeutic results from somatic therapies, they experience a constriction of their emotional world. Some have explained this narrowing as a side effect of long-term treatment with medications, but many depressed persons who've had an unfavorable outcome have striking distrust for most of their negative emotions. They consider them not just unpleasant, but as indicating a disorder in the central nervous system. In doing so, their range of experience continues to constrict.

Others begin to question their feelings even before they accept them. Instead of fully experiencing how something feels, they try to anticipate the feeling with an evaluation. An evaluation, however, can never be entirely personal, for it is usually shaped by cultural views or by theories of what is healthy. People who do not fully trust their own feelings appear to be especially dependent on outside affirmations. Wanting to prove themselves, they feel pressure to comply with the popular view of their illnesses.

As helpful as it can be at the beginning of treatment to attribute a severe, painful state of suffering to an organic disorder, it is important not to restrict oneself to this simplified explanation during the ongoing course of the disorder. Otherwise there is the risk that depressives, as well as other psychiatric patients, could come loose from the anchoring of their emotional lives, and that their fear that certain feelings could indicate the appearance of a disorder would be reinforced. For this reason, it is important to stress – especially with depressed patients – that their feelings are characterized not by an excess, but by a deficiency. (This point will be discussed more thoroughly in the following chapter.)

Nor must the biological aspects of psychiatry mislead us to equate the neural conditions that produce sensations and feelings with the development and triggering of specific sensations and feelings. Otherwise, one ends up concluding all too quickly that brain functions are the emotions, ruling out social conditions and psychological influences. However, relieving feelings of guilt by using the reductionist model points directly to the importance of psychological factors. The more people relate their emotional condition exclusively to neurological processes, the more they come to depend on medical assessments of their functionality, and such dependency can counter the effects of stigmatization only temporarily and only in restricted ways. When suffering becomes chronic, the situation is radically altered. As afflicted persons they are no longer partially, temporarily dependent on an external assessment, but have become that way continuously and comprehensively. Furthermore, they risk frustrating the expectations of the medical approach that tried to repair them, perhaps to be judged failures of the medical system.

After being good, successful, but acutely ill, patients may become unsuccessful, chronic patients. As a result, they are less attractive to both the medical establishment and the money oriented health insurance system. This loss of status tends to result in the very feeling of shame that patients thought was successfully resolved as a result of the somatization of their problematic situation. In other words, the advantage of the temporary somatization during the acute phase of the illness can easily become the disadvantage of the permanent somatization of their condition. Chronically ill patients may then be stigmatized for not having satisfied the expectations of a medicine bent on repairing them.

> Physicians who deal primarily with chronically ill patients tend to avoid reductionist models of illness. Following in Victor von Weizsäcker's footsteps, they maintain the views of a medical anthropology; this signifies nothing but holding fast to the subject in any medical treatment.[1]

One answer to the problem of stigmatization consists of taking seriously any subjective experiences. I believe that real freedom from stigmatization is possible only when shaming is avoided, yet shame is accepted. It is not a matter of fighting shaming along with shame, a procedure similar to throwing out the child with the bath water. Yet that is exactly the case, it seems to me, when campaigns that are financed by the pharmaceutical industry and seek to eliminate stigmatization show only laughing people (or weeping people who become laughing people), as if shame, sadness and rage are not acceptable. Psychiatric patients are shamed when their painful struggles for a meaningful life are pictured as a campaign for universal happiness.

Helping to remove stigma is a delicate affair. It requires that being ill and impaired are accepted, but it must not idealize these conditions. On the other hand, it must show the ability to enjoy life and good health as goals without seeing them as all one can wish for.

Removal of stigmatization is also related to awareness. Psychological suffering must be neither denied nor glorified.

---

1. See J. Rattner / G. Danzer 1997

Awareness also requires that we do not fashion for ourselves an image of psychiatric patients that is firm and fixed. Successful efforts to remove stigmas depends on our willingness to face suffering and again without considering social standing or depriving those affected of their personal dignity. This is the only way we can achieve a reduction of the shaming that is linked to social ties and opinions.

It is probably an illusion to assume that society as a whole can follow this path. Maybe that expectation will have to be limited to professional groups that assist people with psychological problems. Shortly before his death, Martin Buber, in a presentation before a group of physicians, called upon them to teach their patients to accept shame as something that transcends recognized limits.[1] By this he meant to say that accepting the shame that arises in life can lead to freeing oneself from it, and thence to real peace.

However, shame is more easily accepted when there is the likelihood one will be understood and accepted by someone reliable. Shame, the "hidden feeling"[2] that spreads its influence in secret (and in an uncanny way), is a guardian of the ego. The story of Cain points to this. In the biblical narrative, we hear that God placed a mark on Cain not to shame him, but to protect him.[3] If the mark of Cain, as Leopold Szondi thinks, is understood as an expression of shame, then the biblical tradition bears witness that shame was created not for shaming, but for the protection of the being.

1. M. Buber 1962
2. H. B. Lewis 1987
3. Genesis 4.14: "And the Lord put a mark on Cain so that no one who found him would kill him." (International Bible Society)

*Summary*

Shame is not a simple emotion. In contrast to basic feelings of anxiety or happiness, shame presupposes attention on oneself. One is happy about a success or afraid of a test, but one is ashamed of oneself. Shame can be described as a feeling of the self. Shame, not unlike guilt, presupposes some information about oneself; the person who is ashamed is completely focused on herself. One who feels guilty condemns herself for a certain action. Those who are ashamed see themselves as dishonorable. They want to disguise or hide themselves, but are unable to escape their own verdict, which is mirrored back to them by others.

Whereas envy and jealousy result when one begrudges others what one desires for oneself, shame draws attention to one's vulnerability. Shame is evoked when one's self-image is shaken by external events. For this reason, I have also called shame the "Guardian of the Self." Shame protectively shields those who are ashamed, yet unavoidably ties them to the social assessment (see Table 4).

| *Table 4: A simplified overview of Shame and Shaming* | | |
|---|---|---|
| | On the individual plane | On the interpersonal plane |
| Condition: | Consciousness of self (including a developed, specific image of oneself) | Appreciation (having been appreciated as a child by closely related others) |
| Trigger: | Wounding of the image one has formed of oneself. | Withdrawal of love, loss of position (a threat to one's social status). |
| Consequence: | Feeling of shame (sense that the self is being jeopardized) | Shaming (as a tool aimed at making another manipulable) |
| Complication: | "Shamed shame" (or internalized shaming) | |

There is danger in this double reflection: shame can go hand in hand with a demeaning, shaming remark. When one is repeatedly shamed in society, or has internalized earlier shaming so that being ashamed is experienced as identical to a destructive, devaluing shaming, then he will have a hard time accepting the experience of shame. As a result, his feeling of self may be impaired or endangered.

Being shamed and shame are as different as humbling and humility. Shaming, along with other means, can be used as an instrument to devaluate and socially subjugate others. It is the person's being ashamed of herself that is used to disarm her or force her to cooperate.

We must fight against every form of shaming or stigmatizing, both in our work as therapists and in our everyday life, and at the same time offer care and understanding for the experience of shame by others. Effective relief of stigmatization requires that shame not be seen negatively, that is, by shaming the one who is ashamed. Lacking acceptance of the shame, any effort to relieve stigmatization will alienate and degrade the person. Accepting the shame without simultaneously rejecting shaming and stigmatization will deliver to self-destruction those who are affected. Accepting the shame and fighting the stigmatization belong together.

Clearly, the stigmatization of psychiatric patients must be confronted with illuminating educational campaigns. But it is equally important, and considerably more difficult, to accept those who feel shamed.

In this autumn time passed almost without me
and my life stood as still as when, discontent, I
wanted to learn to type, waiting during the evening
in the windowless anteroom for the beginning of the
class...
I had no feeling of myself and no feeling for something else.
I went and stood there undecided
often changing the pace and the direction.
A diary that I wanted to write consisted of a single
sentence...

– Peter Handke

## Chapter 7.
## Depression – The Discouraged Feeling

Depressions are disorders of affectivity. Earlier, they were
tersely referred to as diseases of feelings. One must not, however, conclude that pathological or abnormal affects occur
in the depressive condition; it is far more the case that the
perception of feelings is hampered. Since in depressive blocking feelings are, so to say, throttled, this condition offers an
impressive example of what happens when one's ability to
sense, to feel and to will is restricted, because a gloomy sense
of life has seized the foreground.

In the first part of this chapter, depression will be characterized as a muted feeling level, and there will be references
to the enormous practical and therapeutic meaning of the
elements of feeling that remain present in only a weakened
state. The second part is dedicated to the question of how to
deal with depressive blocking and suppressed emotions. The

painful, residual feelings that are often questioned or disregarded become instead the real anchor points for self-help and therapy. The third, concluding, part presents a plan that integrates the passive suffering of depressed blocking with a lively discussion of painful feelings and limitations.

### *Islands of Feeling in the Depressive Vacuum*

The depressive mood is not consistent with the feeling of wholeness. Being depressed cannot be equated to a state of profound sadness, nor can it be characterized as overwhelming anxiety or rage. Neither disgust with oneself nor guilt are equivalent to a depressive upset. Attempts in earlier decades to define depressive suffering with a single (primary or secondary feeling) have been failures. Much more often, various feelings, such as anxiety, disgust and rage merge to form a tight composite that worries the person and undermines his former clarity, but does not present him with a recognizable adversary.

The loss of one's vitality and resources of experience is more characteristic than the dominance of a specific emotion. Depressed people feel cast down and weighed down; their emotional life is pushed down, and everything seems gray on gray. Life is no longer the way it once was. Ruedi Josuran writes from his personal experience: "Darkness or emptiness is the only truth one still possesses. Truths that once were found in life are now hidden."[1] In one African tribe, depression has been summed up splendidly with: "My heart is in a wooden box," which accurately expresses painful awareness of the absence of warm, cordial feelings.

---

1. R. Josuran et al. 2001, p. 53

There have been repeated attempts to define depression by employing positive criteria (such as guilt feelings and sadness). However, depression is not an accumulation of individual difficulties or complaints, but rather a change in one's experience. Depressive patients lack something that once was normal for them. Often they are frightened, recognizing that they can no longer perceive, experience and think as before. Though modern diagnostic procedures try to identify individual symptoms, we often observe depressed patients straining for metaphors to communicate experiences that differ radically from those of ordinary life. Thus depression might be described as "a forced experience of the desert (in the midst of other people)," a kind of "dark night (in spite of daylight)," as "being frozen (though surrounded by warmth)," or by the expression of "soulish paralysis (without evidence of physical paralysis)." These images include changes of space and time. They attest to the fact that during a severe depression, nothing is the way it was before, yet what is new cannot be considered positive. Viennese psychiatrist Hans Lenz spoke of an "illness of 'less'."[1] Depressed persons experience themselves as devoid of interests, unable to concentrate, sleepless, appetite-less, strength-less and feeling-less.

The experience of "less" makes it extremely difficult to assert oneself or make decisions. In severe cases of depression, thinking is slowed and restricted. Memories are not recalled as easily as before. Romano Guardini has shaped this mode of experiencing into an impressive image: "An inner shackle emerges from the emotional life and weighs down everything that otherwise bounces freely, moves and works… Those affected no longer control life; they can no longer keep up with the forward-pushing movement of life. Events become entangled around them, they can no longer hold on to them.

---

1. Quoted from R. Josuran et al. 2001

They are no longer able to deal with experience. Tasks pile up before them like mountains that cannot be crossed."[1]

In the book "Welchen Sinn macht Depression?" (tr. *What Sense Does Depression Make?*), I spoke of "depressive blocking" and compared being stopped by the depression to a defensive braking maneuver that causes friction: "The brakes are set." Swiss film maker Rolf Lyssy describes the consequences of such "braking" in an autobiographical report, "Swiss Paradise," with these impressive words:

"Every day was defined by lack of desire, drive and ability to decide. I was overcome again and again by despair and ideas of suicide. The only halfway tolerable moments I experienced came shortly before going to sleep, when the medications began to take effect. In the last few minutes of wakefulness, it felt good to know that the endlessly circulating, torturing, brooding thoughts that were wearing me down would stop for a few hours... Yet then came morning, and a new day... I fought against not wanting to get up as well as against not being able to get up. I lay there like a piece of human being deprived of all will... Getting up meant nothing but being delivered to another entirely meaningless day. This torture ended only when the entire body, including my bladder, rebelled and when the walk to he toilet ended my torment in bed. After I took a shower, the next torture occurred: what should I put on? I was utterly incapable of deciding which pants and which shirt to wear... There must have been a culminating point of despair that made me finally reach for a pair of pants and a shirt. This happened, without exception, every morning. When telephoning, I had the same experience... Even what seemed the most inane tasks in the world: lifting the receiver, choosing the number, waiting for a voice at the other end of the line just did not work. To be aware of this was the worst soulish torture."[2]

1. R. Guardini 1996, p. 24f.
2. R. Lyssy 2001, p. 123

Those who suffer with depression, as Lyssy so drastically portrays, lose the ability to deal with life from a firm footing. Their activities are blocked, their ability to make decisions is impaired. This inability to move toward a goal, to be a "self-starter," is linked to the loss of an emotional cornerstone in life. Being emptied of emotions makes it almost impossible to assume a personal viewpoint and to give one's actions meaning. What is external – and thus factual – assumes excessive importance in view of the inner emptiness. Now those who had always been conscientious and focused on performance instead experience themselves as failures. They are exposed to external pressures or moral expectations, and find themselves unable to respond. Close acquaintances and relatives seem unduly powerful to them, while they see themselves as small and insignificant. In this connection, self-blame can be seen as an attempt to counter inner emptiness with something personal, even if, compared to others, it can only seem to be criticism of oneself.

The dissolution of the emotional core in a depression also explains the self-assessment of many of those affected that they are helpless. Psychoanalysts first recognized helplessness and dependence as the central element of depression.[1] Later, behavioral therapists used a similar term, "learned helplessness," to explain depressive conditions.[2] Depressive helplessness, however, is more than an intellectual idea or socially incompetent behavior. It reflects the self's loss of competence that is based in the muting of the physical roots of experience. Depressed people experience themselves as uprooted, falling into depths and lacking solid footing, because they are no longer capable of feeling themselves as they used to.

---

1. S. Rado 1928
2. M. E. P. Seligman 1975. The development of this concept is described by I. H. Gotlib and C. L. Hammen 1992.

The loss of inner security is also related to the fact that their feelings are losing clarity. Sadness becomes concern without limits, disgust becomes empty boredom, rage becomes form-less displeasure and anxiety becomes blurred worry, while shame is experienced as being shamed, guilt as being accused. Only the awareness of one's lack of joy and lack of interest remains unchanged. Not only is the inner state of feeling muffled and flattened, there is also an absence of "dependable insight."

It is therefore all the more important, in treating depressed persons, to see to it that they rediscover their weakened and currently hidden feelings so they can regain their inner orien-tation. One may perceive different feelings from one person to the next: in one, a somewhat veiled sadness, in another, allusions to feelings of disgust, and in a third, hidden rage and shame.

Awareness of these feelings is hampered by the gray veil of depressive numbness. Yet, using highly developed video analyses, expressions of anxiety, rage and sadness can be recognized in the faces of depressed patients. (These feelings are little noticed in everyday life, because the facial muscles' mobility is generally limited.) Awareness of hidden feelings is further impaired when they are seen as undesirable, usu-ally due to a negative judgement. In such situations we find that depressive muting and negative judgements of feelings go together, becoming tangled in a knot that is hard to unravel. The above-mentioned "less" quality of the emotions offers even fewer points of entry. It is therefore quite difficult to discover weakened and suppressed feelings. Often they can be detected only when one remembers that the patient's feeling life in general is toned down, for the residual bits of feelings are even less noticeable without an acceptance of the depres-sive emptiness. The recognition of a broad loss of emotions makes it easier to discover previously overlooked islands of feelings in the depressive vacuum, and to explore them with the courage to do what is difficult.

In the opposite situation, the condition of general "less"-ness, the emotionless state cannot be accepted, so there is a significant danger of the depressed person imagining herself as being seen only negatively. This is because in the experience of emptiness, "one's own" can be assessed only negatively – usually as a loss of earlier potential. At the same time, the negativity of the hidden feelings has a disparaging effect upon one's self-opinion, so depressed persons often judge themselves not only as depressed and unfulfilled, but also as ill tempered and miserable.

As a result, however, a door is opened that lets in shaming, fearfulness and disappointment with oneself. These hidden feelings of shame, anxiety and rage become destructive intruders that cannot be perceived as one's own feelings, but are seen as justified social condemnations. Helplessness is joined by horror and despair over one's own character.

> This is far more than what Aaron T. Beck, founder of cognitive psychotherapy, proposed as the depressive triad of negative self-opinion, negative appraisal of the future and negative expectations of the surrounding world.[1] This triad reflects only the cognitive attitude toward persons suffering from depression; it doesn't consider the assessment of their feelings. The open question is to what extent these cognitive assessments also have a protective character. The fact that they characterize the condition more than the person, and that they decline after the depression clears might speak in favor of this idea. More decisive than the negative assessments of outward reality, however, would be the devaluation of one's personal feelings.

---

1. A. T. Beck 1976. His paper on *Cognitive Therapy of Depression* (1997) was made available in German with some modifications by M. Hautzinger.

## Disillusionment Instead of Self-Devaluations

In this connection, Swiss philosopher Hans Saner suggested an interesting distinction.[1] He differentiates between a cognitive and a sentimental melancholy.[2] He views cognitive melancholy as a kind of disillusioning process of recognition, painful inasmuch as it goes hand in hand with disappointments. Any recognition contains a negative character; it is always based on defining and distinguishing. As an old saying of logicians goes, *Omnis determinatio est negatio* (every definition is a negation). The opposite of recognition is called positive thinking: the illness of an era that wants to flee from itself, the depression that it would like to heal.

In contrast, Saner considers sentimental depression to be a "bitterness of the emotional life," which represents a darkening, inasmuch as it leads to an "alienation from the lived world and from oneself." Sentimental melancholy – easily recognizable as a form of clinical depression – is distinguished from cognitive melancholy in that it closes itself off from the painful loss, and turns away the bitter fruits of knowledge.

Saner qualifies this statement by adding: "The above distinction nevertheless has significance only in attempting to distinguish two ideal types. Where thinking extends beyond objective recognition and assumes existential features, something happens in what people think, and then they are fully absorbed by one thought. It is then that even a cognitive process of disillusionment can be experienced as a catastrophic loss and lead in the end to a sentimental melancholy. This was the case with Kleist after his study of Emanuel Kant. The insight that there is no absolute truth affected him so very deeply that it literally drove him to commit suicide.[3]

1. H. Saner 1998, p. 8
2. Ibid. p. 230
3. Ibid. p. 229f.

Unless it is understood in absolute terms, Saner's distinction can be useful in treating and dealing with those affected by depression, for the purpose is to act against the depressed patents' devaluation of themselves, whether by the power of reflection, or by supporting their willingness to allow experiences that are rich in feelings. This will be illustrated in what follows, using the example of an historical personality.

### About Depression and Melancholy: A Literary Example

Søren Kierkegaard, the nineteenth century Danish philosopher who significantly shaped the existential philosophy of the following century, had been melancholic ever since childhood. He broadened psychological understanding of anxiety and despair.

In 1844, Kierkegaard wrote in his diary: "There was a father and a son, both very gifted, both witty – especially the father... They conversed and entertained each other, but did so only like two fine heads, not like a father and a son. Once, the father, looking at his son and noticing that he was quite worried, stopped before him and said, "Poor child, you are caught in silent despair;" (yet he never inquired further; ah! he was not able to do so, for he himself was stuck in silent despair). Apart from that, no two words were exchanged in regard to this affair. Yet the father and his son were possibly two of the most melancholy human beings that ever lived, as far back as we can think..."

"And the father believed that he had caused the melancholy of his son, and the son felt he had caused the melancholy of his father; this is why they never spoke of it with each other. And that utterance of the father was an utterance of his own melancholy, so that, when making it, he spoke more to himself than to his son."[1]

Kierkegaard describes his oppressive fate elsewhere with a single sentence: "I appear to myself like a galley-slave, chained to death; and each time that life stirs, the chain rattles, and death allows everything to wilt – and this occurs every minute."[2]

Kierkegaard wrote about his melancholy in many other notes. There is no doubt that, in our current terms, he suffered from a severe depressive condition. On one occasion, he even consulted a physician in order not to avoid, as Karl Jasper states, "the human perspective," and because of his desire to see as sick and unavoidable what to him was a sin. Understandably, he was deeply disappointed, for the medical categories probably fit his personal experiences about as well as the speech of the man-eating Botokudes fit that of Platonic philosophy. Yet it would not have ended differently even if he had been offered the most sophisticated levels of psychopathological insight.[3]

This is because Kierkegaard sought another personal, philosophical and religiously characterized discussion with the support of his suffering. He made it the starting point of an intensive exploration of his own life, as well as of his thinking. In the process of trying to comprehend, by reflection, his depressive experiences, and to contain them existentially, he broadened the philosophical understanding of anxiety and despair. At the same time, he found both cognitively and emotionally a way of dealing with the depressive problem.

Kierkegaard was extremely alert in his thinking. He viewed himself with unbelievable acuity: "Again peering at the one who was eyeing himself; standing as the third at the side of the

1. Quoted from P. Rhode 1959, p. 17
2. Diary 1, 83, quoted from R. Guardini 1996, p. 9f.
3. K. Jaspers 1973, p. 355

two, looking at them and so on, a glaring row of reflections of sleepless mirrors of the ego and counter-ego, facing each other..."[1] Kierkegaard attempted to face the threat of losing himself by using this mental effort to make himself transparent. He described the attack upon the kernel of his life that he experienced as "sickness unto death,"[2] probably alluding to the depressive periods that he experienced as living close to an abyss. Yet he confronted these conditions of "less-ness" that weighed down on him by trying to stare into their veiled faces. In doing so, he did not interpret them as positive, but tried to comprehend with maximal, logical acuity what he could define only negatively to free himself from the negativity. Kierkegaard did not quarrel with his situation in life, but attempted to portray and establish his distress as unequivocally as possible, avoiding a sentimental explanation of the difficulties in his life. In the terrible weight of his suffering, he saw an existential attachment that his analytical mind was not capable of solving. On the contrary, melancholia tied him to his body and to his inner experience.

"Death and hell, I'm able to abstract from everything, but not from myself; I cant even forget myself in my sleep."[3] Kierkegaard provided the concept of existence with its specific philosophic meaning, uniting analytic thinking with inner experience. He struggled with the question of how he could realize himself while remaining fully aware of the heaviness of his emotional condition.

In our present way of seeing it, Kierkegaard was thinking in an affective-logical manner[4], alert while feeling, in an existential manner. His suffering took on a surprising intimacy,

1. R. Guardini 1996, p. 73
2. See his publication of 1849 with the same title.
3. Diary 1, 49, quoted from R. Guardini 1996, p. 11.
4. Social psychiatrist Luc Ciompi postulates that affective states (emotions, feelings) are linked to cognitive functioning (thinking, logic) and named that unity "Affektlogik" (*Affect-Logic*) (1982 and 1997).

something that touched on his innermost courage. It is a way of experiencing that never let him go. He deliberately took this suffering upon himself as the starting point for his philosophical wanderings, all the way to his triumphant statement, "It is my conviction, my victory over the world, that a human being who has not tasted the bitterness of despair has missed the meaning of life."[1]

Yet he also knew of that destructive melancholia in which one gives himself up by despairing about self. Employing the finest weapons of logic, Kierkegaard confronted this destructive "illness unto death" with clear hope and existential courage.

### The Particular beyond the Pathological

Out of such intellectual and existential confrontations with depressive suffering – I have presented Kierkegaard as an example – has grown a therapeutic approach foreign to scientific medical thinking. This approach, not content with proving that a depressive condition is an illness, does not restrict itself to the passive experience of depressive blocking, but seeks in depressive suffering what is unique and points beyond the pathological. What is unique is the experience Kierkegaard described: barely tolerable feelings can also become points of support. Those who feel they are drowning because their relationship to the world has been lost and the treasures of life are fading, can cling to the negative and to their suffering. Those who are not able to feel and decide, who fear being lost in a vacuum without experiences, will have to depend on such contradictions. Getting through to them is more difficult when they can find no helpful, firm control, but instead fear even deeper depression. However,

---

1. Quoted from U. Horstmann 1985, p. 83

oppressive feelings such as worry, fear, disgust and shame are not symptoms of the depressive disorder. In fact, they work against the depressive insensitivity by giving witness to robust life in the midst of pathological emptiness. Where these emotions are misunderstood and warded off as dangerous symptoms of illness, the possibility of a liberating approach is replaced by the peril of linking the depression to shaming and a demeaning appraisal. Where shame, rage and disgust cannot be lived actively, they easily evoke the sense of being the passive victim of shaming, aggression and disgust. However, in these cases the depression is not seen and carefully treated as a heavy, limiting obstruction; more likely, a personal element of negative judgement contaminates the analysis of the depression, evoking in the patient either resistance or resignation. Both responses reinforce the tendency to disregard personal experience and instead direct attention to the negative judgement. As a result, one finds that the stigma of the depressive problem, once apparently eliminated by designating depression as a medical illness, is now increasing as the recurrence of deflected negative feelings is disregarded. It is all the more important that therapists not see the necessarily negative description of depressive experience as devaluing one's feelings. Indeed, paying attention to those feelings – islands of melancholy – can be invaluable support on the journey out of the depression.

That journey will be described more closely in what follows. As is clear from the previous description, such a journey must overcome a number of obstacles. One cannot assume that a depressive mood disorder manifests in each case in pure form, or that it can be accepted as fact without regard to the circumstances of those it affects.

How, then, can we accept those deadened feelings in spite of everything else? How can the journey be promoted carefully in psychotherapy?

## Dealing with Suppressed Feelings in Therapy

One might think that dealing with depressed patients depends on having made the right diagnosis, i.e., that therapy is about the diagnosis. In a certain way, this is quite true. However, one cannot be separated from the other. Diagnostic clarifications can have therapeutic effects, and therapeutic progress can lead to new diagnostic insights. Also, in the case of depressed persons, therapy does not begin with a definite diagnosis, but with the first contact between physician and patient. The empathy with which the physician responds to the suffering of the patient will determine to what extent she can express her experience, all of which will affect the way the suffering is handled.

The circumstances and setting within which the diagnosis is established are of fundamental importance for therapeutic collaboration. If the diagnosis is removed from its human, therapeutic connection and becomes merely a thing that can be formally established according to the criteria of the WHO, then their personal suffering will be expressed to patients as something foreign. The more casually the word "depression" passes the lips, and the greater number of those who go to their physicians with a self-diagnosed depression, the greater the risk that the concept of depression will no longer allow access to personal suffering. It seems all the more important that, in the course of medical and psychological explanations, one does not replace the painful experiences of those asking for help with a diagnosis. The diagnosis must, instead, simply bring to the experience a shared language. The diagnosis must not misinform nor direct a depressed person away from his experience. The questions raised during a medical or psychiatric evaluation must instead contribute to the depressed person's feeling that his experiences are, to some extent, being understood, and that the therapist is interested in his experiences even if they diverge from the classic textbook picture.

It cannot be emphasized enough that the diagnosis of a depression ultimately is based on the depressive changes a person experiences, and that the list of physical symptoms serves only to clarify the roots of the depression. It is full participation in the experience of a human who is looking for help that must take precedence over a reduction of their suffering to isolated symptoms, however important those might be.

Unfortunately, this form of therapeutic consideration is often absent. It can be cut short by many influences, such as being under time pressures, overworked and tired; theoretical prejudices also tend to increase blind spots in the eyes of the therapists. The theoretical intent of therapists to work by focusing on problems and psychodynamics can also be misleading if the depressed individual's potentials are regarded too highly. In the worst case scenario, the patient's depressed impotence is interpreted as resistance. A biological viewpoint can make it easier to recognize the actual impairment of patients who are blocked by depression. At the same, that viewpoint can also make it more difficult to do justice to the area of experience and action that is still available to the depressed person.

Therapeutic prejudice of one kind or another is especially disturbing, as when a therapist feels he is being questioned and tries to assert himself against a patient. Here theoretical concepts serve more as shields or walls to offer protection in a struggle with the depressive person rather than helping in therapeutic orientation. Protectively confining oneself to theories lessens the possibility of entering the world of the sufferer, leading to excessive counter-measures that can be avoided by remaining calmer.

In treating depression, the main problem, it seems to me, is the difficulty of remaining fully attentive without tensing up in the face of the depressive person. Depressive moods can affect therapists as well as relatives, sucking them into the depressive maelstrom.[1] The danger of depressive contagion then threatens to restrict perception. The large amount of insecurity that depressive problems commonly create in personal relations can hamper not only a therapeutic relationship, they may also harm the therapy. When unsure, therapists who are excessively concerned about harmony in the relationship can be seduced into excessive caution in dealing with depressive patients, treating them like fragile eggshells. A willingness to yield may sneak into one's attitude, inhibiting direct attention to the feelings of the depressed person. In such cases, rage and disappointment, but also shame and disgust are easily overlooked by the therapist.

Conversely, a rather compulsive therapist who is inclined to formalize the procedure and firmly ward off unpleasant feelings may, if insecure, go on the counteroffensive and establish a plan of therapy that is not individually defined and does not sufficiently take into account the patient's personal experience. In such tense situations it is nearly impossible to properly address the detuned state of a depressive and open a dialogue about their hidden feelings. When they fail to meet in their dialogue, the partners' ability to collect themselves is made even more difficult. The depressed person now feels

--------

1. I have explored this dynamic in my paper "Ehen depressiver und schizophrener Menschen" (tr. *Marriages of depressive and schizophrenic patients*)(1998), and in a book written for the general public, "Welchen Sinn macht Depression?" (tr. *What Sense Does Depression Make?)* (2002)

that she is not understood, and that there is a lack of empathy, and she remains empty and torn up inside.

In this context, it is important to emphasize the idea of collecting. Inner and outward collecting are closely related. When a therapist is able to collect herself inside, to feel herself inside while remaining attentive to the experiences of the other, the chances of a depressive patient turning toward his deadened feelings is greatly increased.

A precondition for therapists' success in collecting themselves is their ability to avoid depressive infection and remain caring and attentive toward the sufferer. The inner collecting of the therapist is a prerequisite for a patient's increasing capability of perceiving their available feelings. It also creates an inner space that provides resonance between both therapeutic partners' feelings, allowing underrated or ignored feelings to be perceived more readily. What was, at first, only a vague feeling of unease can then differentiate itself into intimations of anger and shame. The sense of being hounded, of stress and hatred, can grow into the internal experience of rage. The helpless sense of being pursued and discriminated against may become a feeling of indignation. With the awakening of anxiety and rage, passive suffering develops into active feeling. Out of heteronomy comes a certain amount of autonomy, and in the midst of inner experiences that have been shaped by external factors, enclaves of personal experiences and memories arise. In the thick of feeling driven, one's personal power also begins to be perceptible, and out of passive suffering personal suffering emerges.

The shift from foreign influence towards personal experience, from feeling depressively helpless to experiencing one's personal value, does not happen suddenly. But however and whenever such a change begins, one must not see the "negative" feelings as questionable. Developing rage and beginning sadness are indications that the depressed person is finding a way to herself; the depressive rigidity is beginning to dissolve.

Leo Tolstoy produced an impressive image of the un-prejudiced acceptance of oppressive feelings. In his diaries, he writes that passive suffering cannot be diminished by distrac-tion, but only by turning to face oneself. "When one suffers, one must look into oneself and not rely on matches, but turn off the light that, shining, prevents us from recognizing our true ego. One must take the little doll that is ordinarily kept upright by the lead in his lower part, but who has been placed on his head, and one must turn it around; then everything becomes clear, and a good part of the suffering, namely all that is not physical, eases."[1]

Tolstoy's idea applies to the depressive event, since ac-cepting the depressive burden is more likely of be of help in raising oneself than hitting one's head against the depressive blockage. One must, however, notice Tolstoy's added remark that physical disorders can impede the raising of oneself. One must be aware that in depressive disorders, the brakes may also be locked in terms of their bodily functions. Depressive disorders are not always purely psychological suffering. An ailment of the body often accompanies the mental blockage. Usually there are disruptions of appetite, digestion, sexual function and, most disturbing, sleep. Furthermore, bodily mobility is often diminished. My own examinations at the psychiatric university clinic confirmed that muscle strength and the walking step length of depressive people were sig-nificantly reduced (compared to both a control group and the later, improved condition of the affected patients).[2]

When the physical disorder becomes predominant, and the functional impairment of the mind causes a person

---

1. L. Tolstoi, Tagebücher (Diaries) 2/293
2. J.-P. Bader et al. 1999

to become helpless, then even "raising oneself by oneself" reaches a biological limit. In such cases, physical treatment is unavoidable most of the time. These range from psychotropic drugs to light-therapy and sleep-suppression. This is not the place to present these widely used biological methods of treatment in detail; I have discussed these methods elsewhere[1] in some detail, attempting to fit biological and psychological methods of treatment into a comprehensible discussion of depression in an orderly way. It is important to know about any interpersonal dynamic that triggered a depression, especially when powerful physical treatment methods are being used. Otherwise, there is danger that the therapist will be influenced by the patient's depressive despair, that he will lose his carefulness and inner collectedness and end up treating the patient unnecessarily. In such a situation, therapeutic procedures could be used in an aggressive manner, as if an enemy had to be overcome. Worse yet, repeated failures of chosen therapeutic measures could lead to the attitude that the patient's condition is hopeless.

### Assistance for Self-Help

The world of feeling is continually in motion, and it moves others. During a depression, when feelings are no longer experienced in the usual manner, sufferers greatly need others' support. In this situation, reassurances like "Everything has its good side!" or "There's always a silver lining!" are of no help. Advice such as "Pull yourself together!" or "Just relax!" are experienced mostly as offensive. Impulsive analyses will not break through the depression's drama either, but simply

---

1. In D. Hell, "Welchen Sinn macht Depression?" (tr. *What Sense does Depression Make?*) or in R. Josuran et al. 2001, see also M. Wolfersdorf 2002 and U. Nuber 2001.

aggravate the cheerless thoughts and bitter despair of the severely depressed. When a person experiences depression as an avalanche that buries him and takes his breath away, any remark that implies he triggered the mishap himself could be dangerous. Those who feel traumatized need first the assurance that their connection to the outside world is not broken, and that help is near.

Most depressed people realize that release from their misery will take time, and require patience and perseverance. For this reason, it is critical for them that therapists and others are patient, and do not give up hope.

Depressed persons may eventually achieve enough perspective about their situation to complain about it, even though they may fear that their support system will hear these complaints as accusations. The complaints of a depressed person can be taken as a positive sign, as protests that show they know they are in a dangerous situation.

Their treatment must be carried out knowing that a depressive despair is provoked not only by acute, persistent pressures, but that those who are affected also feel traumatized by the depression itself. It is dangerous to focus exclusively on the biographical and social circumstances that have led to the depression, overlooking the fact that the depressed experience their condition itself as traumatic. Where the traumatic effect of the depression masks earlier traumas, the treatment must find ways to give precedence to the original trauma, without neglecting the primary history in which that trauma has become embedded.

This therapeutic challenge is not always easy to meet. It requires that the patients' previous attitude in life be carefully considered without hastily relating it to the core of the actual depression, thereby making the patient responsible for the depressive trauma. Therapy must be resolute in facilitating self-help, and at the same time remain conscious of the limits of this possibility. In this connection, a therapeutic approach is likely to be helpful if it initially stays in the "here and now," thereby indicating that the therapist understands and accepts the patient's depression as a traumatic experience. Demonstrating interest in the patient's life history may establish a background against which the depression stands out and can be better understood.

This procedure, which also includes the use of medications, is always advisable when the depressed person suffers less from what triggered the condition than from the impairment and exhaustion that accompanies it. Many depressed people must deal with the intimidating thought of no longer being able to cope with their own lives. When everyday life turns into unending torment because even the simplest activity can no longer be performed spontaneously, then each moment becomes a challenge. Now it is not the mastery of one's life that is at stake; everything is questionable. The challenge lies in surviving this day, this hour, or the next few minutes. In such severe cases of depression, it has proven helpful to view the seemingly senseless, ordinary day of the depressed patient from a therapeutic standpoint, assisting these derailed sufferers (with the help of psychosocial and pharmacological tools) in their efforts to endure the current situation.

In his book "Swiss Paradise", Swiss filmmaker Rolf Lyssy, creator of the comedy, "Die Schweizermacher" (tr. *The Swissmaker*), describes how he experienced this kind of therapeutic approach in our hospital. At the beginning of the treatment, Lyssy's condition made it impossible for him even to look at a movie, much less to read or write a script. He was under the impression he had lost himself:

> "It was as if I was constantly looking over my shoulder, as if I was frightened of myself every second." Awake, but completely

unable to make any decisions, Lyssy experienced as helpful a
conversation that essentially did nothing but focus on what
was happening to him at the moment and avoided digging up
the past. Doctor V., "Asked about nothing apart from my quite
ordinary day, yet he did so wanting to know everything accurately, such as the thoughts that preoccupied me during the day,
and my reactions to them. I didn't know what sense that made,
because the variety of meaningless stuff that characterized my
ordinary days for months didn't seem to me to be worth men-
tioning. Doctor V. was interested only in the immediate present
and my ability (or lack of it) to deal that, not in anything that
had to do with the past, and even less anything that had to do
with the future. The inside of my head looked like a telephone
switchboard where all the cables were pulled out and hung free,
and I was disoriented, completely incapable of establishing pri-
orities. Everything had the same meaning for me. Then Dr. V.
helped me to take each telephone cable one by one and plug it
into the proper socket. I felt like a first grader who is patiently
being taught the alphabet. A picture from childhood came to
mind: I was barely nine years old, sitting with my father at the
kitchen table where he asked me, using several yogurt containers,
to solve a simple mathematical problem. Now Dr. V., dressed in
light summer clothes, was sitting in front of me doing much the
same that my father did fifty years before. This is important, this
is not important, this can wait, and here he would recommend
that I respond, here I should not worry. I had the impression that
he would not only return the cables in my brain to their proper
place, but that he would also move the individual fragments to
which the cables were fastened to where they had originally been.
After four therapy sessions, I began to gain new trust in myself
as a result of his logic, his simple, clear arguments, and the small
but perceptible experiences of success. It was the hesitant, but
clearly detectable beginning of a new, positive feeling. At first I
could barely believe it, but it was so."[1]

1. R. Lyssy 2001, p. 201f.

At first sight, it would seem this straightforward therapeutic approach, also used in behavior modification therapy, was skirting the hidden feelings of a depressed patient, but that is not so. This technique takes seriously everyday events that point to the connection between individual adaptation and everyday happenings (including the thoughts they evoke). Following the image of the telephone switchboard whose cables need to be straightened out, it is not a matter of disentangling the thoughts, but of connecting them with emotions, weak as they might be. The thoughts can be likened to cables that trigger feelings when plugged into the proper sockets. A therapeutic approach requires that the ideas become linked to the feelings experienced. When attention is paid to the patient's everyday life, the connections between feelings and thoughts and the events that evoked them are very powerful. The connections elicit many questions: which experiences cause my mood to sink deeper? Which ideas oppress or anger me? Does anything tend to elevate my mood? Are there relationships that put more pressure on me?

This kind of question does not make the person responsible for her feelings. Nor does it demand that painful feelings be suppressed or changed into something positive. Instead, it helps the affected person to recognize her personal feelings as spontaneous responses related to certain thoughts or events. Feelings thereby become what they really are: fundamental elements of life that accompany the thoughts and actions of humans and give personal meaning to the events of life.

Just because emotions and passions can elude personal control, it is the experience of depression as a 'dark night' that reveals both the high value of active perception and the sweetness of life free of depression. Much like a near death experience, in favorable situations it strengthens our attention to our everyday lives and perceptions.

After going through his depression and recovering lively perceptions and feelings again, Lyssy wrote, "I went through something that has made me stronger, and I have reached a range of experience that I did not have before... I have gotten through the depression, and it has made me more perceptive." As an explanation of what he has become more conscious of, he added, "There are three basic things that decisively shape us: solitude, hunger, and anxiety. The older we get, the more we become conscious of it when we are alone. Hunger gives context to everything: hunger for love, for sensuality, for eternal life, for recognition, for power. Then the anxiety: anxiety about failing, anxiety over getting sick, fear of dying. These are the three things that now, after the depression, have entered strongly and sharply into my consciousness. Now I accept being alone, it does not scare me. As far as hunger is concerned, I feel secure. And I am able to face my anxieties."[1] This personal assessment is all the more impressive when Lyssy disagrees with C.G. Jung's comparison of depression to a "woman in black" to which one must listen and hear what she has to say. "No, depression is not a lady in black, it is an octopus that suddenly emerges out of the depths, disconnects the soul from the body and spirit, blocks all entrances to feelings, attaches itself with its tentacles, surrounds the victim with its arms and threatens to choke him. The victim fights helplessly and desperately for air, squirms, tries to speak, but cannot. If a victim succeeds in getting a hold somewhere before being dragged into the depths by this monster, then there is hope for a rescue."[2]

In my experience, those who are sinking into depression usually cannot get a good hold on certain thoughts, on images, nor even on their religious faith. Faith played absolutely no role, even in the most difficult hours, for theologian Ingrid Weber-Gast in her severe depression: "My reason and my will clearly tried to continue to affirm my faith, but for my

---

1. "Sonntagszeitung" (tr. *Sunday Paper*) 25.2.05, p. 31
2. R. Lyssy 2001, p. 199f.

heart, faith was unreachable. Faith was no consolation and no answer to desperately tormenting questions, and of no help when I could no longer cry. On the contrary, the faith did not carry me, I had to carry the faith."[1]

What sometimes makes it possible to hold fast during the fall into depression is the experience that despite emotional barbs that are very bitter and painful, one can have at least a distressing existence.

For this reason, when there are unfavorable developments in a depression, it can be dangerous to judge feelings of anxiety, sadness or disgust that show up as "sick" and try to eliminate them using various methods, including medications. When that sort of suppression becomes fixated in recurrently or chronically depressed patients, then an ever larger range of their lives could become inaccessible, as if it were occupied by enemy invaders. In the end, there may be a condition that leaves no inner room to the person, because contact with their feelings is interrupted. This condition is experienced as exceptionally pitiless, and not infrequently leads to the kind of serious suicidal development known as "balance-suicide."

Ruedi Josuran described the opposite development in his book "Mittendrin und nicht dabei" (tr. *In the Midst, and Not Part of It*). When, after a long time, he succeeded in accepting his depressive condition and some of his residual negative feelings, the blockage seemed to be broken. The more intently and frankly he viewed himself as depressed, and experienced rage in the depressive blockade, the more the depressive events eased in terms of scariness and power. This seemingly paradoxical experience presupposes that there is no irreparable brain disorder, and that the psychological pain stays within certain reasonable limits.

---

1. I. Weber-Gast 1989, p. 32f.

*Healthful Resources*

Up to this point I have pursued the question of how the use of self-help in dealing with suppressed feelings can be enhanced therapeutically. The question of self-help is not linked exclusively to therapeutic efforts; it attracts people outside medical or psychiatric treatment. The danger of independent self-help lies in the possibility of overrating one's abilities. Unrealistic expectations contribute greatly to difficulties in dealing with a depressive blockage. One cannot emphasize enough that an intensification of emotional life, a reduction in the depressive rigidity, cannot be brought about by will alone. Nonetheless, independent self-help is of very great importance. In relatively mild disorders, it can actually supplement professional help, or even replace it completely.

An impressive paradigm change has come about in medicine and clinical psychology during the past thirty years, a change that can be fittingly expressed by the slogan "From pathogenesis to salutogenesis." The concept of salutogenesis (from *salus*, Latin for well-being, health) does not accept illness as the first consequence of unhealthy influences, as does the term pathogenesis (from *pathos*, Greek term pain, suffering). Instead, it sees illness as the result of inadequate health-preserving resources.[1] Viktor von Weizsäcker, one of the pioneers of the term, stated in nineteen thirty, "Health is not some sort of capital one can consume; it is present only when it is created in every moment of one's life. Where it is not created, the person is already ill."[2] This change of view resulted in patients being seen less as receivers of medical procedures, and more as partners in the work to be healthy. As a result, their subjective experiences become more impor-

---

1. Medical sociologist Aaron Antonovsky was an early representative of the concept of salutogenesis.
2. V. v. Weizsäcker 1949

tant, while focusing on a clear, objective pathology became somewhat more relative. A further consequence was to move psychiatric and psychological researchers to seek not only the causes of illness and stress, but also to increasingly bring to the foreground an inquiry into the patient's ability to overcome illness and serious stress. In this regard, it is of special interest to see how patients can deal with heavy burdens and stress without significantly sacrificing their well-being, while also finding out how illnesses and their effects can be controlled. At this point, we are focused on the latter question.

In the nineteen-seventies, English psychologist Vicky Rippere conducted research with which she attempted to develop an "anti-depressive behavior" model.[1] She began by showing that anti-depressive strategies are widely distributed in the general population, and that most people have an idea of how depressive disorders should be curbed. Later research indicated that the application of anti-depressive strategies was greatly dependent on the depth and duration of the depression.[2] What the mildly depressed person is able to do is denied those who are severely depressed. Lengthy research projects have clearly shown that the forms of control depend very much on the nature, stage and momentary situation of the affected patient. Indeed, it has been regularly demonstrated that the more uniform the coping methods, and the more rigidly they are applied (for example, the suggestion that only conversation with friends can help), the less significant the positive effect will be. For this reason, it is helpful when the depressed person, perhaps in a self-help group, is shown different coping strategies and can experiment with one procedure or another. It has been shown, based on careful questioning of depressed patients, that the coping attempts that have been

1. V. Rippere 1976
2. Review by D. Hell 1983

helpful can be divided in three categories: mental attitudes, emotional attitudes, and concrete modes of behavior.

As far as the mental attitude is concerned, it seems that conscious acceptance of the depressed condition is most beneficial. However, it is more difficult for depressed patients than for the physically ill, such as patients with breast cancer, to accept their illness and its consequences. Having said that, when they are successful in accepting their conditions, depressed patients experience impressive relief.

## Burdensome Arguing

The attempt to avoid suffering is the opposite of an accepting attitude. "What must not be, cannot be." One of the most reliable research findings related to coping mechanisms is that any persistent attempt to "think away" a developed depression by brooding and arguing is associated with a severe depression and an unfavorable prognosis.[1] Those who brood ask themselves over and over, "Why me? Why has this misery fallen on me? What if I had behaved differently? How can I turn back the clock and regain my prior condition?" By brooding, one tries to turn what has happened into something that has not happened; instead of accepting the experience, one tries to find an alternative reality. In this way, the course of time is reversed: no longer is today determined by what happened yesterday; what is not permitted to exist today determines the measure of yesterday. In this way, one's own being becomes uncertain. "Why me?" implies, basically: "I'm seeking a reality different from the one that I experience, the one that I am."

1. S. Nolen-Hoeksema, et al. 1993, 1994, 1997

A special contribution of the American research group around Susan Nolen-Hoeksema consists of having shown, in methodically reliable studies, that brooding and arguing in situations of loss is frequently associated with depression, and that arguing prolongs the depression.[1] Nolen-Hoeksema rightly distinguishes the argumentative brooding that can be characterized as "ruminating" from self-critical work focusing on one's shortcomings. In this case, rumination does not meant a critical controversy regarding one's often exaggerated ideals. Also, argumentative brooding should not simply be equated with complaining. By complaining, people often create space for themselves and at the same time call for help. Complaining comes close to argumentative brooding only when the complaint loses energy and turns into self-pitying whining.

Rumination is first a devaluing of one's personal experience. What these people experience is questioned intellectually because it goes hand in hand with suffering. Yet no amount of brooding can relieve their misery. Arguing with reality, however, is linked to the danger of losing contact with one's feelings – or in Lyssy's terms – to the danger of not plugging the cables (thoughts) into the right sockets (feelings).

In depressive conditions, attempts to minimize the brooding are helpful, because arguing and brooding provoke insecurity in one's feelings and weaken one's ability to experience self. Also appropriate in this regard is a procedure used in behavior-modification treatment that analyzes problems (see below). Additionally, distracting patients from brooding by shifting their concentration to television or radio programs, newspapers or books, or even routine activities, has been helpful for those who are not too severely depressed.

Deliberately sorting out the oppressive emotional situation and the islands of feeling contained therein can be of equal help. The more residual emotions that can be elicited, the less

---

1. Ibid.

the fear of aggravating the depression. On the other hand, according to Beckham and Leber's study of one hundred hospitalized depressed patients (1985), suppression of feelings may contribute to aggravating the depression.[1] Also, patients have frequently commented that being able to express feelings has been helpful to them. As R. Josuran noted, "It is good that there are places where one can let go, where one can get rid of rage and sadness, where tears are allowed to flow…"[2]

Management of depressive disorders through concrete modes of behavior occupies a good deal of space in literature. Rippere's research showed that diverse, usually distracting, activities are helpful to depressed patients.[3]

> Doing something that leads to different thoughts, that one experiences as agreeable, and meeting with friends were experienced as especially helpful. M. Hautzinger later validated these finding with German patients. Noted Australian psychiatrist Gordon B. Parker tried to establish the predictive value of coping attitudes for the course of depressions, and thereby developed a special set of instruments.[4] With them it was indeed confirmed that the patient's level of perception and expression of emotions goes hand in hand with a more favorable course of the depression. The studies did not show that there was a similar positive effect in consoling themselves or adopting distracting activities.

The following kinds of behavior were rated as relatively effective by those studied: seeking warmth, listening to music, participation in work, and spending time and discussing problems with friends. That reflects clinical experience that even in severe depressions, taking a warm bath, massages, or hearing music can be of help. Individual senses can be

---

1. Quoted from E. E. Beckham / W. R. Leber 1985
2. R. Josuran et al. 2001
3. V. Rippere 1976 and D. Hell 1983
4. G. B. Parker / L. B. Brown 1979

stimulated without great effort, and the sensory experience offsets compulsively circulating thoughts.

Available studies show that what provides relief for a short time, but is unfavorable in the long run, are attitudes that go hand in hand with recklessness and carelessness. Attempts to blot out up the unpleasant experience with alcohol, medications or drugs are of little help, instead aggravating the patient's condition.

Extensive review of pertinent literature[1] gives one the impression that relaxation, distraction, attempts to solve problems, and talks with friends have favorable effects, but that depressives, because of their illness, rarely resort to them. Instead, social withdrawal and passive adjusting are prominent in depressive behavior.

Recently, religious approaches have found greater attention. Religious thought and spiritual practices like meditation and praying have assumed an important role in the lives of many depressed people, though various psychiatric treatments and psychological studies have, essentially, not paid attention to that. More than anything else, depressions have to be endured and lived through by those affected. In this regard, there is a difference between those who view life primarily as a source of pleasure and opportunity to fulfill themselves, and those who – speaking in biblical terms – see themselves as "strangers in the world" who may have to journey through the "Vale of tears."

Religious traditions embrace many stories of suffering and the mastering of suffering. One can, to a large extent, read religious texts – from Job to the Psalms and the stories of the passion of Christ – as instructions on how to deal with privation and suffering. Christian literature began quite early

---

1. D. Hell 1983 and J. Gotlib / C. Hammen 1996

to address the proper way of dealing with certain forms of depression.

In the early history of Christianity, the so-called "desert fathers," hermits living in the Egyptian desert in the third and fourth centuries, described a kind of pathological spiritual inertia called *acedia*.[1] Many edifying books and theological treatises have been dedicated to the question of how to deal with *acedia*. It is interesting to read that a hermit of the fourth century, Evagrius Ponticus, recommended that one try to tolerate the condition of *acedia* as much as one could, while at the same time observing one's inward experiences. "Simply accept what the temptation brings upon you. Mainly, look into the eye of the temptation of *acedia*, for she is the most evil of all, but she is also followed by the greatest purification of the soul. To flee such conflicts, or to avoid them, causes the spirit to be clumsy, cowardly and fearful."[2] In contrast, yielding would lead to the temptation to hang on to the past. Thus Evagrius warned especially against fleeing from the present into the past and clinging fast to something that is gone forever and can never be real again. He consistently recommended to those who were filled with the listlessness and circulating thoughts of *acedia*, to hold fast where they were, and to fight the longing for the past as something seductive. To be able to shift to other thoughts, "The person who is seized by the midday demon" was to turn to simple tasks and to read specific texts in the bible to find distraction and renew a firm stance.

Translated into today's language, he recommends an attitude that accepts the disagreeable present as a challenge and avoids arguing with destiny. At the same time, some kind of occupational and biblical therapy is recommended, which is not unlike what we find in today's self-help literature.

---

1. *Acedia* has been interpreted as an illness of monks that can affect all people. This idea shaped the understanding of depression during the Middle Ages. In my book "Die Sprache der Seele verstehen – Die Wüstenväter als Therapeuten" (tr. *Understanding the Language of the Soul: The Desert Fathers as Therapists*) I have explained this in considerable detail (D. Hell 2002).
2. Quoted from D. Hell 2002, p. 125

## Special Psychotherapeutic Possibilities

Where self-help has reached its limits, dealing with depressive moods can be supported with psychotherapy. Depressed people are often unable to initiate active self-help because of the blocking of their drives. Yet what is difficult to do alone by personal initiative may be possible with the help of a "pacer." With the support of an experienced psychotherapist or a physician familiar with psychotherapy, self-help activities are possible that otherwise would have been abandoned. During the last few decades, three psychotherapeutic procedures have emerged that have proven effective with mild to moderately severe depression. Each of the procedures aims both to help and to facilitate self-help. They are also intended to reduce the argumentative brooding of depressed people, and to reinforce their sense of self. Though different in certain ways, they all agree that one must work against the tendency of depressed individuals to see themselves as unworthy, and that the patients' sense of self must be strengthened. In controlled studies of different treatment modalities for depression, the effectiveness of these three special psychotherapeutic procedures proved similar to the effectiveness of psychotropic medications. Each will be briefly discussed. (For further information, see the book "Welchen Sinn macht Depression?" [tr. *What Sense Does Depression Make?*], and other professional literature.[1])

*Cognitive behavioral therapy*[2] consists of questioning accumulated negative thoughts such as "I'm incapable," "Others despise me," or "Nothing will ever change" and trying to influence mood by modifying thinking. At the same time,

---

1. An up-to-date review of psychotherapeutic possibilities (and their combination with biological methods) is presented in H. Böker and D. Hell's book, "Therapie der affektiven Störungen" (tr. *Therapy of Affective Disorders*) (2002)
2. A. T. Beck 1976, Beck et al. 1981, M. Hautzinger 1997

using step by step demands related to everyday activities, it is made clear to the patient that those who become ill with depression are capable, even against their own expectations, of some accomplishments.

*Interpersonal psychotherapy*[1] seeks the same effect through different means. It attempts to open for the depressed person a new way of looking at his problems with relationships, thereby strengthening his ability to socialize. During treatment, issues such as the immediate consequences of the experience of losses may be discussed. The procedure, as in behavior therapy, is pedagogic, for example when explaining the process of mourning intending to further the patient's acceptance of temporary lessening of performance, and the need to lower excessive demands on himself.

The *psychoanalytic method*[2] is more directly oriented toward feelings, and attempts, on the basis of everyday happenings and dreams, to direct the patient's attention to hidden feelings of anger, rage, or sadness. At some point, the discussion turns also to those issues that prevent the conscious perception of these feelings. The principal aim, for the development of the person, is the gradual integration of repressed feelings. This form of therapy seems particularly suited to the processing of a depression that has already been resolved. Feelings such as sadness and rage are often accepted only with difficulty by depressed persons, because they were taught as children to suppress their feelings. "Boys don't cry," or "Girls must be nice." Knowing her history can make it easier to explain a defensive attitude toward emotions to a depressed person, and to help her express them. It is especially interesting that it is crying that may indicate the waking from depression.[3] Tears

1. G.L. Klerman et al. 1984
2. H. Böker 2000
3. (Translator:) Goethe knew this when he caused Faust, who had been utterly depressed about Gretchen's fate and death and his crucial role in all of it, to utter the beautiful words, "The tears run down, the earth has me again."

seem to soften things and to dissolve bitterness. Indeed, tears can, in the poetic words of David's psalms, turn into "Bread by night and day."

But rage is often required in order to detach oneself from false attitudes. Surprisingly, however, it may be the tricky complex of feelings expressed in disgust that has the strongest effect of freeing one from the "false self."

One major difficulty of the psychotherapeutic process consists of finding an appropriate verbal expression for certain emotional problems. An inner restlessness may be difficult to describe. One nevertheless can attempt to open a conversation with that restlessness, and then listen to what it has to say. Here I offer an example taken from psychoanalytically oriented therapy:

> Fritz S., a fifty-five-year-old bank director who suffered from a persistent depression, localized his restlessness in his abdomen and chest; one day he labeled the tension "rumor" (Latin meaning: restlessness, tension). Once he had localized and named it, he tried to get it to talk. He tried to hear what the rumor would say if it could speak: "You're not allowed to work less, because then you would be a loser. You must perform as expected. If you allow them to give you a pension prematurely, I will call you a loser. After all, what would you do without your work? Even financially secure, your life would be without content, a pile of rags."
>
> It is self-evident that this rumor kept the man awake and left him panicked and in despair. Yet when he managed to give the restlessness a name and a voice, the earlier anonymous suffering, i.e., the "anxious restlessness and depressive blockage," gradually became an inwardly confronting other with whom he was able to argue. Eventually, favorable family and social conditions made it easier for him to reorient his life and to become friends with the idea of an early retirement. The more he succeeded in separating himself from earlier ideas of what was valuable, and confronting

the "inner rumor" with a new sense of what was of real value, the more the compulsion to brood and the depressive blocking disappeared. The inner dialogue of this patient brought forth a hidden dynamic.

This interior aspect of the depressive happening is increasingly threatened with being ignored in today's medicine. Discounting of and opposition to the fundamental sociobiological model of depression have significance for the further development of the person, and must not be underestimated. Of similar importance is the creation of an inner space that offers us a counterbalance against the centrifugal forces of our modern, everyday lives. While that inner space may contract under the weight of a depressive development, it can also expand again during the healing process, provided that enough attention is focused on one's personal experience.

*An Attempt to Integrate*

I shall conclude these comments related to psychiatric practice with a model of depression in which my basic position regarding to the interplay of experience (first person perspective) and bio-social events (third person perspective) finds a schematic expression.[1]

The popular notion of a steady condition of health that is interrupted by illness (depression, for example), is inaccurate. First, being sick and being healthy cannot always be clearly separated, as there are mixed conditions. Second, one must recognize that humans constantly keep changing in sickness and in health, so that any later illness, as well as any subsequent condition of health, are not an exact copy of the earlier conditions. The direction of time in human life is irreversible.

1. Data drawn from several of my psychiatric articles (D. Hell 1993, 1995, 1998, 2002).

As Heraclitus said, "One does not step twice into the same river."

It is also important to consider the factor of constant change when noting the waxing and waning of depressive disorders. It is not enough, as the model of "predisposition-stress" presupposes, to start from a certain tendency that later, as a result of stress, becomes a disorder. One must also consider that any disturbance evokes multiple counter-reactions, all of which can then either inflame or retard that disturbance. I prefer to replace the linear "predisposition-stress" model with a circular version that also considers feedback cycles. However, the "predisposition-stress" model is well suited to emphasize the connections between personal conditions and oppressive life situation that fit like key and keyhole.

In principle, one can draw distinctions between (a) *risk factors* that statistically increase the likelihood of a depression developing, (b) *triggering factors* that immediately precede the depressive experience, and (c) *ongoing influences* that reinforce or weaken the depressive disorder.

Genetic predisposition and biographical experiences fall under risk factors. A growing number of depressive disorders are found in the families of depressed persons. In such situations, there is a far greater risk of becoming ill than in the rest of the population. Nevertheless, an inherited vulnerability does not automatically lead to a depression. Indeed, sixty percent of uni-ovular twins whose womb mate has come down with a depression do not share their fate. Furthermore, there is no familial increase of depression in the majority of those who develop depressive disorders.

Along with the hereditary predisposition, there are biographical experiences (such as deprivation and anxiety in childhood) that can increase the risk of a depressive disorder at some time during one's life. Those who experienced painful losses as children, or who constantly felt they were helplessly exposed to excessive demands, turn out to be more vulnerable when faced with separations or ongoing, oppressive demands. As a result, when they are grown, heavy demands may become so magnified as to be unbearable, perhaps triggering a depressive pattern.

The connection between loss and deprivation in early childhood and increased sensitivity to stress is found not only in humans. It has also been firmly established in repeated studies of depressions among animals on the higher rungs of phylogenetic development. Experimentally forced separation of young apes results in patterns of behavior and biological changes in their later lives that correspond to neurobiological findings in depressed humans.

Depressions are usually accompanied by an increased level of the stress hormone cortisol, due to the hyperactivity of a relatively complicated system involved in stress, namely the axis that links lower parts of the brain (especially the hypothalamus) with the adrenal cortex. Both clinical findings and results based on animal experiments indicate that this regulatory system can be altered by genetic and biographical influences to the point of responding to heavy demands with unusual intensity and for a long time. In such cases, stress triggers an increase of the stress hormone, resulting in diminished ability to deal with stress.

Among the triggering factors of depression, socially stressful situations must be highlighted most of all: professional difficulties, continuing marital difficulties, and loss, especially of partners, parents, or children. These triggering factors have in common the fact that they strike people in their most vulnerable areas, and that the triggering event and the personal predisposition fit like key and keyhole. The triggering factors, being different from one person to another, therefore must always be determined individually. A social snub might deeply hurt one person, while another who is less ambitious might react far more calmly. Triggering factors may in fact be difficult to recognize, since they usually seem trivial to others. Moving away from home can be a trauma that triggers a depression in one person, while that response might seem incomprehensible to others who are less sensitive to separation. Relatively small injuries or stressful problems may add up so that the triggering "last straw" seems insignificant, and the affected individual herself cannot understand why it had such a profound effect. Most difficult to understand as triggering factors are pleasant events, such as a professional promotions, but these, too, can lead to increased worry and, eventually, feeling overworked.

Along with psychosocial problems, whose significance must be evaluated individually, physical illnesses and intensive treatments (e.g., cortisone therapy) can also trigger depression. There are physical illnesses that can affect specific brain functions, such as the central executive function, or the stress-regulating function. They may do so directly, or indirectly, because of enervating demands. Infections, strokes and tumors of the brain are examples of direct effects, while indirect effects are such issues as thyroid deficiencies, painful chronic illnesses, or other debilitating physical ailments. Drug addictions, too, frequently result in depressions. Finally, disturbances in one's circadian rhythm, or light deprivation syndrome (popularly known as Seasonal Affective Disorder, or SAD) can also contribute to the appearance of a depression.

Besides these triggering issues, there are other factors that exert significant influence in the development of a depression. Ongoing influences are usually underestimated, and they are barely mentioned in textbooks, yet they are important elements that coexist with an established depression and contribute to either the exacerbation or weakening of the developing depressive blockage. Just as fear of fear affects the development of an anxiety neurosis, being depressed about being depressed effects the course of a depression. Awareness of a depressive blockage thus can lead to an alarmed counter-reaction that adds to the existing problem. However, it can also accompany an unburdening intervention (see *Figure 3*)

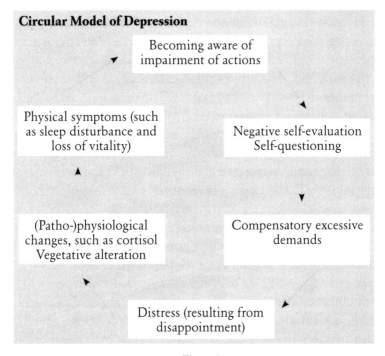

*Figure 3*

Understandably, it is especially those who have gone through severe depressions who recoil most violently from the first indication of a developing depressive blockage. On the other hand, it is easier for those who have so far experienced only minor depressive undulations to face an oncoming depression with more equanimity. One's reaction to the first indication of an oncoming depression depends on a one's inner attitude (self-confidence or self-critical tendency), as much as on external circumstances (such as the understanding of one's surroundings and the obligations one faces). People who, for example, feel that they are personally responsible for the occurrence of the depression, or those whose strong sense of duty does not allow them to let go of certain tasks, will push themselves when the depression develops, eventually overdoing it. This also applies to those whose external circumstances do not allow them to slow down, such as mothers with small children and no partner to help out.

Broadly designed research in England has shown that frequently this latter group is especially at risk for becoming ill with depression. Overworked mothers with small children are emotionally and socially burdened, but lack the opportunity to retreat from the burden of the children and restrict their activities to what their depressive condition allows. As a result, they get caught up in a vicious cycle of depressive blockage and continual discouragement, and stress fuels the depression.

The negative feedback loop of depressive exhaustion and willful rationalization goes hand in hand with turbulent thoughts and feelings, though the feelings progressively lose potency during the depression, and the thoughts flow ever more clumsily. Yet mutually interlocked feelings and judgments can result in an especially persistent negative effect.

The problems of depression are exacerbated by depressive changes that affect physical and verbal expression and may lead to a profound alteration of communication, and thus also human relationship. Indeed, the term depression is derived from the Latin *deprimere*, or pushing down. The term indicates that depression has physical form; sagging or bent posture, a rigid facial expression and a weak voice bear witness to the depressive condition as much as the invisible inner experience that affects the sufferer to her very core. The word emotion suggests a person's mobility, deriving from the Latin *emovere*, or moving toward the outside. Thus the mobility of the body expresses one's condition to others. Depression goes hand in hand with sending exceptionally strong messages, so the depressive process must not be seen as restricted to the depressed person, as is implied in *Figure 3*. To do justice to the depressive happening, in many cases it is important to understand the environment and its manner of reacting. In *Figure 4*, the inner circle that indicates the singular happening in the affected person is completed by an external circle that reflects the behavior of those to whom he is closely related. Encouragement, empathic participation, tactful suggestions and offers of help have a positive effect upon depressed people. Though it is probably not possible to constantly maintain a positive stance, it is essential to retain at least a basic, positive attitude that will defuse the critical or self-condemning tendencies that are likely to be present.

Criticism, hostility and withdrawal have negative effects. A difficult relationship is likely to develop, especially when there have been significant problems in relating to others before. When uncertainty arises from changes in communication that are due to the depression, and the affected person's mate displays a defensive, reproachful attitude, it can be compound the problem. There is also danger that relatives will worsen the situation by criticizing or discounting the depressed person. Frequently, threats of separation will magnify an already difficult communication situation. Such responses contribute to the depressed person seeing herself as even more untrustworthy, and her self-esteem may fall even farther.

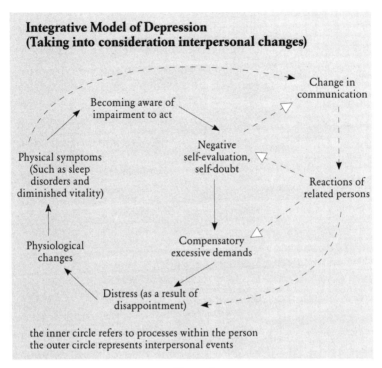

**Integrative Model of Depression
(Taking into consideration interpersonal changes)**

Change in communication

Becoming aware of impairment to act

Negative self-evaluation, self-doubt

Physical symptoms (Such as sleep disorders and diminished vitality)

Reactions of related persons

Physiological changes

Compensatory excessive demands

Distress (as a result of disappointment)

the inner circle refers to processes within the person
the outer circle represents interpersonal events

*Figure 4*

These negative interactions can frequently be improved with the therapeutic support of relatives, or a couple of joint meetings with the family. The fact that a patient is essentially set apart by relatives does not necessarily indicate deeply rooted hostilities. The relatives could be stumbling under a heavy burden. If so, they might benefit from thinking more about themselves. It could be useful to observe their own lives and give themselves time to collect themselves. Faced with a family member absorbed in a depression, those close to him are truly challenged to listen to their own inner voices to avoid becoming confused. A temporary stepping back need not have negative effects on the depressed person.

An elderly teacher once related to me how, during a depression, he had the insight that something was separating him from even those who were close to him. Before his depression, he was inclined to seek the fullest possible agreement with his wife. As a result of being depressed, he came to realize that in the final analysis, he could not be completely understood by other people. It was the depression that helped him to, as he put it, a kind of individuation, the discovery of a personal self that also contained shadowy aspects.

## Summary

It is precisely by such examples of depression that one can demonstrate how emotions are essential in organizing one's life. When emotions grow weaker in the beginning of a depression, or when they are locked up during a severe depression, those afflicted, to some extent, lose access to themselves. The flow of life stops and the world seems foreign and inaccessible. Depression clearly reveals that feelings are not accidental, and certainly not harmful. Rather, they are indispensable elements of a life of meaning and value. Their suppression and devaluation in the depressive state leads to "death in the midst of life."

The journey out of depression is, on the contrary, characterized by the strengthening and acceptance of feelings. In the depressed condition of "less-ness" (joyless, meaningless, sleepless, etc.) one generally can still recognize hidden feelings that float like "islands of melancholy" in the emotionless vacuum. One must treat these remnants of emotion with great care; they represent the seeds of new life. Feelings that are especially difficult to accept, such as shame, rage and sadness, can eventually provide those who have been uprooted by depression a new foundation. One must support depressed persons in accepting these surviving, often negative feelings, and in resisting the fear that they might pull others down even farther. Anti-depressants may simultaneously assist in the strengthening of their reduced self-motivation, and in easing the depressed mood.

The following are road signs for one's orientation in the landscape of depression.

1) Every depression has a different face. Though there is a wealth of different symptoms, overall expression is typically suppressed, and the initiation of action is inhibited.

2) In a condition of acute depression, there is a change in brain activity that goes hand in hand with impaired feeling, thinking, remembering and acting. Nobody can be held responsible for this condition

3) Once a depression has subsided, or even when it is lifting, it is often possible to discover individual risk and triggering factors, and to obtain a picture of what has contributed to the depression. An acquaintance with therapeutic experience can be of help in this regard. Physical causes like chronic illness or drug dependence (for example, on alcohol or cocaine) must be ruled out medically.

4) Once it is established, a clinical tendency to react with a depression is not easy to remove. Most of the time, however, it is possible for such persons to deal better with stresses that have led to a depression, or to avoid them.

5) Inasmuch as no two depressions are the same, one must always deal with its meaning in an individual way. Exchanges with others who have suffered from depression are helpful in learning to better accept one's own depressive experiences. Accepting one's depressive condition is the prerequisite for dealing with the depression either as a "beast" or listening to it as the "Lady in black." Both attitudes exclude a third

option, namely transcending the depressive experience as
though it consisted only of symptoms and was not personal.

I can be reduced to nothing, reiterates the highest
subversive message of the fourth commandment.
(You must not draw a picture nor any kind of likeness.)

                        – Georges Arthur Goldschmidt

You must not make a picture, it says, of God. This
might also be taken in this sense: God as what is
alive in each human being, that which cannot be
comprehended.

                                  – Max Frisch

# Conclusion: Where are we now?
# A Summarizing Challenge[1]

*The Quiet Revolution of the Natural Sciences*

Right into the eighteenth century, psychiatric illnesses were
linked to medicine as a disequilibrium of bodily fluids (blood,
phlegm, yellow and black bile). Melancholia was related to
an excess of, or the overheating of black bile. During the
past two centuries, neurology has almost completely superseded the theory of these four fluids. Established theory says
that psychological functions are dependent on the nervous
system. One hundred and fifty years ago, an internist, and
later professor of psychiatry, Wilhelm Griesinger, declared
categorically that "Mental illnesses are illnesses of the brain."[2]

The enormous advances in the neurosciences during the
last few decades have made it abundantly clear that functions

---

1. This challenging argument represents an abbreviated and thoroughly analyzed
   version of the article "Are psychiatric illnesses exclusively illnesses of the brain?",
   that was included in a book by G. Rager, tr. *Me and My Brain* 2000.
2. D. Hell 1993

of the brain have a decisive role in psychological experience
and behavior. Mental processes imply intact functioning of
the brain. Restricted, disturbed functioning of the brain leads
to disturbances in memory, attitude, perception, speech and
many other cognitive skills. In the nineteenth century, French
surgeon Pierre Paul Broca discovered the speech center in the
third left frontal gyrus of the brain. Injuries of this center, by
hemorrhage, for example, lead to speech impairments affecting grammar. Later it was found that other nerve centers and
linkages are also decisive in the formation and understanding
of speech.

Of special interest to psychology and psychiatry are
disturbances in motivation, in planning for action and in
the control of drives. These "higher functions" are of fundamental importance in regulating emotions, thinking and
social behavior. They require certain functions of the frontal
lobes, as well as of some adjoining areas. Lesions of the orbito-
frontal cortical areas, situated just above the dome of the
orbit, result in unstable moods and social disinhibition. On
the other hand, lesions on the side of the convex frontal lobe
will, among other things, produce inhibition of initiative.
Left-sided brain infarcts of the lateral convexity have been
connected with descriptions of genuine depressions. On the
other hand, lesions of the medial frontal regions typically
result in the flattening of emotional responsiveness. Modern
neuroscience has, on the basis of such connections, tried to
develop an ever more detailed image of brain functioning.
Using modern imaging and neuropsychological procedures, it
has tried to develop an ever more detailed depiction of brain
functions. One hopes thereby to also find a way to trace the
collaboration of brain and spirit.

The case of Phineas Gage[1] illustrates this particularly well. In 1848, this man was the victim of an extraordinary accident in which an iron bar penetrated his head. What can we learn from the sad story of Phineas Gage? While the neurological injuries of other victims clearly showed that the brain is responsible for speech, perception and motor functions, Gage's history drew attention to the fact that there are systems of the human brain that serve as the ground of thinking and personal judgement. "Phineas Gage was no longer Phineas Gage after the accident," wrote his treating physician; while he had been considerate and dependable before, he now was irritable and antisocial.

The anatomical explanation for this change in personality remained open until a few years ago, when Hanna Damasio was able to reconstruct the changes in Gage's brain by employing modern imaging methods. The injury had, in the first place, affected the anterior medial and orbito-frontal parts of the frontal lobes that were close to the midline. These structures are required for planning the future and conforming to accepted social rules. Other centers remained intact, including the lateral part of the frontal lobes, which we know, thanks to other patients, are responsible for attentiveness and mathematical skills. Because of this, Gage could continue to do business, though he was socially disinhibited and acted in ways that harmed himself.

## The Meaning is not located inside the Head

Even though there are currently no doubts that human behavior is based on physicochemical processes in the brain, the question nevertheless remains whether it is sufficient in understanding human personal soulish experience to recognize neuronal processes, or if additional conditions of biological, psychological and social nature are required. One principal argument in favor of this wider inquiry comes from the field

---

1. A. R. Damasio 1997

of brain research itself, because the development of the brain (within genetic limits)has been shown to depend on environmental influences and life experiences. The brain is in no way a static organ; it is an adaptable organ that accommodates its exquisite structure to outside influences. Thus it has been possible to show, first with apes, then with human beings, that persistent stimulation of the fingertips, or ongoing finger movements (such as playing the violin), leads within several weeks to the enlargement of those areas of the cortex that are responsible for movements of the fingers. Other studies have shown that damage to the speech centers in childhood can be partially compensated, as long as the speech functions of the damaged areas were not yet fixed.[1]

We must remember that the sprouting and interconnecting of brain cells depends on biographical developments and learning experiences, and that taxing environmental factors (such as stress) have an enormous influence on the microanatomy and neurophysiology of various brain-centers. Because of this, it would be premature to casually conclude that mental illnesses are diseases of the brain, since the changes in the brain that produce illness could also be expressing the circumstances and experiences in the affected person's life.

Even more important than expanding the scope of the neuroscience to include environmental influences is the recognition that personal soulish experience cannot entirely be reduced to neurophysiological processes. Subjective experience contains an additional meaning, and this can be understood only by reflecting on the cultural background. As American philosopher Hilary Putnam puts it, "Meaning is not located inside the head."[2] Meaning is contained in language, which

1. W. Hartje / K. Poeck 1997
2. H. Putnam 1975

comes from the relationship of people and the dialogue with their surroundings.

Psychological disorders have the unusual quality of being characterized mainly (sometimes exclusively) by subjective experience and the meaning given to it. They manifest as anxieties, compulsions, depressions, deceptive sense perceptions, confused speech, excitement and – more and more frequently – self-inflicted injuries or eating disorders. This is the kind of suffering that leads one to psychiatrists.

*Relation to Oneself and Psyche*

The theory of knowledge suggests that psychiatric problems are characterized by being focused on the self. They differ from physical problems in that in psychiatric problems, it is the experience of the self that is first affected. This intentional relationship to the self is unique in psychiatric disorders.

A patient with a diseased heart might well interpret a heart disorder symbolically, but a disorder in the heart's rhythm never experiences itself directly; rather, it is perceived, apart from other ego experiences, as a bodily change. It is different in most psychological disorders. Depressed people experience themselves as being different in their thinking, feeling, remembering and acting. They don't just have symptoms like disturbed appetite or sleep, but experience themselves as changed in their awareness. Time seems to be arrested, space is more confining, and their opinion of self and others changes.

In depression, as in most other psychological disorders, one runs into a problem that does not noticeably affect the rest of medicine: the question of a disorder's relation to the self, and its intentionality. This question also interests the neurosciences and the research into artificial intelligence; so

far, it has not been answered conclusively. One might begin
with the assumption that certain instrumental functions of
the brain are essential to intentionality and relating to oneself. Nevertheless, feeling and thinking do not only express
cerebral functions. There is support for the idea that our
environmental experience, as well as our experience of ourselves, would be impossible without the peripheral nervous
system and other bodily functions, and that human speech
– and thinking, in terms of talking with ourselves – would
be unthinkable without cultural assumptions. The experience
of anxiety, for example, requires a healthy amygdala nucleus
as well as other cerebral structures. Yet vegetative changes
in other organs, such as the skin and the heart, and in more
complicated cases, the evaluation of one's situation in life as
dangerous, also play a role. This has clearly been shown by
the research of Damasio,[1] LeDoux[2] and others.

Roald Dahl's fantastic story *William and Mary*, in which
the brain of a scientist connected to a heart-lung machine
continues to live independently, is poor science fiction, unfortunately. An isolated brain is no longer capable of distinguishing perceptions, feelings and thoughts in the same way
as can a living person who interacts with others and with the
environment.

Psychiatry is involved in a very special way with the complex relationships of inner experiences and outer perceptions.
Psychiatry's methodological problem is marked by the fact
that inner perception (first person experience) and perception
of the outside world (third person experience) are difficult
to connect. While a few decades ago, a psychoanalytically
oriented psychiatry left the outer, objective view (and with
it, the complex, technical contributions of the brain) almost

---

1. See footnote 1 page 333
2. J. LeDoux 1998

unnoticed, today we are menaced by a neurobiological psychiatry that neglects the inner side of psychiatric problems.

However, there is a difference between viewing the experience of a toothache as coincidental and medically unimportant, and ignoring the experiencing of depressive distress. Depression may in fact be related to technical dysfunction of the brain, such as the inhibition of the central executive function, but the experience may also have a supportive, self-referential trait, such as the feeling one is a failure. Therapists (in cognitive behavior work, for example) have, with real success, systematically included this aspect in the treatment of depressive disorders. One can influence the mood of depressed patients by challenging their negative self-opinions. When one can replace a negative self-opinion with a neutral or positive opinion, the mood frequently brightens. Scientific observation demonstrates that one's opinion of an experience has a lasting effect upon mood.[1]

The kinds of problems psychiatrist are called on to consider are, in a unique way, linked to cultural and social suppositions. This has been recognized by leading American neurobiologists like Nobel laureate Eric Kandel. In 1998, Kandel offered an excellent, often cited contribution to the scientific understanding of psychiatry.[2] The question is, can social or cultural phenomena be fully integrated in the history of nature, as Kandel sees it, or are natural science and cultural science two independent areas, different in methodology, that must not be merged prematurely?

1. M. Power / T. Dalgleish 1997
2. E. R. Kandel 1998. The reference is to the first of two contributions in the American Journal of Psychiatry.

*Are Psychological Problems Conditioned by Culture or by Nature?*

Kandel began with the assumption that all mental processes – even the most complex psychological perceptions – can be reduced to functional events in the brain.[1]

> In short, he established the following series of arguments: Our modes of behavior and experience depend on neural circuits, interconnected nerves within the central nervous system. Genes and proteins are important determinants of the pattern of neural connections. The forms of genetic messages, their characteristics, are influenced by environmental factors. Failing the influence of these environmental factors, many genes remain inert and ineffective. For these reasons, it is possible that even a learning experience (through the activation of genes) could alter the links between certain neurons, and these alterations could cause disordered behavior. Effective psychotherapies and pharmacotherapies can lead to changes in the characteristics of genes, resulting in structural changes in the brain.

Kandel also includes in his neurological understanding of psychiatry the environment and the effects of learning, but only in the sense that they have an influence on the characteristics of genes and thereby on the functions of the brain. Consequently, he largely reduces psychiatry and psychology to the role of applied natural science, being convinced that in the last analysis, all culture expresses itself as nature. With that, he turns upside down von Weizsäcker's position that, "all natural science is, in the last analysis, cultural science,"[2] by concluding that, "All culture is, in the last analysis, natural science."

1. (Translator:) Even more radical, perhaps, is the book by Nobel laureate Francis Crick, *The Astonishing Hypothesis: The Scientific Search for the Soul* (Scribner's, N. Y., 1995), which implies that, considering the enormous progress in investigating the cerebral processes involved in human experience, everything will eventually be expressed in terms of these complex functions, thereby providing a complete description of what has been called "soul."
2. C. F. v Weizsäcker 1984

This position is strongly reminiscent of the writings of an aging Eugen Bleuler,[1] whose views on schizophrenia, at the beginning of the last century, exerted a major influence on psychiatry. Bleuler fought, with different words and less adequate data, for a universal psychology within the framework of the natural sciences. His opinion was that all life was a combination of genetics and experience. He did not find any room for free will, or for a subjective viewpoint.

### Dangers contained in Naturalism

More than half a century has elapsed between Bleuler's later publications and Kandel's essay. During this period, psychiatry has been misused by various political systems. The equating of biology and society – that is, explaining social phenomena with biological and social-darwinistic theories – has been partially responsible for that misuse. With the equating of biological abnormality and social abnormality, psychologically ill people were caught in a tragic tautology: the social devaluation of human beings was justified by biology, and biological abnormalities seemed to justify the social consequences. During the Nazi era, these circular conclusions contributed first to stripping psychiatric patients of their ability to reproduce, and eventually to their murders as "worthless eaters."

Today's molecular biology has nothing to do with eugenics; in fact, it has been able to contradict the claims of that so-called science. Nevertheless, considering the history of science, we must emphatically warn that the individual and society must not be explained by biology alone.

Psychiatry is involved here on at least three levels, each of which demands an individual approach, even if they overlap:

---

1. See A. Möller / D. Hell 1999

the biological level, the social level, and the personal level. Most people feel the strongest affinity for the third level, so it's understandable that most patients want, first of all, to feel understood as individuals.

## *The Concept of "Person"*

The term "person" emerged in the thirteenth century.[1] While Aristotle's teachings, which were then prevalent, had included naturally given conditions (*ens naturale*) and logical legitimacy (*ens rationale*) the possibility of making personal decisions (*ens morale*) was now added. From then on, a person was no longer just the wearer of a mask (Latin: *persona*, mask) who performed according to prescribed laws, but was someone allowed a certain degree of freedom of action.

In the potential of "to want," there is always contained the potential of "not to want." The person is thereby introduced to the experience of an "inner distinction."[2] Consciously experiencing this inner distinction, one may regret that. He may also want to make himself different. He can create images of what he desires and reject what deviates from those images. Quite apart from the fact that his plans may or may not be successful, he gains the inner experience of being able to take a position about an external object or a sensation, and of being in a position to judge something as wanted or not wanted.

It is impossible to overestimate the psychological significance of that inner experience. The person who wants something always embraces with that wanting the not wanting of something else. A world of opposites is revealed, one that extends well beyond moral questions of good and evil, or

---

1. The concept "person" arose up in connection with the doctrine of the Trinity, thus having from the very beginning an interpersonal connotation.
2. R. Spaemann 1996

the aesthetic matter of beauty and ugliness. As "persons," people find themselves, intentionally or not, in certain social positions (such as poverty), certain emotions (such as sadness), certain moods (such as depressed), or certain physical experiences (such as anorexia). In all this, the question of whether or not the will is truly free is not the decisive issue; what is decisive is that one is able to experience "wanting" or "not wanting" as an internal distinction. That experience makes possible an internal discussion between wanting and not wanting, or, in the archaic case, between a good and bad voice. Finally, with the help of language, this leads to detachment and self-reflection.

> Therefore, what is ultimately personal in the human being is not something systematic that can be reproduced through cybernetics, as an orderly, logical sense of meaning about oneself. What is primary is instead the experience of simultaneously being able to want and not want. It is only out of that experience that the possibility of self-reflection can develop.

However, this inner dynamic can be observed only from the first person perspective; it cannot be objectified. This is why the personal approach needs special attention in conveying understanding and empathy for the individual's experience. Understanding based on the first person experience is different from the objective methods of the natural and social sciences, which imply the third person perspective, an external view. It would, however, be shortsighted to play these two different starting approaches against each other, because while they involve different viewpoints and perspectives, they can also complete each other. This is especially clear in the case of depression.

*Multiple Dimensionality seen in the Example of Depression*

Depression affects the sufferer's entire being, involving significant biological, psychological and relationship changes.

At the onset of a depressive episode, one usually finds a punishing interpersonal experience, perhaps the loss of a partner, a professional disappointment, or deep hardship.

Typically, physical functions are altered during a depression. There are changes in brain activity (especially in the frontal lobes and the limbic system), in the vegetative nervous system (for example constipation), in hormonal balance (especially an increase of the stress hormone cortisol) and in psychomotor features. On the whole, these changes place the body in a state of rest and inhibit all outwardly directed activities,[1] all of which reduces one's ability to function and communicate.

However, these bio-social changes alone are not enough to define a depression. Psychological changes in experience and behavior must also be present before a depression that fits the WHO's definition can be diagnosed. That is so because, while biological and social impairments are indeed found in the majority of cases of depression, they may be absent in many forms of depressive suffering. Furthermore, they may appear in different psychiatric disorders that are not accompanied by a depressive mood.

A diagnosis of depression therefore continues to be based primarily on psychological criteria that include the subjective experience of an oppressive mood, a general loss of interest, and diminished drive. One must accept that so far, no one has found a satisfactory biological marker for depression. The biological changes that have been identified simply are not the material reflection of the subjective experience of "depres-

---

1. D. Hell "Welchen Sinn macht Depression?" (tr. *What Sense Does Depression Make?*), 2002

sion." In other words, today's understanding of depression does not include clearly defined functional components, such descriptions as: "elevated cortisol of central origin," or "transmitter deregulation." On the contrary, it is based exclusively on dimensions of experience that so far cannot be translated into a functional organic model.

Depression is still defined in terms of how people experience themselves: dejected, lacking interest, easily fatigued, etc., definitions that correspond to the first person perspective. If, in the future, a neuroscientific model based on a third person perspective is created, then experiencing oneself as dejected, etc., would no longer play a primary diagnostic role. Its place would have been taken by those specific disorders of brain function that would be considered decisive in the diagnosis.

That change would be as radical as the Copernican revolution in astrophysics, in which the belief that the sun circulated around the earth was replaced by the discovery that the earth rotates around the sun. In contrast to astrophysics, it is the human being who occupies the center of interest in psychology and psychiatry. It is difficult to imagine that a human's inner experience could ever be grasped or precisely predicted by any diagnostic method. Yet reducing the comprehension of psychiatric illness to a bio-social viewpoint is ruled out on methodological grounds, and by the theory of knowledge, as long as the spectrum of human experience – feelings, will and action – is given a dominant position.

> Psychological influence is unfathomably important in depressive events. Only the shocking awareness of an unwelcome reality, or the lack of success in reaching a specific goal, can provide an understanding of depressive misery. It is the psychological dynamic, combined with the bio-social pattern of a depression that makes biological and relational limitations a painful affliction.

In a profound depression, one's range of action is so limited that, while a question might be contemplated deep inside, an active decision is not possible. In such a case, thinking seems to turn backward and contract into the question of whether the torment could have been avoided if one had acted differently. However, even in one's deepest doubt and ambivalence, the human capacity to want or not want is still alive. It is this incompatibility in one's freedom of choice that makes the depressive suffering so horrible, because while one's ability to act is impaired during a depression, the awareness of options and the demand for a decision remain.

This discrepancy is certainly experienced by modern people, because ever since the Age of Enlightenment, the image of the individual has grown into the ideal of an autonomous and responsible actor. Modern people – in contrast to those of the Middle Ages, when a person's destiny was still determined by cosmic events – now must discover their fates all by themselves. This image of an individual with no one to turn to conveys fairly well the tragic situation of depressive blockage. Because modern people have internalized an enlightened self-image, they cannot led go of it, even in a depression. The theory of evolution's claim that only the fittest survive, and that human strength lies in our power and prestige, is now deeply rooted in the populace. As a result, modern individuals, their thinking oriented toward efficiency and adaptation, are hit in their most vulnerable places by a depression, for the autonomous person is expected to take the initiative in thinking and acting, but it is just those skills that are impaired. What the modern person can least tolerate is what happens in a depression: restriction of the ability to make decisions and exert influence. It's hard to get in touch with thoughts and memories. The planning and making of decisions are frustrated, as are the execution of ideas or physical forms of communication. At the same time, depressed people – unlike unconscious or deranged people – are aware of their predicament. The modern ego feels it is faced with nothingness. There is no longer a way out, as there was in the *melancholia* of history, when people saw themselves as part of the universe and derived some meaning and comfort from the idea. Depressed persons now fall back on themselves, unable to find a supportive rationale in the cultural values that predominate.

## From Isolated Subject to Integrated Subject

However, subjective experience does not come to a stop during a depression. Depressed people experience themselves as suffering, utterly helpless and dependent. Having lost autonomy, they are often left with only a feeble experience of their corporeality. This experience cannot be turned into something positive, but it is the only thing of their own they have left. Even though the individual as such may be indifferent to nature or the scientific viewpoint, it is impossible for individual humans to withdraw from themselves. As Manfred Stark remarked, the individual cannot be deceived into being someone else. (She cannot step behind herself and hide.) Her individual worth is not given by nature, but is couched in herself.

Depressed persons may feel all lost at sea as a result of their exaggerated subjectivity and their cutting sense of personal shortcomings. Yet sometimes, because of their depression, they discover unexpected avenues of experience. They may sense that what made that possible was a first person perspective that others don't know. As Wolfgang Welsh once said, "Having been 'strong subjects,' they can be 'weak subjects,'" which means that they were independent, and then became only conditionally independent persons. They can take better care of themselves just because they have experienced being dependent on a broad variety of things, and thus are able to not have control over everything. A deeper understanding of depression may help in developing a passion for the "weak subject," that is, to discard the image of a person who is weighed down by excessive demands. Seeing a totally independent and isolated ego as questionable, the subject must not perish. It may come to understand itself as a creature that, as a natural "living being," depends on many necessities, but still senses that it has personal value or – in the ancient way of speaking – a soul.[1]

## Conclusion

Summing up, we find that experience from the first person perspective cannot simply be shifted to an observation from the third person perspective. This is not just because the complexity of feeling, thinking and willing make it impossible to produce an accurate picture with computerized calculating of individual data. Transferring a first person perspective to an objective image that is seen from the outside is limited also by the presence of a degree of inner freedom. After all, the spontaneity of experience precludes a contrived approach.

Many psychological problems are characterized by the fact that they not only represent disorders of the brain, in the sense of organic dysfunction, but that they also go hand in hand with taking a position opposed to that functional loss. They also express a self appraisal.

---

1. "Those who initially are naïve children eventually discover that what we call 'nature' is something that possesses them, but does not cause them to feel emptied out. This is one of the great experiences." (C. F. von Weizsäcker 1997, p. 34)

While various forms of psychological misery are accompanied by altered cerebral function, this does not adequately explain the personal experience: it is not a brain that is ill, but a person. "In the language of the neurosciences, the concept 'person' is frequently replaced with 'brain,' but it is not the brain that is in touch with the surrounding world, it is the human being whose existence thrives or falls apart."[1]

The meaning and importance of psychological suffering is not found in the brain, but in the attitudes people have in evaluating their experiences and in the verbal communication between people and their culture.

---

1. J. Willi 1999

# Thanks!

As I finish this book, I realize that what was initially to be a professional discussion of basic psychological and psychiatric questions has turned into a personal stance. Instead of leaving it as an uncommitted viewpoint, I have, in the four years of this endeavor, been led to a most definite perspective that has an intrinsic, a biographical, and a local starting point. However, such an endeavor cannot be limited to what is usually meant by "subjective." The concept "person," as opposed to "subjectivity," presupposes other persons to whom I am related. Thus my personal stance must also be seen as a reply that is cognizant of the viewpoints of other authors, and tries to come to grips with the experience of other people. My own viewpoint is personal only to the extent that it was possible only thanks to many other people.

First, it was the patients I treated in the hospital or as outpatients who have helped with the ideas in this book. Several of their experiences have been mentioned herein with their consent to publication in the form in which they were presented. For this, too, I warmly thank those patients.

Many who worked with me at the Psychiatric University Clinic of Zürich have supported the development of this book with excellent suggestions. I'm in dept to Prof. Jerome Endrass, Prof. Heinz Böker, Dr. Hans Martin Zöllner, Dr. Vera Koelbing, Dr. Jean-Pierre Bader and especially to Dr. Jacqueline Dutli. Others close to me have followed this work for years, and have contributed significantly to its final format. I owe the structure of the book to a suggestion from Barbara Küchenhoff. Along with her husband, Dr. Bernhard

Küchenhoff, she read the preliminary phases of it and made enthusiastic suggestions for its further development.

I would like to express a warm "Thank you" to my former secretary, Mrs. Margrit Milz. In a certain sense, this book is also hers, for she accompanied its development from beginning to end, always with the greatest care and continually thinking of ways in which it could be improved.

I want to thank cordially Dr. Julius Heuscher, an American psychiatrist, for initiating the translation of this book in English. I am very sorry that Dr. Heuscher died unexpectedly after finishing the translation, so that I cannot thank him personally for his splendid work. The publication in English was supported by a generous grant of the Dr. Margrit-Egner-Stiftung.

Last but not least I would like to thank Daimon Publishers, namely Dr. Robert Hinshaw, for the beautiful form of the book and making the translation even better. Dr. Jacqueline Dutli gave the book its final touches. Many thanks.

May 2009
Daniel Hell

# Bibliography

Ackerknecht E. H.: Kurze Geschichte der Psychiatrie. 3. Aufl. Ferdinand Enke Stuttgart 1985

Agamben G.: Bartleby oder die Kontingenz. Merve Berlin 1998

Alexander F. G., Selesnick S.T.: The History of Psychiatry. New American Library New York 1968

Allen G. E.: The social and economic origins of genetic determinism: a case history of the American Eugenics Movement, 1900-1940 and its lessons for today. Genetica 99:77-88, 1997

Anders G.: Die Antiquiertheit des Menschen. Bd. 1. Beck München 1956

Andreasen N. C: Das funktionsgestörte Gehirn. Einführung in die biologische Psychiatrie. Beltz Weinheim und Basel 1990 / The Broken Brain. Harper Paperbacks, New York 1985

Andreasen N. C: Linking mind and brain in the study of mental illness: A project for a scientific psychpathology. Science Vol. 275 1586-1593, 1997

Antonovsky A.: Salutogenese. Zur Entmystifizierung der Gesundheit. Deutsche Gesellschaft für Verhaltenstherapie Tübingen 1997 / Unraveling the Mystery of Health. Jossey-Bass Inc Pub, Hoboken 1987

Bader J.-P., Bühler J., Endrass J., Klipstein A., Hell D.: Muskelkraft und Gangcharakteristika depressiver Menschen. Nervenarzt 7: 613-619, 1999

Bader J.-P., Hell D.: Der psychische Schmerz als Symptom der Depression – Phänomenologie und Neurobiologie. Fortschr Neurol Psychiat 2000; 68: 158-168

Barlow J. P.: Unabhängigkeitserklärung des Cyberspace. «Telepolis» 0, 1996 / A Declaration of the Independence of Cyberspace. Published online: http://www.eff.org/~barlow

Bartlett E. S., Izard C. E.: A dimensional discrete emotions investigation of the subjective experience of emotion. In: Izard C. E. (ed) Patterns of Emotion. Academic Press New York 1972

Beck A. T., Rush J. A., Shaw B. F., Emery G.: Kognitive Therapie der Depression. Urban & Schwarzenberg München 1981 / Cognitive Therapy of Depression. Guilford Press, New York 1987

Beck A. T.: Cognitive Therapy and the Emotional Disorders. International Universities Press New York 1976

Beckham E. E., Leber W. R.: Handbook of Depression. Treatment, Assessment and Research. Dorsey Homewood IL 1985

Böker H. (Hrsg.): Depression, Manie und schizoaffektive Psychosen, Psychodynamische Theorien, einzelfallorientierte Forschung und Psychotherapie. Psychosozial-Verlag Giessen 2000

Böker H., Hell D.: Therapie der affektiven Störungen. Psychosoziale und neurobiologische Perspektiven. Schattauer Stuttgart New York 2002

Brown G. W., Harris T.: Social Origins of Depression. Tavistock London 1978

Buber M.: Schuld und Schuldgefühle. In: Werke Bd. 1. München 1962 / in Buber J.: Martin Buber on Psychology and Psychotherapy. Syracuse University Press, Syracuse 1999

Ciompi L.: Affektlogik. Klett-Cotta Stuttgart 1982

Ciompi L.: Die emotionalen Grundlagen des Denkens – Entwurf einer fraktalen Affeklogik. Vandenhoeck & Ruprecht Göttingen 1997

Clark D. M.: A cognitive approach to panic. Behaviour Research and Therapy 24 461-470, 1986

Crick F.: The Astonishing Hypothesis: The Scientific Search for the Soul. Charles Sribner, New York 1995

Dahl R.: Three Tales of the Unexpected. Reclam Stuttgart 1987

Damasio A. R.: Descartes' Irrtum. Fühlen, Denken und das menschliche Gehirn. (Übers. Kober H.) 2. Aufl. dtv München 1997 / Damasio, A.: Descartes' Error: Emotion, Reason and the Human Brain. Avon Books New York 1994

Darwin Ch.: On the Origin of Species by Means of Natural Selection. Dover Giant Thrift Editions, Mineola 2006

Dennett D. C.: Consciousness Explained. Penguin Books 1993

Descartes R.: Discourse on the Method of Rightly Conducting the Reason, and Seeking Truth in the Sciences. Forgotten Books 2008

Diagnostic and Statistical Manual of Mental Disorders. DSM IV. American Psychiatric Association Washington 1994

Diels H.: Fragmente der Vorsokratiker. Hrsg: Kranz W. Weidmann Zürich 1985

Dörner K.: Bürger und Irre. Zur Sozialgeschichte und Wissenschafts-soziologie der Psychiatrie. Europäische Verlagsanstalt Frankfurt am Main 1984 / Madmen and the Bourgeoisie: A Social History of Insanity and Psychiatry. Blackwell Publishers, Oxford 1981

Ekman P.: Facial expression of emotion. Psychological Science 3 34-38 1992

Ernst C.: Eugenik und Nationalsozialismus. Wurzeln in der Geschichte von Wissenschaft und Sozialpolitik. NZZ Fernausgabe No. 252: 31.10.1990, 11

Ernst C.: Lebensunwertes Leben. Die Ermordung Geisteskranker und Geistesschwacher im Dritten Reich. Schweiz. Monatshefte 65 (1985) 489-504

Felsman J. K., Vaillant G. E.: Resilient children as adults: A 40-year-study. In: Anderson J. E., Cohler B. J. (Hrsg.) The Invulnerable Child. Guilford Press, New York 1987

Fink P. J., Tasman A. (ed): Stigma and Mental Illness. American Psychiatry Press Washington 1991

Foucault M.: Wahnsinn und Gesellschaft. Suhrkamp Taschenbuch Wissenschaft Frankfurt am Main 1973 / Madness and Civilisation. Routledge Classics, Taylor & Francis Ltd., Abington 2001

Foucault M.: Mental Illness and Psychology. University of California Press; Revised edition, Berkeley 1987

Frank M.: Die Unhintergehbarkeit von Individualität. Edition Suhrkamp Frankfurt am Main 1986

Freud S.: Studien über Hysterie. Frühe Schriften zur Neurosenlehre. In: Gesammelte Werke, 4. Aufl., S. Fischer Verlag 1972 / Freud, S. & J. / Trans & edit James Strachey et al.: The Standard Edition of the Complete Psychological Works of Sigmund Freud: Vol. II. (1893-1895): Studies on Hysteria. Breuer 1955. And: Freud, S.: Studies in Hysteria. Penguin Classics 2004

Freud S.: The Problem of Anxiety. The Psychoanalytic Quaterly Press and W. W. Norton & Co., New York 1936

Frisch M.: Tagebuch 1946-1949. Suhrkamp Taschenbuch 1148 Frankfurt a.M. 1985 / Sketchbook 1946-1949. Harcourt, Oxford 1983

Fromm E.: Haben oder Sein. Hrsg.: Funk R. Wilhelm Heyne München 1997 / Fromm, E.: To Have or to Be? Rev. Edition, Continuum 2005

Gierer A.: Die gedachte Natur. Ursprünge der modernen Wissenschaft. Rowohlt Reinbeck 1998

Gilbert P.: The evolution of social attractiveness and its role in shame, humiliation, guilt and therapy. Br J Med Psychol 70 113-147 1997

Goldbrunner H.: Trauer und Beziehung. Systemische und gesellschaftliche Dimensionen der Verarbeitung von Verlusterlebnissen. M. Grünewald Mainz 1996

Goldschmidt G. A.: Der bestrafte Narziss. Ammann Zürich 1994

Goldschmidt H. L.: Freiheit für den Widerspruch. Novalis Schaffhausen 1976

Goleman D.: Emotionale Intelligenz. Carl Hanser München 1996 / Emotional Intelligence. Bantam, New York 1997

Gotlib I. H., Hammen C. L.: Psychological Aspects of Depression. John Wiley & Sons Chichester New York 1992

Grawe K.: Psychologische Therapie. Hogrefe Göttingen Bern Toronto Seattle 1998

Guardini R.: Vom Sinn der Schwermut. 6. Aufl. Topos Taschenbücher Band 130 1996

Guscott H. R., Grof P.: The clinical meaning of refractory depression: A review for the clinician. Am J. Psychiatry, 148, 695-704, 1991

Hänsli N.: Der sich selbst schädigende Mensch. Huber Bern 1994

Hartje W., Poeck K.: Klinische Neuropsychologie 3. Aufl. Thieme Stuttgart 1997

Hartmann H.: Essays on Ego Psychology. International University Press, New York, 1964

Hasenfratz H.-P.: Die Seele. Einführung in ein religiöses Grundphänomen. Theologischer Verlag Zürich 1986

Hautzinger M.: Kognitive Verhaltenstherapie bei Depressionen. Psychologie Verlags Union Weinheim 1997

Hawton K., Salkovskis P. M., Kirk J., Clark D. M.: Cognitive Behaviour Therapy for Psychiatric Problems, A Practical Guide. Oxford University Press 1991

Healy D.: The Antidepressant Era. Harvard University Press Cambridge, Massachusetts and London 1999

Heisenberg W.: Quantentheorie und Philosophie. Vorlesungen und Aufsätze (Hrsg.: Busche J.). Reclam Stuttgart 1994 / Physics and Philosophy. Prometheus Books, Amhurst 1999

Hell D., Scharfetter Ch., Möller A. (Hrsg): Eugen Bleuler. Leben und Werk. Verlag Hans Huber Bern Göttingen Toronto Seattle 2001

Hell D.: 100 Jahre Ringen um die Schizophrenien. Schweiz Arch Neurol Psychiatr 146 189-194 1995

Hell D.: Das «vierte Bein» der Psychiatrie. Krankenpflege 11 52-55 1983

Hell D.: Die Sprache der Seele verstehen. Die Wüstenväter als Therapeuten. Herder Spektrum, Freiburg Basel Wien 2002

Hell D.: Ethologie der Depression. Gustav Fischer Stuttgart Jena 1993

Hell D.: Gibt es die Schizophrenie? Schweiz Arch Neurol Psychiatr 149 51-52 1998

Hell D.: Klinische Psychiatrie – woher? wohin? Schweiz. Ärztezeitung 13 503-509 1993

Hell D.: Welchen Sinn macht Depression? Ein integrativer Ansatz. 8. Aufl. Rowohlt Reinbeck 2002

Hell D.: Bleulers Seelenverständnis und die Moderne. In: Thomas Sprecher (Hrsg.): Das Unbewusste in Zürich. Literatur und Tiefenpsychologie um 1900. NZZ Verlag Zürich 2000

Hell D.: Ehen depressiver und schizophrener Menschen – Eine vergleichende Studie an 103 Kranken und ihren Ehepartnern. 2. Auflage, Springer Berlin Heidelberg New York 1998

Hell D.: Praxisorientierte Depressionsbehandlung heute. Schweiz. Rundschau Med No. 22, 659-666, 1995

Heller A.: Theorie der Gefühle. VSA-Vlg. Hamburg 1987 / A Theory of Feelings. Lexington Books, Lanham 2009

Heraclitus / Haxton, B. (Trans.) Fragments. (English and Greek Edition) Penguin Classics, New York 2003

Hillman J.: Emotion. Northwestern University Press Evanston 3rd ed. 1997

Hinterhuber H.: Die Seele. Natur- und Kulturgeschichte von Psyche, Geist und Bewusstsein. Springer Wien New York 2001

Høeg P.: Der Plan von der Abschaffung des Dunkels. Rowohlt Reinbeck 1998

Hohendorf G., Roelcke V. und Rotzoll M.: Innovation und Vernichtung – Psychiatrische Forschung und «Euthanasie» an der Heidelberger Psychiatrischen Klinik 1939-1945. Nervenarzt 67: 935-946, 1996

Holsboer F.: Nervenheilkunde als angewandte Neurowissenschaft. Jatros Neurologie 1: 16-25 1996

Horstmann U.: Der lange Schatten der Melancholie. Die blaue Ente Essen 1985

Izard C. E.: Die Emotionen des Menschen. Eine Einführung in die Grundlagen der Emotionspsychologie. Beltz Verlag Weinheim und Basel 1981 / Human Emotions. Plenum, New York 1977

Jaspers K.: Allgemeine Psychopathologie. 9. Aufl. Springer Berlin Heidelberg New York 1973 / General Psychopathology. University of Chicago Press, Chicago 1963

Jaspers K.: Gesammelte Schriften zur Psychopathologie. Springer Berlin Heidelberg New York 1963

Jaynes J.: Der Ursprung des Bewusstseins durch den Zusammenbruch der bikameralen Psyche. Rowohlt Reinbeck 1988 / The Origin of

Conciousness in the Breakdown of the Bicameral Mind. Houghton Mifflin, Abington 2000

Jonas H.: Das Prinzip Leben. Suhrkamp Frankfurt am Main 1997 / The Phenomenon of Life: Toward a Philosophical Biology. University of Chicago Press, Chicago 1982

Josuran R., Hoehne V., Hell D.: Mittendrin und nicht dabei. Taschenbuch Econ Zürich 2001

Jung C. G.: Gesammelte Werke. Solothurn 1994 / The Collected Works of C. G. Jung. Vol 1-20, Princeton University Press, Princeton

Kalberer G.: Ist der Mensch ein Auslaufmodell? Tages-Anzeiger, 8.9.2000 S. 2

Kandel E. R.: A new intellectual framework for psychiatry. Am J Psychiatry 155: 457-469, 1998

Käser E.: Kultiviert und überflüssig. Neue Zürcher Zeitung, 21./22.3.1998 S. 81

Kemper P. (Hrsg.): Die Geheimnisse der Gesundheit. Suhrkamp Taschenbuch Frankfurt am Main 1996

Kielholz P., Adams C.: Die Vielfalt von Angstzuständen, Deutscher Ärzte-Verlag Köln 1989

Kierkegaard S.: Werke I, Der Begriff Angst. Rowohlt Taschenbuch Reinbeck 1960

Kierkegaard S.: Sickness unto Death. Penguin Classics, New York 1989

Klee E.: "Euthanasie" im NS-Staat. S. Fischer Frankfurt a.M. 1983

Klerman G. L., Weissman M. M., Rounsaville B. J., Chevron E. S.: Interpersonal Psychotherapy of Depression. Basic Books Inc. New York 1984

Klibansky R., Panofsky E., Saxl F.: Saturn und Melancholie. Studien zur Geschichte der Naturphilosophie und Medizin, der Religion und der Kunst. Suhrkamp Taschbuch Wissenschaft Frankfurt am Main 1992 / Saturn and Melancholy: Studies in the History of Natural Philosophy, Religion, and Art. Basic Books Inc., New York 1964

Kornhuber H. H., Deecke L.: Pflügers Archiv für Gesamte Physiologie. 284 1-17 1965

Küchenhoff B., Hell D.: Angsterkrankungen, Klassifizierung und Therapiemöglichkeiten. DIA-GM 12 920-929 1995

Küchenhoff J. (Hrsg.): Selbstzerstörung und Selbstfürsorge. Psychosozial Giessen 1999

Kurzweil R.: Homo sapiens. Kiepenheuer und Witsch Köln 2000 / The Age of Spiritual Machines. Penguin, New York 2000

Laing R. D.: The Politics of Experience. Pantheon New York 1967

Lazarus R. S.: Emotion and Adaptation. Oxford University Press 1991

LeDoux J.: The Emotional Brain – The Mysterious Underpinnings of Emotional Life. New York 1998

Lévinas E.: De l'évasion. Fata Morgana Paris 1982 / On Escape. Stanford University Press, Palo Alto 2003

Lewis H. B.: The Role of Shame in Symptom Formation. Erlbaum Publishers London 1987

Lewis M.: Scham – Annäherung an ein Tabu. Ernst Kabel Hamburg 1992 / Shame: The Exposed Self. Free Press, New York 1991

Lieberman J. A., Rush A. J.: Redefining the role of psychiatry in médecine. Am J Psychiatry 153: 1388-1397, 1996

Littlewood J.: Aspects of Grief: Bereavement in Adult Life. London 1992

Lyssy R.: Swiss Paradise – Ein autobiographischer Bericht. R+R Verlag Zürich 2001

Margraf J., Schneider S.: Panik – Angstanfälle und ihre Behandlung. Springer Berlin Heidelberg 1989

Marks L.: Ängste verstehen und bewältigen. 2. Aufl. Springer Berlin Heidelberg 1993 / Living with Fear: Understanding and Coping with Anxiety. McGraw Hill Higher Education, Maidenhead 2005

Mead G. H.: Mind, Self, and Society: From the Standpoint of a Social Behaviorist. Charles W. Morris ed. University of Chicago Press, Chicago 1962

Meier-Seethaler C: Gefühl und Urteilskraft. Beck München 1997

Meister Eckehart: Deutsche Predigten und Traktate (Hrsg. J. Quint). Diogenes Zürich 1963

Melville H.: Bartleby. Reclam Stuttgart 1985

Menninghaus W.: Ekel: Theorie und Geschichte einer starken Empfindung. Suhrkamp Frankfurt am Main 1999 / Disgust: Theory and History of a Strong Sensation. State University of New York, Albany 2003

Mentzos S.: Depression und Manie – Psychodynamik und Therapie affektiver Störungen. Vandenhoeck & Ruprecht.: Göttingen Zürich 1996

Metzinger Th. (Hrsg.): Bewusstsein. Beiträge aus der gegenwärtigen Philosophie. Ferdinand Schöningh Paderborn 1996

Miller W. I.: Anatomy of Disgust. Harvard University Press 1997

Möller A., Hell D.: Das allgemeinpsychologische Konzept im Spätwerk Eugen Bleulers. Fortschr. Neurol. Psychiat. 67: 147-154, 1999

Müller C.: Wer hat die Geisteskranken von den Ketten befreit? Skizzen zur Psychiatriegeschichte. Das Narrenschiff Bonn 1998

Müller-Hill B.: Die Philosophen und das Lebendige. Campus Frankfurt New York 1981

Musil R.: The Man without Qualities. Macmillan, New York 1997

Nagel T.: Der Blick von nirgendwo. Suhrkamp Frankfurt a. M. 1992 / The View from Nowhere. Oxford University Press, Reprint, New York 1989

Nagel T.: Die Grenzen der Objektivität. Reclam Stuttgart 1991

Navratil L.: Schizophrenie und Religion. Brinkmann und Bose Berlin 1992

Neumann J. M.: Gesundheit, Krankheit und Therapie im Mittelalter. In: Kemper P. (Hrsg.): Geheimnisse der Gesundheit – Medizin zwischen Heilkunde und Heiltechnik. Suhrkamp TB Frankfurt a. M. 1996

Nolen-Hoeksema S., McBride A., Larson J.: Rumination and psychological distress among bereaved partners. J Pers Soc Psychol 72 No. 4 855-862, 1997

Nolen-Hoeksema S., Morrow J., Fredrickson B. L.: Response styles and the duration of episodes of depressed mood. J Abnorm Psychol 102 No. 1, 20-28, 1993

Nolen-Hoeksema S., Parker L. E., Larson J.: Ruminative coping with depressed mood following loss. J Pers Soc Psychol 67 No. 1 92-104, 1994

Nuber U.: Depression. Die verkannte Krankheit. Kreuz Stuttgart 2001

Parker G., Brown L. B.: Repertories of response to potential precipitants of depression. Australian and New Zealand Journal of Psychiatry 13: 327-333, 1979

Pauen M.: Grundprobleme der Philosophie des Geistes. Fischer TB Frankfurt am Main 2001

Percy W.: The Message in the Bottle. 19th printing, the noonday press New York 1995

Pfau B.: Scham und Depression – Ärztliche Anthropologie eines Affektes. Schattauer Stuttgart New York 1998

Phillips M. L., Senior S., Fahy T., David A. S.: Disgust – the forgotten emotion of psychiatry. Br J Psychiatr 172: 373-375, 1998

Pichot P.: Das Problem der Angst in historischer Sicht. In: Kielholz P. und Adams C. (Hrsg.): Die Vielfalt von Angstzuständen. Deutscher Ärzteverlag Köln 1989

Popper K. R.: Conjectures and Refutations. The Growth of Scientific Knowledge. London Routledge and Kegan, 1963

Power M., Dalgleish T.: Cognition and Emotion. From Order to Disorder. Psychology Press Publishers Sussex UK 1997

Prigerson H.G., Frank E., Kasl S.V., Reynolds C.F., Anderson B., Zubenko G.S. et al.: Complicated grief and bereavement-related depression as distinct disorders: Preliminary empirical validation in elderly bereaved spouses. Am J Psychiatry 152: 22-30, 1995

Putnam H.: The Meaning of «Meanings». In: ders., Philosophical Papers, Bd. 2, Cambridge 1975

Rado S.: The problem of melancholia. International Journal of Psychoanalysis 9, 420-438, 1928

Rager G. (Hrsg.): Ich und mein Gehirn. Grenzfragen Bd 26. Alber Freiburg 2000

Rapoport J. L.: Der Junge, der sich immer waschen musste. Wenn Zwänge den Tag beherrschen. MMV Medizin Verlag 1993 / The Boy Who Couldn't Stop Washing: Experience and Treatment of Obsessive-compulsive Disorder. New American Library, New York 1990

Rattner J., Danzer G.: Medizinische Anthropologie – Ansätze einer personalen Heilkunde. Fischer Frankfurt am Main 1997

Rippere V.: Antidepressive behaviour. Beh. Res. and Therapy Vol 14, 289-299. Pergamon Press 1976

Rohde P. P.: Kierkegaard. Rowohlt Reinbeck 1959

Roth G.: Das Gehirn und seine Wirklichkeit. Kognitive Neurobiologie und ihre philosophischen Konsequenzen. Suhrkamp Taschenbuch 1997

Rousseau J.-J.: The Confessions. Classics of World Literature, Wordsworth Editions, Hertfordshire 1996

Rozin P., Haidt J., Me Canley C. R.: Disgust. In: Lewis M. and Haviland J. (eds.) Handbook of Emotions. Guilford New York: 1993

Rudolf G.: Der Organismus als Maschine bei Descartes. In: Kemper P. (Hrsg.): Medizin zwischen Heilkunde und Heiltechnik. Suhrkamp TB 2521 Frankfurt 1956

Saint-Exupéry A. de: Der Kleine Prinz, Arche Zürich Hamburg 2000 / Saint-Exupéry, A. de / Howard, R., Transl.: The Little Prince. Mariner Books 2000

Salkovskis P. M. und Kirk J.: Obsessional disorders. In: Hawton K., Salkovskis P.M., Kirk J., Clark D.: Cognitive Behaviour Therapy for Psychiatric Problems. Oxford Medical Publications 1991

Saner H.: Melancholie und Leichtsinn – Grenzstimmungen der Vernunft. Schweiz Arch Neurol Psychiatr 149: 229-235, 1998

Sarasin Ph., Tanner J. (Hrsg.): Physiologie und industrielle Gesellschaft, stw 1343 Suhrkamp Frankfurt am Main 1998

Sartre J.-P.: Nausea. New Directions Publishing Corporation, New York 2007

Sass L. A.: Madness and Modernism. Basic books New York 1992

Scharfetter C.: Allgemeine Psychopathologie – Eine Einführung. 4. Aufl. Thieme Stuttgart New York 1996 / General Psychopathology: An Introduction. Cambridge University Press, Cambridge 1980

Scharfetter C.: Was weiß der Psychiater vom Menschen? Hans Huber Bern 2000

Schmid Ch., Hochstrasser B., Hell D.: Selbstbeschädigung als Symptom psychischer Krankheiten in der PUK Zürich zwischen 1987 und 1995. Schweiz Arch Neurol Psychiatr 151: 184-9, 2000

Schulte G.: Neuromythen: Das Gehirn als Mind Machine und Versteck des Geistes. Zweitausendeins Frankfurt am Main 2000

Searle J. R.: Die Wiederentdeckung des Geistes. Suhrkamp TB Frankfurt a. M. 1996 / The Rediscovery of the Mind. The MIT Press, Cambridge 1992

Seidler G. H.: Der Blick des Andern. Eine Analyse der Scham. Verlag Internationale Psychoanalyse Stuttgart 1995

Seligman M. E. P.: Helplessness. W. H. Freeman San Francisco 1975

Sennett R.: Der flexible Mensch. Berlin Verlag Berlin 1998 / The Corrosion of Character. W. W. Norton & Company, London 1998

Shorter E.: Von der Seele in den Körper. Die kulturellen Ursprünge psychosomatischer Krankheiten. Rowohlt Sachbuch Reinbeck 1999 / From the Mind into the Body: The Cultural Origins of Psychosomatic Symptoms. Free Press, New York 1993

Spaemann R.: Personen. Versuche über den Unterschied zwischen «etwas» und «jemand». Klett-Cotta Stuttart 1996 / Persons. The Difference Between Someone and Something. Oxford University Press, New York 2007

Starobinski J.: Geschichte der Melancholiebehandlung von den Anfängen bis 1900. Acta psychosomatica. J. R. Geigy S.A. Basel 1960

Steinmann H.: «... dieser geniale Lästerer» Achillos: Der Dichter, der das Ich entdeckt. Neue Zürcher Zeitung 21./22. März 1998, No. 67 S. 69

Stern R. und Drummond L.: The Practice of Behavioural and Cognitive Psychotherapy. Cambridge University Press 1991

Szasz Th.: The Myth of Mental Illness. Harper Perennial; Revised edition, New York 1984

Taureck B. H. F.: Emmanuel Lévinas zur Einführung. Junius Hamburg 1997

Taylor C.: Quellen des Selbst – Die Entstehung der neuzeitlichen Identität. (Übers. Schulte J.) Suhrkamp Taschenbuch Wissenschaft 1233 Frankfurt am Main 1996 / Sources of the Self. Harvard University Press, Cambridge 1992

Teasdale J. D., Barnard P. J.: Affect Cognition and Change – Re-modelling Depressive Thought. LEA Publishers Hove UK 1995

Tellenbach H.: Psychiatrie als geistige Medizin. Verlag für angewandte Wissenschaften München 1987

Thich Nhat Hanh: Lächle deinem eigenen Herzen zu – Wege zu einem achtsamen Leben. Herder Spektrum. Freiburg im Breisgau 1998 / Peace is in Every Step: The Path of Mindfulness in Everyday Life. Bantam, New York 1992

Tolstoi L.: Tagebücher Bd. 2 1885-1901. Ges. Werke hrsg. von E. Diechmann und G. Dudeh. Rütten und Loening Berlin 1971 / Tolstoy's Diaries. Charles Scribner's Sons, New York 1985; The Complete Works of Leo Tolstoy. Kindle Edition, O'Connor Books 2009

Tomkins S. S.: Affect imagery consciousness vol. 2: The negative affects. Springer New York 1963

v. Braun C: Versuch über den Schwindel. Pendo Zürich München 2001

v. Weizsäcker C. F.: Die Unschuld der Physiker? 2. Aufl. Pendo Zürich 1997

v. Weizsäcker C. F.: Die Einheit der Natur. 4. Aufl. dtv München/Wien 1984 / The Unity of Nature. Farrar Straus & Giroux, New York 1980

v. Weizsäcker C. F.: Ein Blick auf Platon. Ideenlehre; Logik und Physik. Reclam Stuttgart 1988

v. Weizsäcker V.: Arzt und Kranker. Köhler Stuttgart 1949

van Doren C.: A History of Knowledge – Past, Present and Future. Ballantine Books New York 1992

Völker L.: «Komm, heilige Melancholie». Eine Anthologie deutscher Melancholie-Gedichte. Reclam Stuttgart 1984

von Avila T.: Die innere Burg (Hrsg.: Vogelsang F.). Diogenes Zürich 1979

Wallace E., Radden J., Sadler J. Z.: The philosophy of psychiatry: Who needs it? J Nerv Ment Dis 185:67 1997

Wasserman G. S.: Neural/mental chronometry and chemotheology. Behavioral and Brain Sciences. 8, 556-557, 1985

Weber-Gast J.: Weil du nicht geflohen bist vor meiner Angst. 8. Aufl. Matthias-Grünewald-Verlag Mainz 1989

Weltgesundheitsorganisation: Internationale Klassifikation psychischer Störungen (ICD10 Kapitel V(F) Klinisch-diagnostische Leitlinien, Hrsg.: Dilling H., Mombour W., Schmidt M. H. Hans Huber Bern 1991

Wieland W.: Diagnose. Überlegungen zur Medizintheorie. Walter de Gruyter Berlin New York 1975

Willi J.: Die patientenbezogene Tradition der Schweizer Psychiatrie. Neue Zürcher Zeitung No. 127 1999 S. 95

Wittgenstein L.: Werkausgabe Bd. 1, (Tractatus logico-philosophicus. Tagebücher 1914-1916, Philosophische Untersuchungen. Suhrkamp Frankfurt a.M. 1984 / Wittgenstein, L., Anscombe, G.E.M.: Philosophical Investigations: The German Text with a Revised English Translation. Third Ed. Blackwell 2001

Wittgenstein L.: Werkausgabe Bd. 7 (Bemerkungen über die Philosophie der Psychologie ...) Suhrkamp Frankfurt a. M. 1984

Wittgenstein L.: Vermischte Bemerkungen. Suhrkamp Frankfurt a. M. 1977

Wolfersdorf M.: Depressionen verstehen und bewältigen. Springer Berlin 2002

Wurmser L.: Die Maske der Scham. Springer Berlin 1990 / The Mask of Shame. The Johns Hopkins University Press, Baltimore 1981

*Heinrich Karl Fierz*

## Jungian Psychiatry

C.G. Jung spent the first ten years of his career working in a psychiatric clinic, an experience which had a powerful influence on his lifelong endeavors. Now the psychiatric-analytic observations of a highly respected Jungian, the Swiss Heinrich Fierz, who devoted his life to psychiatry, are available in English at last. Jungian Psychiatry is rich with the insights of a rare therapist and teacher in the world of the psychiatric clinic.

Heinrich Karl Fierz worked as a psychiatrist at the famed Binswanger Clinic, Sanatorium Bellevue, for many years before co-founding the Jungian "Klinik am Zürichberg" in 1964, where he was medical director until his recent death. A son of one of the first Jungian analysts, Linda Fierz-David, he also became a training analyst and lecturer at the Jung Institute in Zürich. His sensitive and innovative contributions to the realm of psychiatry are well-known in the German-speaking world; *Jungian Psychiatry* is the first major publication of his work in English.

420 pages, numerous illustrations, ISBN 978-3-85630-521-5

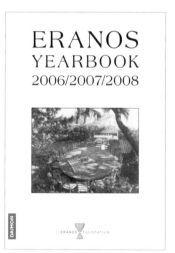

## Eranos Yearbook 69

*2006 / 2007 / 2008*

This Eranos Yearbook covers the events of the first three years since the relaunching of the Eranos Foundation in 2006. The themes of the conferences – 'The Modernities of East and West' or 'Perspectives on Violence and Aggression', for example – reflect both the long and prestigious tradition of the Eranos Foundation and the relevance of Eranos to the present. The prominent international speakers succeeded in making fruitful contributions in addressing some of the most pressing questions of our times.

524 pages, hardbound, illustrated, ISBN 978-3-85630-734-9

## C. A. Meier

## Healing Dream and Ritual

*Ancient Incubation and*
*Modern Psychotherapy*

C. A. Meier investigates the ancient Greek understanding of dreams and dreaming, Antique incubation and concomitant rituals. In this greatly expanded version of his classic work, Ancient Incubation and Modern Psychotherapy, Meier compares Asklepian divine medicine with our own contemporary psychotherapeutic approaches to dreaming. He elucidates how the healing cure was found in the very core of illness itself – a fact of invaluable significance today in both medicine and psychology. In helping us to recognize the suprapersonal aspects of illness, the dream is shown to reveal a transcendental path to healing.

*Healing Dream and Ritual is one of the most significant and lasting witnesses of how far beyond immediate psychology the implications of Jung's work stretches. This book is, in my feeling, as important for today's healers as was the early work of Paracelsus to the redirection of medicine in the Renaissance.*
- Sir Laurens van der Post

168 pages, ISBN 978-3-85630-629-8

## Aniela Jaffé

## The Myth of Meaning

Aniela Jaffé explores the subjective world of inner experience. In so doing, she follows the path of the pioneering Swiss psychologist C.G. Jung, whose collaborator and friend she was through the final decades of his life. Frau Jaffé shows that any search for meaning ultimately leads to the inner "mythical" realm and must be understood as a limited subjective attempt to answer the unanswerable. Any conclusion drawn from such a quest is one's very own – its formulation is one's own myth.

186 pages, ISBN 978-3-85630-500-0

# English Titles from Daimon

## English Titles from Daimon

Laurens van der Post - *The Rock Rabbit and the Rainbow*
Jane Reid - *Jung, My Mother and I: The Analytic Diaries
of Catharine Rush Cabot*
R.M. Rilke - *Duino Elegies*
Miguel Serrano - *C.G. Jung and Hermann Hesse*
Helene Shulman - *Living at the Edge of Chaos*
D. Slattery / L. Corbet (Eds.) - *Depth Psychology: Meditations on the Field*
D. Slattery / G. Slater (Eds.) - *Varieties of Mythic Experience*
David Tacey - *Edge of the Sacred: Jung, Psyche, Earth*
Susan Tiberghien - *Looking for Gold*
Ann Ulanov - *Spirit in Jung*
- *Spiritual Aspects of Clinical Work*
- *Picturing God*
- *Receiving Woman*
- *The Female Ancestors of Christ*
- *The Wisdom of the Psyche*
- *The Wizards' Gate, Picturing Consciousness*
Ann & Barry Ulanov - *Cinderella and her Sisters*
- *Healing Imagination: Psyche and Soul*
Erlo van Waveren - *Pilgrimage to the Rebirth*
Eva Wertenschlag-Birkhäuser - *Windows on Eternity:
The Paintings of Peter Birkhäuser*
Harry Wilmer - *How Dreams Help*
- *Quest for Silence*
Luigi Zoja - *Drugs, Addiction and Initiation*
Luigi Zoja & Donald Williams - *Jungian Reflections on September 11*
Jungian Congress Papers - *Jerusalem 1983: Symbolic & Clinical Approaches*
- *Berlin 1986: Archetype of Shadow in a Split World*
- *Paris 1989: Dynamics in Relationship*
- *Chicago 1992: The Transcendent Function*
- *Zürich 1995: Open Questions*
- *Florence 1998: Destruction and Creation*
- *Cambridge 2001*
- *Barcelona 2004: Edges of Experience*
- *Cape Town 2007: Journeys, Encounters*

*Available from your bookstore or from our distributors:*

| | |
|---|---|
| AtlasBooks | Gazelle Book Services Ltd. |
| 30 Amberwood Parkway | White Cross Mills, High Town |
| Ashland OH 44805, USA | Lancaster LA1 4XS, UK |
| Phone: 419-281-5100 | Tel: +44(0)152468765 |
| Fax: 419-281-0200 | Fax: +44(0)152463232 |
| E-mail: order@atlasbooks.com | Email: Sales@gazellebooks.co.uk |
| www.AtlasBooksDistribution.com | www.gazellebooks.co.uk |

*Daimon Verlag - Hauptstrasse 85 - CH-8840 Einsiedeln - Switzerland
Phone: (41)(55) 412 2266   Fax: (41)(55) 412 2231
email: info@daimon.ch*
*Visit our website:* **www.daimon.ch** *or write for our complete catalog*